FINDING HOME

FINDING HOME

A war child's journey to peace

Frank Oberle

Heritage
House

Heritage House Publishing Co. Ltd.
#108-17665 66A Ave.
Surrey, BC, Canada   V3S 2A7
greatbooks@heritagehouse.ca
www.heritagehouse.ca

Edited by Laurel Bernard
Cover design by Nancy St.Gelais
Book design and layout by Darlene Nickull
Cover photos courtesy of City of Rheinstetten Archives

Printed in Canada

Library and Archives Canada Cataloguing in Publication
Oberle, Frank, 1932-
    Finding home: a war child's journey to peace / Frank Oberle.

ISBN 1-894384-76-8

    1. Oberle, Frank, 1932-   2. Immigrants—Canada—Biography.   3. German Canadians—Biography.   4. Cabinet ministers—Canada—Biography.   5. Peace River Region (B.C. and Alta.)—Biography.   I. Title.

FC601.O24A3 2004   971.064'092   C2004-905028-1

Heritage House acknowledges the financial support for its publishing program from the Government of Canada through the Book Publishing Industry Development Program (BPIDP), the Canada Council for the Arts, and the Province of British Columbia through the British Columbia Arts Council.

The Canada Council | Le Conseil des Arts
for the Arts | du Canada

BRITISH
COLUMBIA
ARTS COUNCIL
We acknowledge the support of the Province of British Columbia
through the British Columbia Arts Council

This book has been produced on 100% post-consumer recycled paper, processed chlorine free and printed with vegetable-based inks.

This book is an attempt, inadequate as it will be, to make up for the many opportunities that I surely missed throughout my life to say thank you to the people who helped me in so many ways to dispel the clouds of chaos and despair that have cast such a heavy shadow on my life, my childhood, and early youth and who helped me find my place in the sun.

It is dedicated to my children and grandchildren to help them trace their roots, but most of all it is dedicated to Joan, my partner and friend, my love, without whom my life would have been ordinary at best.

Acknowledgements

This is the first of a two-volume exposé of my life story that was never intended to be shared with any audience other than my immediate and, perhaps, some of my extended family, as well as a small circle of friends and benefactors to whom I owe a special debt of gratitude.

Special mention must go to Anemone and Martin Schliessler, who helped to inspire the effort in the first place, and to our daughter Ursula, who, once it was taking shape, recognized the story as a unique perspective on a certain period in the history of the 20th century—a period that shook the world to its very core—and an important reflection on the lives of millions of our fellow citizens. Throughout history, they felt drawn to the shores of our great land to escape hunger, misery, and social upheaval and have helped shape a society that has become the envy of all the world. It was Ursula who convinced me to commit my story to the public domain, and it was Laurel Bernard, my editor extraordinaire, who with great sensitivity and tireless effort helped me to refocus my effort in that direction.

To all of them I am eternally grateful.

Contents

Publisher's Note

When Frank Oberle was born in 1932, much of Germany was rooted in values and social structures that had changed little since the Middle Ages. People in the countryside lived as they had for generations, farming a few patches of land, celebrating the seasons, going to church, and obeying the local representatives of God and man.

Frank's birthplace, Forchheim on the Rhine near the Black Forest, was typical of such rural communities. Cattle pulled wooden-wheeled wagons, water was hand-pumped from the village well, and the only sign of the Industrial Revolution's onset was a steam-powered thresher. Social status was rigid, and change unheard of. As the son of an "outsider," and a respectable family's poor relation, Frank grew up with few prospects. By birth, the best he could expect was to learn a trade or find work in one of the nearby cities' factories.

Instead, Frank Oberle crossed the Atlantic to North America and carved out a living as a logger, a gold miner, and an entrepreneur. By the time he was 30 he had started a successful business, a family, and a career that eventually took him from municipal politics in British Columbia to the House of Commons in Ottawa, where he served as the MP for Prince George–Peace River and as the Minister of State for Science and Technology and Minister of Forests in Brian Mulroney's government.

Prior to that, before taking one step on his remarkable journey, he lived through some of the worst horrors of the Second World War, witnessing through a boy's eyes the Great Trek out of Poland and the Dresden fire-bombing. Separated from his parents, he saw and learned things about war and human nature that irrevocably changed his character and the course of his life.

This first volume of Frank Oberle's memoirs records his childhood in Forchheim and those terrible wartime years. It follows him into Canada, from his landing in Halifax to his wild frontier adventures in B.C. and his reunion, long awaited, with his sweetheart and lifelong partner, Joan. Finally, it takes him to a tiny B.C. town and that moment when he and Joan wonder if at last they have found home.

Introduction

Who knows whether in retirement I shall be tempted to the last infirmity of mundane minds, which is to write a book.

—Geoffrey Fisher, Archbishop of Canterbury

It wasn't an ideal day for playing golf, but then at Fairwinds we don't abandon golf just because of the less than perfect conditions that prevail throughout most of the winter. It was Mark Twain who said, "Golf is a good walk spoiled," which indicates how unfamiliar he must have been with the disease. George McMulkin, one of my regular partners, and I were coming down the steep slope off the sixteenth green, I perhaps just a bit annoyed at having missed a two-foot birdie putt. It had been raining hard, and the spikes on my left foot failed to take hold of the rain-soaked turf, leaving my right foot trapped under the rest of my body as it came crashing to the ground.

My first concern, of course, was having to forfeit the sizable lead I had accumulated, which, providing I was able to hold onto it for the last two holes, would net me the princely sum of 75 cents, most of it coming from another regular, Bob Dorion, who had skinned us mercilessly for the last few games. At first it felt like a bad sprain, but as I made my way off the last green I knew I was in deep trouble. I did manage to protect my lead, but the satisfaction I gained from that did little to compensate for the tongue-lashing my wife, Joan, laid on me on the way to the hospital.

I knew the leg was broken even before I was shown the results of the X-rays. I would be laid up for at least three months, deprived of my last excuse to delay what several of my friends and other influential people had been urging me for some time to do: preserve some of the stories about the trials and tribulations that shaped Joan's and my lives and made us who we are.

Faced with the prospect of being housebound for several months and watching from my window as other members of the club strutted their stuff on the golf course, I saw the accident as an omen and an opportunity.

I would not only find distraction from such torture, but would also face up to what I had long considered to be an obligation owed, first, to all our children and, second, to the many people who touched our lives and helped us along the way. I hoped to give them some insight into that past which may have shaped my character and Joan's.

I knew from the beginning that a journey back to the early days of my youth and childhood would be painful and that I would risk irritating some of the many scars that have never quite healed. I would be reminded of the pain and of the suffering that for all the years of my adult life I have been trying to shut out of my mind—so many bad memories that I felt best to be denied or forgotten.

Modern psychology may prescribe exposing and airing psychological scars of the kind my contemporaries acquired during those years when civilization remained suspended and the nations of the world engaged each other in a conflict from which none could emerge a winner. But I think there are altogether too many examples where whole tribes and nations of people have embraced a culture of persecution that forces them to constantly relive their past and be reminded of the horrors and injustices inflicted on them and their ancestors, sometimes thousands of years in the past. For some individuals, it has become a singular obsession to seek redress or revenge.

Joan and I have chosen not to burden ourselves or any of our offspring with such fruitless thoughts or pursuits. I am not weighed down with any feelings of guilt for the sins of our fathers, nor do I bear malice against any of the characters who will be featured in these pages. In fact, I have changed the names of certain people in some cases or have chosen to introduce them in the abstract rather than offend the sensitivities of their friends and families.

The beginning of the story dates back more than half a century. While I can attest to the accuracy of the historic facts and the account generally, I have no doubt that time may have eroded my memory of some of the details I have described, which may therefore be at variance with the recollection others may have of the same events. If I have offended anyone, I offer my sincere apologies.

Some of the people who inspired this effort are featured in the book. Among them is my grandfather, with whom the reader will become much better acquainted. There are many stories about him, but none that help me understand what there may have been in his past to make him the man I so much loved and respected, yet later learned to despise. Perhaps if he had been moved to tell the story of his life I might have been spared the torment I suffered trying to unravel the mystery.

I have no illusion that the passage of time can ever erase the heavy burden of guilt the world has placed on the shoulders of those German people who perpetrated or sought to benefit from the horrors Hitler's racist policies inflicted on the world. Perhaps by writing about my experiences during the 20th century's darkest days I can afford those who are born into my family the comfort of knowing that their ancestors were not among them. Instead, like the vast majority of the German people and other Europeans, they were themselves innocent victims.

GERMANY

1932-1951

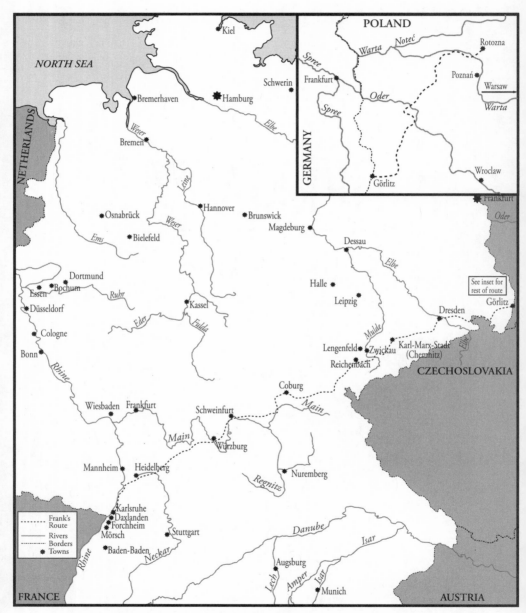

"Frank's Route" refers to his personal journey at the end of the war, which is described in detail in Chapter 4: The Great Trek. In the early 1980s, Forchheim and Mörsch, along with Neuburgweier, were amalgamated to form the city of Rheinstetten.

CHAPTER 1

The Roots

The deepest definition of youth is life as yet untouched by tragedy.
—Alfred North Whitehead, English mathematician and philosopher

The grand old sandstone structure where Joan and I started school together in 1938 is still in use today. It was called the New School, the Old School across from the *Rathaus* having become too small to accommodate all the new citizens that the townsfolk, obedient to their Catholic creed relating to family size, brought into the world.

Neither school suffered much damage during the war, and together with the other older buildings, including the 150-year-old church, they stand as a solid foundation on which a most intricate, highly regulated social structure was built. The social order and the rules governing it were as intractable as the institutions to which they were anchored.

Forchheim's recorded history dates back a thousand years. The early settlers were no doubt attracted to the area by its proximity to the Rhine, which in its timeless quest to find its way to the North Sea has carved a wide channel through the mountainous regions in the south. Its often cataclysmic floods levelled the landscape, depositing fertile soil over a wide area along its path. It was the lifeblood of the region and became a natural border separating the Germanic tribes from their western neighbours, the French.

The area's people tended to regard the Rhine as the instrument by which God delivered his boundless blessings to his faithful and obedient children, as well as his curse and punishment for their indiscretions and sins. The town's present-day location is about two kilometres from the main channel, on sufficiently high ground to shelter it from the ravaging floods

Lorenz Albecker, his wife Anna, and brother Wilhelm are part of a typical farm family in Forchheim. This picture was taken in 1946. The upper right-hand corner shows part of the Leibold family's ancestral home.

that were all too common before it was possible to construct an elaborate network of dykes to confine the water to a more regular channel.

The Romans actually traversed the area 2,000 years ago on their way to Britannia, the name they used for England and Wales. Understandably, perhaps, they left few signs of their presence in the neighbourhood of Forchheim. After all, they had regular stopovers in Baden-Baden, 30 kilometres to the south, where they had established elaborate spa facilities connected to the hot springs there. Incredibly, these facilities are still in use today. So it's reasonable to assume that after a change of socks and underwear they would march 150 kilometres farther down the Rhine, lured by the golden-haired siren sitting atop the Lorelei.

During my early childhood years, Forchheim was a tranquil, sleepy little village. Its citizens engaged mainly in subsistence farming. The *Hauptstrasse* [main street] branching off the regional highway was lined with stately chestnut trees giving shade to the bakery, the butcher shop, the *Gasthouses* [inns], and a few other commercial establishments that the sparse local population was able to sustain. It came to a dead end at the

Rathaus [the town hall], which like the church was perched at the edge of the high ground overlooking the lowlands separating the town from the river. The burghers were used to a pace and rhythm dictated by the seasons and by the livestock on which they depended. Only a few of the local farmers could afford the use of horses to cultivate their fields. Most relied on their cows to do double duty, providing the family with milk and other dairy products as well as pulling the wagons and still somewhat primitive farm implements.

A number of strategically placed wells, the pumps of which were operated by hand and anchored to a three-metre trough carved out of a solid block of sandstone, served as the source of water for man and beast alike—and as the fountains of the latest gossip and secrets to which only the priest, Pfarrer Dorer, ought to have been privy. For the womenfolk, gathering around these sites as part of the daily ritual of fetching water was a major part of their social life.

I spent only the first eight years of my life and another two or three years after the war in Forchheim, but if there are places where people have roots, mine would be planted there. That's because my mother's family tree has been rooted there from time immemorial. Grandfather Leibold, the patriarch of the family, was the forester charged with the custodianship of the *Rheinwald* [forest along the Rhine], which ranked him among the town's elite, right behind the priest, the mayor, and the school principal, in that order. A sergeant in the Kaiser's army during the First World War, he retained his moustache and the authoritarian demeanour befitting the rank and the hero status to which he felt entitled after his honourable discharge from the service. He was a stern, almost draconian disciplinarian, demanding slavish obedience from his wife and children.

Of these, by the time I was born in March of 1932, my mother Rösel's siblings, Otto and Wilhelm, were well established in business: Otto with his print shop and a toy and stationery store, and Wilhelm as the local painter. Another brother, Anton, had chosen to pursue his fortune elsewhere, moving to Daxlanden, the next village down the Rhine, where he married Frieda.

My father, on the other hand, was an immigrant, an outsider, who came from Mörsch, where his family, the Oberles, settled after they had been chased across the Rhine, victims of the ethnic cleansing that followed the Thirty Years War in the mid-17th century. His siblings, brother August and sisters Barbara, Marie, and Sofie, together with my grandparents, still lived in Mörsch, less than a kilometre away. Dad participated actively in the affairs of Forchheim, but he was deprived of an important birthright. Local citizens were entitled to a share of the wealth produced by the forests and the agricultural lands, which were either owned outright or held in common by the town. Dad, as an outsider, had no such entitlement. For the same reason, people never referred to him by his surname or by his given name of Adolf. He was simply Leibold Rösel's husband, and my siblings and I were known as Leibold Rösel's offspring.

That was not altogether bad because very few people were known by their proper names anyway. Most had earned a nickname by distinguishing themselves in one way or another in a past that could date back several generations. My uncle Herman, for instance, was known as Keller Herman, even though his proper name was Herman Winter. Keller is a common enough name in Germany, but in his case it identified him for what he was: a packrat who had his *Keller*—cellar—packed full of a lifetime's collection of junk that he guarded with his life. Such nicknames were passed on to the offspring and could only be shed by earning notoriety greater than that of the elder.

Now I don't want to be unfair to Onkel Herman; his habit proved useful. Years later, when I began to assemble my first bicycle after the war, I had to rely on the charity of relatives and friends for old bicycle parts. After the most exhausting search, I was still short a drive-chain and a seat for my new "street-rut racer." My brother Erich suggested the obvious: a visit to Onkel Herman's basement. That was easier said than done, but after some coaxing, I was allowed a visit to this treasure house and discovered at least a dozen bicycle seats perfectly suitable to my needs and just as many drive-chains. However, Keller Herman pointed out that his own children would be thinking about getting mobile themselves, so he couldn't determine whether any of these items were surplus to his needs at that time. Fortunately, Tante Barbara, Dad's sister, had anticipated this verdict, and she whispered to me to come back on a certain day a week hence for another try. As it turned out, Keller Herman was away that day and Tante Barbara simply told me to help myself, confident that he would never know the difference.

Such was Forchheim in 1932, with its web of relatives and rigid social structures. My immediate family fitted in at the bottom of this social scale. Dad was a carpenter by trade, working, as I first remember, at a factory in Karlsruhe. Prior to my arrival, like everyone else, he had been unemployed. In North America everyone was affected by the recession of the 1930s, but

Adolf Oberle's family lived in Mörsch. This photograph shows (left to right, front row) his adopted sister Marie, his mother, his sister Sofie, his father, and his sister Barbara. Adolf himself stands in the middle of the back row with his brother August (right) and Marie's father.

Rösel Leibold's family. In the back row (from left) are Wilhelm, Otto, Anna, Anton, and Rösel. Seated in front (from left) are Frank Oberle's maternal grandmother, his Tante Johanna, and Grandpa Leibold.

in Europe, and more particularly in Germany, that period was preceded by economic disaster. In Germany, the economy and, in the end, the entire monetary system collapsed under the weight of the worldwide recession and the heavy burden placed on the shoulders of its citizens by the Treaty of Versailles, which divided the spoils of the First World War among the victors.

The southern regions of Germany were in the main still dependent on subsistence farming and, until the First World War, had not been touched by the Industrial Revolution that awoke the rest of the world from its sleep. It took much longer in that region to heal the lingering effects of those terrible times, and the cost throughout Germany was high.

It was in the same year I was born that Hitler and the Nazi party came to power, setting in motion events that would leave indelible scars on our souls and shake the world to its very foundation. That was also the year Roosevelt was elected president in the United States and construction was started on the Golden Gate Bridge in San Francisco.

For our family the 1920s and '30s were particularly hard, and Mom and Dad had to rely on the charity of their relatives to feed their children. Rösel had been brought up in an affluent household, but it was Johanna, her younger sister, and Otto Albecker, Johanna's husband, who for unexplained reasons, and against all tradition, inherited the family fortune. Perhaps Otto and Wilhelm, having had the good fortune of learning a trade, showed little interest in being shackled to the primitive way of life of their ancestors.

Grandfather presumably was able to assist each of them in getting their careers established as part of their inheritance, but there would have been precious little, if anything, left over to help my parents get started. With Dad unemployed, they had a lot of time on their hands and, to make things worse, they allowed themselves to be talked into building a house—on the strength of some promised help from Grandfather and their relatively well-to-do siblings along the way. To make ends meet, they had to resort to all kinds of desperate measures. Mother, as I recall, took in laundry and, three times a week, walked eight kilometres to Karlsruhe to help a well-to-do Jewish family with some of their domestic chores. In the main, she helped out with the field work on the family farm, with only scraps of food as her remuneration.

I was born in the new house, which still stands in its original form. But, understandably, my memories from my early childhood were not very happy ones. Mother tried hard to accept her station in life, but she never really found solace in the priest's assurance that a camel would find its way through the eye of a needle before a rich man would find his way to heaven. For one thing, no one she knew had ever laid eyes on a live camel to appreciate how difficult it would be; for another, she would have gladly traded her own salvation in heaven for the happiness of her children and for sufficient wealth to feed them properly.

Ludwig, 10 years my senior, and Lina, 8 years older, attended school. Erich went to kindergarten, leaving me to either accompany mother on her chores or take shelter with friendly neighbours.

Rösel never attempted to control her anger and frustrations, which all too often she took out on her children. I was her favourite, but she had strange ways of expressing her love and affection. As I got older, she insisted on taking me wherever she went, sometimes exposing me to scenes in which she publicly accosted town functionaries or her siblings, whom she blamed for some of her misfortune.

I wanted to start this story with the New School because that's where Joan—or rather Hanna, as she was then—and I met for the second time in

Grade 2 in 1938 at Forchheim's school. The teacher at the back is Herr Kraus, killed on the eastern front early in the war. Frank is the third boy from the right, second row from bottom.

our short lives. The first was during our baptism. I have no recollection of that event, but I am told that we disappointed both the Kistners, Emil and Berta, who had been hoping for another boy, and my parents, who would have much preferred to balance out the family with another girl.

Hanna behaved as if she were being offered as a sacrifice to God. She exercised her vocal cords to test the acoustics in the alcove behind the altar at St. Martins in a manner that would have overshadowed the combined volume of the organ and the 30-person church choir. Being a week older and therefore much more mature, I, according to people attending the ceremony, acted in a more restrained manner.

Normally, of course, it would have been in kindergarten where Hanna and I met next, but when Rösel took me there to be put in charge of the nuns, fearsome-looking creatures that they were, I coined the phrase later to be uttered by our youngest son, Peter. When faced with the same traumatic experience of being liberated from his mother's apron strings and put in the care of a kindergarten teacher, he said: "I am not staying here and that's final!"

So I missed out on the all-important first part of a good Catholic education. For instance, I did not know, until much later, that looking at oneself in the mirror without first covering certain parts of the body was a serious offence. I probably escaped 10,000 years of purgatory by the mere fact that we didn't have a mirror sufficiently large to reflect the full dimensions of a person's anatomy. Instead, I spent much of my time as a child sitting at one end of a field or another, observing my mother weeding or hoeing Tante Johanna's crops.

In any case, Hanna and I did meet again, and while I don't remember the occasion exactly, it could well have been during recess on our first day of school, having a drink of water at the pump that dominated the centre of the schoolyard. It would have been the kind of thing to which she was attracted because it provided ample opportunity for all kinds of mischief. The pump was a huge contraption that also served as the watering hole for the neighbouring houses and cattle. (A central water system for the town had to wait another 10 years until after the war.) The big spout had a hole on top from which one could coax a squirt of water by blocking the main flow. So it required one person to operate the pump handle, another to block the end of the spout, while the third took nourishment out of the top hole. With about 60 six-year-olds standing in close proximity awaiting their turn, not even the most scrupulous of the supervisors could detect all the misdeeds committed in such a scrum.

Hanna was a tiny little sprout. Her Onkel Otto, Berta's brother-in-law, called her *Pfutzen,* meaning pimple. Even at the age when we started school together, she was always in a hurry, always involved with some scheme that seldom conformed with any agenda the teacher had in mind. With just the slightest move of her head, she had a way of making the braids that contained her beautiful black hair fly through space as if they had a mind of their own.

Hanna's Tante Anna, Berta's sister, and her Onkel Otto actually became her second set of parents. They operated a small convenience store that was an ideal outlet for her boundless energy. Once properly channelled, it earned her room and board, relieving Berta not only of that burden, but also of the challenge of taming the little tiger, something that had seemed to be a fruitless effort.

Since both of us were born with the healthiest instinct for curiosity, Hanna and I could also have met at the moment when someone in the classroom sitting closest to the window observed a Zeppelin cruising by on the horizon. Normally, looking out of the window would have met with a very stern warning or even the strap, but I suppose Herr Kraus, the teacher, whom I remember so fondly, had his own curiosity aroused enough to let us all run outside to observe this phenomenon. How sad I was to learn a short time later that he had given his life for the "Fatherland," being among the first to be summoned by the Führer to serve on the eastern front during the Second World War.

Life in Forchheim was still very agrarian, much as it had been for hundreds of years. The Wright Brothers had accomplished the previously impossible feat of free flight 40 years earlier, and the Red Baron and his contemporaries brought warfare into the modern age with their exploits during the First World War. By 1935 air passenger and mail service was well established in various parts of the world. However, in our part, even the conventional use of automobiles was still in its infancy, and it was a rarity to see an airplane or an airship. Gotlieb Daimler had built the first four-wheel motor-driven car 45 years earlier, and I can recall only two or three privately owned cars in town.

My Leibold uncle Otto had one of them. I recall my first ride in it at the age of five. He used to make it a practice, imposed on him by Tante

Gretel, to take me or one of my siblings or cousins along on his weekly business trips to the city. This, Tante Gretel speculated, would prevent him from making too many unscheduled stops at various bars or other places of questionable repute along the way. She was always most curious to know how we had enjoyed the trip and where we had all been. I could not aspire in my wildest dreams to breaking out of the station God had allocated for my family, but there was nevertheless a certain comfort and prestige to being related to Onkel Otto and his family.

Such luxuries were enjoyed very seldom. The school year was planned to coincide with the rhythm of the place. There was a recess in the spring and fall to free up extra hands for work in the fields. Certain fieldwork had to be timed to coincide with the religious holidays. For instance, no one would plant anything before certain saintly observances in the spring. Once a year, cow barns and pigpens were painted and whitewashed, and this, too, had some religious connection since the work was done only on Good Friday.

The Sabbath was strictly observed. It was obligatory to attend church service twice on Sundays. Any work except that which was absolutely necessary, like caring for the livestock, was strictly taboo. An infraction would invariably result in sudden and severe retribution. I recall the time Onkel Otto Albecker, my mother's brother-in-law, set about on a Sunday evening to sharpen the scythe the men would be using for harvesting hay the following morning. He ended up, to no one's surprise, with a nasty cut to his hand. I remember Tante Johanna praising the Lord for His leniency in not striking him dead on the spot.

Not having any fields ourselves, we were nevertheless kept busy with Mom's family estate and its livestock. The animals were often treated with greater respect, tenderness, and care than members of the family. The place was totally self-sufficient. There was enough land to grow all the feed needed for the livestock, which included two or at times three cows, several pigs, chickens, geese, and ducks. Grandpa kept several hives of bees. The farm also produced all the grain (which was ground into flour), potatoes, and vegetables needed throughout the year.

I recall these early years and the time spent at Grandpa's place fondly. For one thing, my four cousins Lore, Hilde, Veronika, and Christa, all about my age, were a lot of fun to be with and never showed any reluctance to participate in all kinds of mischief, be it an expedition to discover where one of the cats was hiding a new batch of kittens, or exploring the wonders hidden in the forbidden grounds of Grandpa's workshop and private domain.

Once a year there would be a *Schlachtfest* [sausage festival]. It, too, was scripted by the rules of time-honoured tradition. The butcher, who only made house calls, came to preside over festivities. It was a production planned and timed to the last detail, and it involved the extended family and the immediate neighbourhood. By the end of the day, everything but the squeal of the pig had been converted to sausages, hams, pails of lard, and a year's worth of other delectables.

Another great event of the season was the thrashing of the grain after the harvest. There was a commonly owned thrasher in town, which was made available to everyone. It was driven by a monstrous steam engine and innumerable belts and sprockets. During the harvest season it operated 24 hours a day. Everyone would bring their harvest stacked as high as possible on farm wagons and would park in a lineup that could stretch for half a kilometre along the road back to town. Some of the men would collectively operate the machine while others would keep the line moving by hand.

For the kids this was always a great time. For the parents, who had just finished the back-breaking harvest, all of it done by hand of course, it was a festive time as well, with everyone usually in the best of spirits. The noisy monster worked away at a steady pace, leaving lots of time for tasting and comparing some of the new fruit wines the season had produced. The women would outdo themselves in supplying regular meals and snacks to the site, and they contributed their laughter and songs to the festivities.

Nothing was wasted. No one had ever heard of artificial fertilizer. Human waste was preserved and collected and mixed with the cow and pig manure to be spread on the fields in the fall as additional nutrients for the soil. The size of the manure piles in front of the farmer's house was seen as a measure of wealth and prosperity. Liquid sewage was stored in large underground pits and hauled onto the fields in wooden tanks the size of a regular wagon. Not everyone could afford to maintain such a conveyance, so it had to be rented from a more enterprising establishment. To get this equipment returned to its source as quickly as possible, the work started early in the morning, and it often happened that the last load was dumped after dark.

This was the case on the occasion when I, together with my cousin Lore, came perilously close to meeting our maker or at least suffering most grievous punishment. We were assigned the critical role of tending the cows and coaxing them to periodically move the conveyance so that the precious cargo would be evenly spread. Onkel Otto was standing on top, near the rear of the tank, discharging the smelly contents with the aid of a specially crafted wooden shovel. Meanwhile, the cows, past their mealtime, in desperate need of milking, and tortured by swarms of mosquitoes and other flying objects attracted by the aroma of the enterprise, had become ever more restless. The sun was setting over the Rhine, and worse, the wagon was facing in the direction of the barn. This was a recipe for disaster.

When the cows decided to lunge forward, Lore and I hung on for dear life, but Onkel Otto lost his balance and, with his arms flailing, disappeared into the sewage tank. Lore and I, hoping to assist in the rescue, ran to the rear, leaving the cows unattended. They saw that as a signal to beat a hasty homeward course. We found ourselves chasing the carriage, which was only half discharged. Otto's hands showed first at the top, then his head, dripping with the smelly wet. Then the whole of Otto hit the ground running—and not in the direction of the disappearing cows.

Lore took off in one direction, I in another. This way, I reasoned, he would not get us both. The chase went on long enough for the cows to reach the barn well before we did, and Otto came close on several occasions. However, he ended up sneaking through one of the town's back streets, Lore and I through another, all the while contemplating whether we should consider running away from home for good. We were ushered to bed without supper and were told not to show our faces in the morning until Otto had gone to work. Tante Johanna assured us his disposition would improve in time; 24 hours might persuade him to render a more lenient punishment. In fact, this turned out to be not much more than several days of silent treatment

At first sight, Forchheim's agricultural way of life might seem rather primitive. However, looking at it from the perspective of the end of the 20th century, it is amazing how sophisticated a social structure had evolved, and how rich its benefits were even by today's standards.

In 1883, when Canada's Confederation was only 16 years old, the popular German chancellor Otto von Bismarck established the world's first modern universal social benefits system. The benefits from it were meagre, of course, and the system was sorely tested during the wars and the bad economic times, but it survived and became the model for most Western countries to follow.

The greatest benefits flowed from the church, which was the centre of all activity in rural Germany. Supported by the government through taxation and other sources of public funding, and supplemented by its own resources, the church offered a rich menu of social services and amenities. It was the focal point of most cultural activities, such as organized sports, drama clubs (I starred as Escamillo in a production of *Carmen* at the age of 18), and a host of stimulating activities aimed at youths, seniors, and other special interest groups. The nuns provided daycare for children and infants and, even by today's standards, rather sophisticated home care, including palliative care and other health services.

Forchheim had about 2,800 inhabitants in the 1930s. They were served by one doctor who made his regular house calls, leaving the rest to the nuns. The busiest among the health professionals was the midwife. Like the doctor, she practised her trade in the expectant mother's bedroom, assisted only by a kindly neighbour, whose main function it was to keep the menfolk at bay and the water boiling. The system was primitive only in the sense that penicillin did not come into use until 1943 and few of the drugs and hospital facilities we now consider indispensable had been developed.

The church was also key in education. The priest and his aides were part of the formal school curriculum. Schooling was, of course, compulsory and, apart from an isolated case of mental disability, there was no illiteracy.

Other responsibilities were divided between the town and the church. The single policeman doubled as the town crier. There was no need for a lawyer. Births, marriages, and deaths were recorded by the church. The town's municipal officials kept all other demographic data. They had all the necessary authority to probate wills and settle any disputes arising from the succession of property and the allocation, or use, of the assets held in common.

With regard to political events outside the community, it was the priest to whom the people looked for elucidation and guidance. His judgement was delivered from the pulpit during High Mass every Sunday, giving the parishioners the comfort and trust that he and God would guide and protect them from any evil.

There were no telephones. Television arrived long after the Second World War. At his print shop, Uncle Otto operated a printing press and a modest publishing business. He also published a weekly newsletter. The business is still in the family, connected to modern stationery and toy stores.

Naturally, the First World War and the economic chaos had disrupted the tranquillity of the place. There were few families whose lives had not been affected. The leaders of the National Socialist German Workers' Party (the Nazi party) inspired hope that turned to euphoria when this new populist movement, to everyone's surprise, delivered on the promises which had earned it a mandate in 1932. In no time at all, the regime restored full employment, helping it win the fatal plebiscite that gave Adolf Hitler his dictatorial powers in 1934, when I was two years old.

Economic recovery brought the pride, self-confidence, and respect that comes with ascent to full membership in the family of the world's industrial nations. Massive public works projects were started almost immediately. Work began on building the autobahn bridges and modern infrastructure projects that heralded the dawn of a new industrial age. It was easy at first to ignore the fact that some of the enterprise was geared to military purposes. Most people were much too preoccupied with rebuilding their own lives and learning to reconcile new and old ways of doing things. In most cases, they were just grateful to be working and glad to have some hope for the future restored.

I remember how happy Mom was to prepare for Christmas at the end of 1935, the first year Dad was back working full-time. It had been a long while since we'd had ample supplies for cooking and baking and even a few pennies to spare, which aroused faint hope regarding the prospect of presents. Mom and Dad always took us on an annual window-shopping trip to Karlsruhe before Christmas. We would spend hours looking at display windows and watching with fascination the electric trains, moving toys, and elaborate arrangements of toy soldiers, all of which we could only dream of ever owning.

However, this year, after supper on Christmas Eve, everyone adjourned to the *Guten Stube*, the living room, which apart from Christmas Eve was only used for weddings, first communions, or funerals. After the visit of the Christ child (a neighbour in a white dress and veil) and the obligatory prayers and songs, Santa arrived to lecture us on the virtues of being good rather than bad and to announce that, on balance, in this house, he was able to observe more of the former than the latter. He then stepped outside, just long enough to create some doubt, before returning with a large package, which he asked Dad to help him open.

Mom was pretending to be busy with something behind the tree in an attempt to hide her tears. Looking at my siblings, I thought she was probably afraid our eyes would roll out of their sockets. And there it was, a medieval castle complete with a drawbridge, several towers, and parts for building a moat. But that was not all. Lina got a little doll, and each of us boys got an additional present as well. Mine was a clay soldier on horseback, who was obviously the king of the castle. It had to be the happiest day of my life.

To show just how unusual this was, even today Joan laments the fact that she never wanted anything more in all the world than a simple little doll, but, despite her two sets of parents, she never got her wish. Perhaps she might take comfort in the fact that my gift that special Christmas was accompanied by a lot of grief and disappointment later. During a visit by a neighbour's boy two years my junior, my most precious possession, the proud clay horse and rider, ended up broken. So heartbroken was I that when I was introduced to the boy—now a senior executive of a large corporation—many years later in Forchheim, I blurted out without thinking: "You are the guy who broke my horse soldier!"

The following year we got even more accessories to fill in the dreams and fantasies we had built around the castle, including new toy soldiers. These should have been our first warning of things to come, but their contemporary uniforms held no significance for us. There was also a windup *Panzer* [tank], able to climb up the steepest hurdle we could build and not dissimilar to the images we had seen of weapons the Führer was having built to restore Germany's military strength. We were told this was necessary if Germany was never to fall prey again to the forces that had enslaved us for so long.

The Nazi message was not accepted without question. Our elders had begun to worry. I remember Dad, one day in about 1937, being one of the first among our neighbours to get his *Volks-Empfaenger*, a radio allotted to every industrial worker tied to a payroll deduction scheme. One could sign up for ownership of a Volkswagen, as well, but Dad felt that to be just a little too pretentious for someone of his status in the community. Erich and I were dispatched to invite the neighbours to listen to the Führer speak at six o'clock that very night. To us kids it was pure magic, but the older folks spent much time afterwards, not so much discussing the new technology as the ominous message contained in the speech. Everyone looked deeply concerned. I knew because Dad's tobacco pipe emitted its puffs in rapid succession, which always indicated some extraordinarily deep cerebral activity.

They didn't have to wait long for other signs of the events that were to unfold. Forchheim was invaded by an army of contractors commissioned to build military installations, and their workers had to be billeted in private homes. To our great delight, our worker was a truck owner-operator who parked his noisy monster in our yard and gave us the occasional ride. Work started on the construction of the Siegfried Line, which was intended to guard against hostility by the French across the Rhine. There was a flurry of activity in our area: massive bunkers and pillboxes were constructed all along the Rhine and at other strategic locations inland. This, of course, was a clear indication that the powers that be in Berlin were intending to allow history to repeat itself.

I was much too young to understand or be concerned about these developments, and whatever views my siblings held at their age would have echoed those of our elders. Hitler justified the invasion of Austria and Czechoslovakia as an attempt to reintegrate the millions of German ethnics whose cultural links to the Fatherland remained strong and who were sympathetic to the new regime in Germany. People in Forchheim, at first at least, seemed to be persuaded by these arguments.

Then there were all those rumours about the Jews, which were puzzling to Forchheim's inhabitants. Everyone knew that the Nazis laid much of the blame for the crisis Germany had to endure during the '20s and '30s on the Jewish establishment. But there were no Jewish people in Forchheim, nor did our contact with them on the outside support such a claim. Apart from the occasional salesman or money lender, who made his annual rounds selling implements and the like or helping farmers add to their livestock, mostly on credit, the only direct contact we had was with the family Mom worked for in Karlsruhe. They were kind and charitable people who quite often sent home little presents for us. I remember how distraught my mother was when she learned in 1938 that they'd had to flee to Switzerland, leaving behind their business, their home, and most of their belongings. But not even then, at least in our part of Germany, did anyone have any idea of the terrible plans Hitler had in mind for his Final Solution.

I suppose the drafting and the mobilization of the army finally brought home the reality of imminent war. Of course, for us kids it seemed exciting. Brother Ludwig, 10 years my senior, just missed the first draft, but we were all caught up in the gaiety and the enthusiasm of the young men as they marched through town, singing songs proclaiming their intention to take on the world. The scene I remember most is their final assembly at the soccer pitch where, now all decked out with their new uniforms, they swore an oath pledging their lives to the Fatherland. The priest was on hand to remind them that God had chosen their cause as the righteous one; it was, after all, engraved on their belt buckles: "*Gott mit uns*"—"God is with us." As I have often reflected, God must have had a very special affection for that first crop of Forchheimer youth because he allowed only a very few to return home.

Some of them, including Hanna's dad, Emil Kistner, were among the first to march into Poland in September 1939. In response, the English and the French declared war, removing any doubt that there would be a western front as well and that our part of Germany would be involved. The war was on.

CHAPTER 2

The War Years

What difference does it make to the dead ... whether the mad destruction is wrought under the name of totalitarianism or the holy name of liberty or democracy?

—Mahatma Gandhi, Indian nationalist and spiritual leader

As if it happened just yesterday, I can see our neighbour running up the street, people shouting questions at him as he went from house to house telling everyone that war had broken out with France and the town had to be evacuated before midnight. It was early September 1939 and Hitler had just launched his *blitzkrieg* [lightning war] against our neighbour over the Rhine. I was in Grade 2 and had come home from school to a scene of utter chaos and confusion.

All women and children, except boys over the age of 16, were ordered to assemble at the *Bahnhofsplatz*, the main square, by six o'clock that same evening to await transport. We were allowed to take only the most essential things, and in any case not more than we could carry. Mom went into hysterics; Dad and Ludwig, now 17, were not yet home from work. In several houses along our street, where husbands and sons were already away at war, women were crying, trying to arrange for someone to tend to their livestock. To top it all off, it started to rain, which turned into a ferocious thunderstorm.

Luckily, it wasn't long until Dad got home to take charge of the situation. We found shelter in Onkel Otto's store, which was right across from the little streetcar station where we would be picked up. The women without menfolk were told to set their pigs, goats, chickens, and geese free in their yards, and the men would organize themselves to look after them as much as possible. Finally, late in the evening, a fleet of open trucks arrived. People were packed like sardines into the backs of these trucks, and no one had any idea where we were going, except of course that is was in an easterly direction.

We were delivered to a small town in the Württemberg area, near Stuttgart. For the first night, Mom, Lina, Erich, and I were fortunate enough to be billeted in the local priest's house. Most were taken to school halls, where loose straw had been spread on floors as bedding. The following day, arrangements were made for more permanent quarters, with efforts to keep families together to be billeted with local farmers or business establishments. Not all the locals greeted us with open arms, but in the main, most people were generous and sympathetic to our plight.

Mercifully, the experience only lasted for about two weeks, but it was just the start of the disruption and sweeping change that war inflicts on ordinary people's lives. Hitler's blitzkrieg against France was over in 35 days, but for neither the victor nor the conquered would the world ever be the same again. We no sooner got home than we were jolted with even worse news. Dad had been told that the entire factory in which he worked would be converted to war production and that much of it would be relocated to Poland. He himself would be among the first to be dispatched to the new site. He was given no more than a few days to arrange his affairs before he had to leave. The family was to follow as soon as the aftermath of the Polish conflict had stabilized. Temporary arrangements for living quarters would be made for us, and we could anticipate generous assistance in acquiring permanent housing in or near the city of Poznań. For Mom and Dad the word "permanent" must have had a very ominous ring.

They were encouraged to dispose of the house into which they had invested so much of their sweat and blood, but which, on the other hand, must have still been a serious burden on them. There were many heated arguments with the relatives, who my parents hoped would help, either by carrying the load or at least by looking after the place until it became more certain what the future had in store for us. But in the end they walked away from it and, I am sure, left it all to the bank.

We arrived in Poland early in 1940, and were allocated an apartment that had been requisitioned from a Polish family. It was equipped with running water, flushing toilets, and even some form of central heating, something Mom thought she would not have any difficulty getting used to. Work had already started, just outside the city, on a subdivision that would provide us with our own permanent home.

It might seem odd, but all in all I have only happy memories of those early years in Poland. In 1941, a year after we had arrived in Poznań, we moved into our new house. It was not big, but it was comfortable. It was equipped with running hot and cold water, a bathtub and shower, a sanitary sewer, and a big garden. There were lots of friends to play with and lots to do. Dad started to raise rabbits that we had to feed and look after. I was even allowed to keep a little dog, my *Dackel* [dachshund] with his short crooked legs.

What's more, we had never seen our parents more happy and content. Dad, who back in Forchheim was never known to be quite as faithful in his church attendance as God—according to Pfarrer Dorer—demanded, even accompanied us to church every Sunday, usually for the special military service that featured a military band. Food was scarce, but we were better off than most. There were four categories of ration coupons. Germans from the Reich were rated highest. Next came the Germans who had been liberated in Poland (the *Volksdeutsche*), then the Germans from the Baltic States who had migrated to Poland to work in the factories. Finally, the Poles themselves were given some meagre rations that must have allowed them to just barely exist unless they had some connection to the rural farming areas, where presumably people managed much the same way they did at home in the Black Forest.

School was fun. Like all the kids my age, I responded with great enthusiasm to the attention that Hitler afforded the children and youth of the Reich. We were Germany's most precious resource. The authorities spared no effort or resources promoting youth activities. I was allowed to enrol in the *Jung Volk*, the precursor to Hitler Youth, in 1941, a year ahead of the enrolment age, which was 10. Membership in the Hitler Youth started at the age of 14.

When Hitler visited the factory in Poznań, all of us kids were wildly excited. Perhaps because I was the shortest and youngest member of our scout troop, I was chosen to present him with a bunch of flowers on his arrival. He was standing next to his car and talked to me briefly, but I was much too excited to remember what he said.

It would be wrong to compare the first stage of the Hitler Youth movement with anything other than the Boy Scouts or to think that Lord Baden-Powell was any less a hero than Hitler was to us at the time. Activities were very similar. There were the same outdoor jamborees, the pledges of allegiance, much the same hierarchy and order of advancement. There were differences, of course. The Jung Volk shirts were brown instead of green, and Hitler's Brown Shirts were already notorious for their attacks on Jews and ethnic minorities.

How proud I was the night I brought home my first uniform, complete with leather belt, shoulder strap, and tie. Dad took one look at me across the dinner table and asked if I knew where my new overcoat was. From the way the question was put, I had to assume that the coat must have suffered some grievous damage during one of the war games that had become our favourite pastime. The coat being brand new loden, this would have spelled ominous consequences.

"Go and get it please," he said. To my relief, I did find it in its proper place, and it did pass a quick inspection before I presented it to the assembly around the kitchen table.

"Perfect," he said. "Now I want you to put it on and eat your supper. I just don't want you to be cold, that's all."

Instead, I stormed out of the room in tears, humiliated by the laughter around the table. Everyone except me had been well aware of the purpose of the exercise. It was only much later that I understood Dad's aversion to brown shirts.

There was another occasion when Dad clashed with Hitler or his henchmen on philosophy. He often complained about how the Polish workers in the factory were treated. There were beatings and worse. The Gestapo rewarded anyone even slightly suspected of sabotage or treason with the death penalty. As a deterrent, the sentence was administered in public.

Whatever benefit the authorities expected from having the 10-year-olds in our Jung Volk troop attend such events, Dad was not visionary enough to recognize it. I recall him reacting with horror and outrage to the colourful account of my terrifying experience at such an event. "This time they have gone too far," Dad exclaimed, and he set out to confront the leaders of our troop, in spite of how dangerous it was to question the Führer's orders. Whatever he did, together with some of the other parents, it remained the one and only time we were treated to the spectacle of a public hanging.

I was much too young to understand what was happening, particularly to the Poles. They were treated perhaps no better than black people were still treated in the southern United States at the time. Poles were not allowed to ride in the same streetcar with the Germans, were under strict curfew and could not attend public gatherings of any sort. Perhaps worst of all, many of the men were interned in forced labour camps to make up for the labour shortages caused by the general mobilization of German troops. The Nazi rationale was to avenge the atrocities that were committed against the German ethnic minority before and after the outbreak of the war. Much, no doubt, was Hitler's propaganda, but we had first-hand accounts of some of the atrocities the Poles inflicted on the German ethnic minority after the hostilities had started.

Because of his position at the factory, Dad was under constant pressure to participate in and conform to the Nazi party's activities and policies. But he remained steadfast and loyal to his beliefs in a different brand of social democracy. Like everyone else, he supported Hitler's ideas at first, but once the extent to which Hitler was prepared to go to achieve his vision of a "workers' paradise" became obvious, Dad quickly lost his enthusiasm.

Risking his own situation, he tried to shelter his work crew, which later on included Russian prisoners of war, from the harsh treatment they were given at the factory. It was not unusual for some of his workers to spend their spare time helping out in our garden, even helping us dig the elaborate bomb shelter that became our playhouse. They would always leave with bags of garden produce, some of Mom's baking, and even the odd rabbit Dad had butchered and skinned for them. These acts of kindness and generosity did not remain unrewarded when the shoe was on the other foot at the end of the war, and the Germans had to flee the area in advance of the Russian "liberators."

Hitler ended the non-aggression pact with Stalin and mounted another blitzkrieg across the Russian plains in June of 1941. The German army took Kiev in September 1941 and moved on Leningrad and Moscow before the Russian winter, which had defeated Napoleon 130 years earlier, stalled the advance. For the German army, it was the beginning of the end.

In Poznań, the war was beginning to reach the city. There were two major bomb attacks on the city during the time we lived there. I was spared the second one, but the first was sufficient to leave me with permanent scars. The intention of the Allied air force was to target transportation infrastructures so as to interrupt the supply routes to the eastern front and to destroy industrial installations in and around the city. Instead, most if not all of the bombs fell on residential areas, both German and Polish. The attack itself was scary enough, even from the relative safety of our "playhouse." However, it is the images of the aftermath that will remain with me always, even though they pale in comparison to what was yet to come.

Late in the afternoon following the attack, Erich and I ventured into the city to see if we could find Dad, who had left for the factory as soon as the alarm was sounded to fight fire if necessary. He had not come home, but Mr. Kappes, perhaps the best friend our parents had in those days, had arrived in the company of his wife earlier in the day to report that Dad had stayed to help rescue people still buried under the rubble of the Kappeses' house, which had taken a direct hit. We knew Mr. and Mrs. Kappes as kind and generous people. They had no children of their own and had adopted us as nephews and nieces.

Mrs. Kappes was in desperate shape. She was delirious and in some kind of shock from which she never fully recovered. Their house had been totally destroyed, but worse, their basement, designated as a neighbourhood bomb shelter, was refuge to about 30 of their neighbours. As the house collapsed above them, it burst both the water and sewer pipes running through the basement. The rubble had blocked all the escape routes.

Mrs. Kappes spoke of the ordeal later. One of the neighbours, the only man at the scene, was trapped under a cupboard that had fallen over. The women, unable to extricate him, had to watch him drown in the rising sewer water.

Dad and Mr. Kappes arrived at the scene in time to help with the rescue. They had managed to dig through the rubble, opening a hole just large enough to pull out one person at a time. Only about a dozen people were pulled to safety before water filled the cavity. They stood helplessly by as the rest drowned, listening to their inhuman cries for help. By the time we arrived, the hole had been enlarged enough to permit the salvage of the remaining bodies, their faces grotesque masks of human suffering. I remember that, like Mrs. Kappes herself, most of them had lost the ends of their fingers as they tried to claw their way out of their brick and concrete tomb.

Dad, his face covered with mud and soot, was hardly recognizable when Erich and I met up with him at the site of the rubble that had been his friend's home. Both he and Mr. Kappes were still frantically engaged in the grisly task of retrieving the bodies of those who had drowned.

Just a short time later, as if the scars were not deep enough, I got another taste of what it was like to be part of the target for hundreds of bomber aircraft indiscriminately discharging their cargo on helpless victims, mostly old men, women, and children. It was during the night of September 2 in 1942, back in Forchheim. Mom had received special permission to travel, presumably for the purpose of winding up some unfinished business with the house. As usual, I was allowed to come along for the trip. We were only there a short while, but it was during one of the fiercest bomb attacks on Karlsruhe.

Several nights prior, the population in the area around Karlsruhe had been showered with leaflets dropped from planes with the message: "*Karlsruhe, Mannheim, Ludwigshafen ihr habt jetzt lang genug geschlafen*" ["Karlsruhe, Mannheim, Ludwigshafen, you have now slept enough"]. So one can't say they weren't warned. The basement of one of Grandpa Leibold's neighbours was the designated shelter. Mindful of my experience with bomb shelters, I literally had to be dragged there. Thankfully, Forchheim still did not have a central water or sanitary sewer system, so there was no fear of drowning, but the scene was nevertheless chaotic. Women were trying to console their frightened children, who were screaming after being ripped from their beds in the middle of the night.

It didn't take long before we heard the drone of the engines of what must have been more than 500 bombers directly overhead. The sound, even in the basement, was deafening. It even overpowered the noise of the flak battery, which was positioned just outside the town.

Incredibly, as the noise started, the basement fell silent. Then someone started to pray, and everyone fell in. It got louder and louder, as if they wanted to make sure God could hear them over the drone of the engines and the exploding bombs. The prayers spoke of the hour of our death, but I did not want to die. They reminded God of His promise of resurrection and His promise for life everlasting, but I couldn't figure out how He would ever find us under all that rubble.

Mercifully Grandpa, the only man there, must have shared my thoughts, because he took me by the hand to go outside where we could breathe. The target was eight kilometres away, and, Grandpa assured everyone later, apart from the shrapnel, screeching and whistling as it rained down and smashed the clay roof tiles, there was little danger.

The sky over the city was red, as if the devil had opened the gates to hell. I had never been more frightened. Grandpa told everyone later how proud he was of me because I didn't even cry. The danger having passed, I couldn't think of any reason to tell him that I had peed my pants instead.

CHAPTER 3

A Different Kind of Residential School

Never think that war, no matter how necessary nor how justified, is not a crime.

—Ernest Hemingway, American author

The 1942 bomb attacks on Poznań gave authorities the excuse, as if they had needed one, to close some of the schools in the city and send the boys to boarding schools in the outlying countryside. Girls, presumably, were more impervious to bomb attacks. Early in 1943 I was among half a dozen or so boys from my school who were sent from Poznań to the tiny village of Luckland near Oborniki, some 35 kilometres north of Poznań. Ludwig, by that time a journeyman tool-and-die maker, was working in Dad's factory. Lina had a job in the city as a sales clerk, and Erich had just started his apprenticeship training with the regional newspaper. I found it particularly hard to say goodbye to my little dog. He and I were inseparable. Dachshunds can be stubborn little creatures, and my Rex was no exception in his relationship to the rest of the family. But he had attached himself to me with all his devotion and obedience. I was never to see him again.

Luckland was a small village of about 300 people who were totally dependent for their livelihood on the *Rittergut* [Knight's Estate], a type of aristocrat-owned manor that pervaded the countryside in that part of eastern Europe. The village and the fields the villagers worked were all the hereditary property of a Prussian baronial family. The chateau at the farm housed four generations of people. The baron himself was in command of the regional *Volksturm* contingent, an army of 50- and 60-year-olds who were recruited toward the end of the war. He came home only on rare occasions and was unaccounted for at the end of the war. His son served as an officer on the eastern front and had been reported missing in action.

That left the baroness, one of the baron's elderly aunts, and his daughter-in-law in charge of the estate. There were also two girls, somewhat younger than ourselves, rounding out the family. There must have been at least a hundred dairy cows, hundreds of pigs, and other assorted livestock on the estate. It extended as far as the eye could see, growing everything from several varieties of grain to corn, forage crops, and potatoes. It even had its own distillery, where they produced their special brand of Kartoffel Schnapps, the local form of vodka.

The school, apart from the chateau and some of the farm buildings, was the only substantial structure in town. It was a two-storey sandstone building that in the past might have served as guest house for the Rittergut. There were 38 of us, all about 11 years old, who had been transplanted from different schools in the city and the surrounding area. The parents of most of the boys were East and West Prussians from the part of Poland annexed by King Friedrich Wilhelm II in 1795 and wrested from Germany after the First World War. Other boys, who had been relocated to Poznań, came from the German ethnic communities of the Baltic States. Only a few of the students, like myself, were "Reich's German," a designation given those who, like my parents, had come from Germany proper. Everyone seemed to speak a different dialect, with mine being the most convoluted and least understood. I was among the smallest of the group, and since I'd never been separated from my parents before, no one could possibly have been more homesick or shed more tears crying himself to sleep than I did during the first few weeks of our stay.

The school was operated under the auspices of the KLV *(Kinder Land Verschickung)*, an innocent enough program to remove children from harm's way to a safe and wholesome environment in the countryside. I am certain that there must have been a rationale for affording this protection only to boys, but I am not aware that it was ever explained.

In terms of modern facilities, such as running water or sanitary sewer, the school was no less primitive than the one to which I was accustomed in Forchheim. At first there was only a two-holer outhouse, which had to accommodate both students and staff, including two female members. The sign on the door proclaimed a strict two-minute time limit on any visitor's residency time. *"Zwei minuten wird geschissen—wer länger scheisst wird rausgeschmissen."*

The bedrooms were small and very crowded, with 6 to 10 of us sleeping in bunk beds nailed together with rough lumber and equipped with large, burlap, straw-filled sacks. Among the fun activities was the periodic changing of the straw, which allowed us a day of terrorizing the farm.

All attempts at hygiene centred on the well in the backyard, not unlike the one in the Forchheim schoolhouse. Only in the wintertime were we allowed inside to wash in a zinc tub with moderately warm water. Once every two weeks, again only in winter, we used the same tub to take a bath. In the summer, bathing was done once a week in the Warta River, about four kilometres away.

It was a Spartan, isolated existence. The program of studies and physical education was tailored to the Hitler Youth creed of "*Hart wie Krupp-Stahl—Zäh wie Leder—Flink wie ein Windhund*" ["Hard as Krupp manufactured steel, tough as leather, swift as a greyhound"]. We were taught endurance and self-reliance to an extreme. We were the hope of Germany, the new breed. Our destiny was to be among the leaders of a nation that would dominate the world. But at age 11 we knew very little of what that meant, other than the need to become superior in physical strength, smarter in everything that was demanded of us, and unwavering in our belief in the ideals, whatever they might be, to which the Führer had committed the Fatherland.

I had little trouble holding my own in the classroom and was quite adept in the use of my wits to talk myself out of the occasional fight, but when it came to sports, apart from my skills as both a fast sprinter and long-distance runner, I had a long way to go to qualify as a worthy member of a master race. For one thing, I was the only one among the group who had never learned to swim, a major flaw for someone who was destined to rule the world, parts of which could only be reached by crossing an ocean.

The problem was solved during our very first outing to the Warta River for our swimming program. Once I had mustered up the courage to admit to my shortcomings, I was treated to the instructor's special attention. The first lesson turned out to be as simple and basic as it was effective. I was ordered to lie on my back in shallow water with my head tilted back as much as possible. He then put his hand under my chin and towed me out to the middle of the stream, at which point he released me to the elements. Somehow I made it to the other side, to the cheering of my friends. For the rest of the afternoon I was excused from the other activities so I could practise my new-found skills, because I was told that on the way home I would be on my own. I have been a reasonably good swimmer ever since.

Despite his disability, Lieutenant Boronovski personally supervised our sports activities and managed the phys-ed program. He was a veteran of the eastern front, to which he had contributed his left leg, earning him the Iron Cross First Class and the rank of lieutenant. Although he needed the help of a walking stick to get around, he was an imposing figure of a man, conducting himself with the discipline and precision befitting an officer of his rank. He was a trained teacher in his civilian life, but until the very end, we never saw him without his uniform.

It was not unusual for Lieutenant Boronovski to conduct a roll call in the middle of the night to inspect our clothes and personal belongings, which had to be properly maintained, folded with great precision, and stored at all times. Anybody caught with shoes that didn't reflect his image, or pants that weren't pressed, would spend the rest of the night bringing things in line for inspection before the early morning assembly. Incidentally, the pressing was a simple enough procedure. One just put whatever item had to be pressed between the straw sack and a sheet and slept on it.

On one occasion we had barely gone to sleep when we were ordered to assemble within 15 minutes and in full uniform. We were about to be examined and rated for bravery. The drill was simple enough. Every three or so minutes, one of us would be dispatched on a route that led along a little creek lined with willow bushes to the graveyard. There we had to find our way to the wooden cross, at the base of which we would deposit a slip of paper bearing our name. To return home we had to cut across the fields. I left in about the middle of the pack. The night was dark, cold, and scary. If curing fear of the dark was the purpose of the exercise, it failed miserably. I was chilled to the bone, least of all from the cold. About halfway to the graveyard I heard voices coming from the willows that sounded very much like those of two of my friends.

One of them had injured his foot stepping into a rut and was unsure whether he could continue. We decided to carry on together, and it wasn't long until the pain had miraculously disappeared. We stuck very close as we dredged our way through the graveyard. We crossed the fields together, but it says something about our obedience to school discipline that we were careful to stagger the final few metres back to the school in the same order we had left to give the appearance that we had made the trip alone.

Our nickname for Boronovski was "Old Shatterhand," after a prominent hero in Karl May's North American Indian novels, indicating the respect all of us had for him. He was no doubt the best teacher I ever had. Despite his tendency to be distant and aloof, we nevertheless felt drawn to him, perhaps because he was the nearest thing to a father. As we were cut off from any ties to family, the school quickly became a substitute to which we transferred our reliance and trust.

We were left with little time during the course of the day to reflect on our situation or feel homesick. Wake-up time was 6 a.m. The day started with a flag-raising ceremony attended in full uniform at 6:30. It was always a challenge to fight your way to the well or tub in order to get washed and dressed on time. The ceremony was preceded by an inspection, not only of the uniform and boots, but quite often of the inner workings of one's ears. Any signs of deposits there were removed immediately with the help of two comrades—one holding your head in the right position under the pump, while the other operated the handle.

Breakfast was served at 7 a.m., with school starting at 8, six days a week, year-round. Lunch was served in a common lunchroom at 12, followed by an hour downtime, meant for sleep, but which was usually occupied with horseplay. Then it was either back to the classroom for homework or out into the countryside for sports activities or war games or a combination of both.

The school curriculum itself varied little from what I had been accustomed to, except that the time set aside for homework and leisure activities was highly structured and included compulsory reading of certain books, such as those written by Karl May that featured tales of rugged outdoor men and adventurers. The school library boasted all 36 volumes Karl May had authored. After supper, unless we were involved with the choir or some other organized activity, we were allowed some private time to read, write letters, or build model airplanes or ships. Eight o'clock was lights out.

There was very little private space or time, but there was always lots of encouragement for individual initiative and personal development. The friendships we developed among ourselves in this highly structured and intense environment became as close as bonds between brothers. Thomas, whose parents came from Estonia, Albert, and Joachim were among my closest friends. Thomas could amuse us with his uncanny ability to blow a loud fart any time, anywhere. He reminded me of a story Dad liked to tell of a colleague he'd had during his years working on construction. This colleague had once made a bet, for two pints of beer, that he could climb a ladder, blowing a fart on every rung right to the top. The ladder had 14 rungs, and he would have won his bet had he not squeezed another one as he stepped onto the platform on top.

Thomas was like that. Any time we were out marching, it was customary for someone, often Thomas himself, to shout *"ein Lied"* ["a song"], which was a signal for him to blow his horn to the rhythm of the marching feet. No one would ever start singing until he had blown himself out.

There was never any shortage of ideas and interesting things to do. One such inspiration came from a female member of the staff, a teaching assistant who took pleasure in spending her weekends bathing nude in the Warta River under the hot summer sun of the Polish steppe. Albert, Thomas, two or three others, and I, for some reason, enjoyed her special confidence and affection. We were assigned special duties to guard her secret not only from the other students, but from the other two staff members as well.

No doubt *Schneewitchen,* or Snow White, the nickname we had affectionately attached to her, knew we could be counted on to thoroughly investigate just what she expected us to guard. We did not disappoint. This was an opportunity to put into practice our well-honed war game skills to sneak up on an unsuspecting enemy on our bellies and elbows. There were no close encounters or any physical contact, but we knew that she knew and she knew that we knew, which apparently was all that was required to satisfy everyone's needs. By today's standards, her well-tanned body was much too ample, but for us it became the model to which we attached our embryonic sexual fantasies.

How heartbroken we all were when she was replaced by a much older woman, who made it her mission to compete with Old Shatterhand in finding ever more innovative ways to make life miserable for us. Nobody, I am sure, remembers her real name. She was a witch in the truest sense of the word, so we named her *Die Hexe*—The Witch.

Perhaps surprisingly, unlike the more conventional schools, there was no corporal punishment backing up school discipline. However, the social penalties were no less severe and thorough. Any infraction of the rules resulted in the whole class being punished, with extra hours in the classroom or the withdrawal of certain privileges. Thus, tied to the dictum "one for all and all for one," it was an absolute rule never to squeal on or abandon anyone who was guilty of an infraction against the establishment. Instead the guilty party was liable to suffer a punishment much more severe than either Die Hexe or Old Shatterhand could ever have invented.

There was one occasion, however, when it was deemed necessary to make an exception to this rule. Someone had liberated a fancy leather-bound writing pad from another student for his own use. The thief was reported to Boronovski as having committed so grievous an infraction against the group that we had to insist that special arrangements be made to administer what we considered an appropriate punishment. We all refused to share a table with him at mealtimes and in the classroom. We asked that he not be allowed to participate in any formal ceremonies, including the raising and lowering of the flag.

Old Shatterhand promised to take the matter under advisement, but we decided to proceed with the administration of the first part of the penalty—shaving the offender's head—without his verdict. Things got out of hand as he was being tied to a bedpost to have his hair removed. There were fisticuffs, with him getting the worst of it. But for him, no doubt, the worst punishment of all was being ostracized by the entire school. Frau Herter, who worked in the kitchen, took pity on him and arranged to have him sleep and take his meals in her quarters. He was excused from attending school, and two days later Die Hexe put him on the train in Oborniki that would return him to Poznań.

We never saw him again, but there were some repercussions. His father was some kind of functionary with the Nazi party and had sufficient clout to launch an investigation into the affair. Some time later we were visited by an official-looking character in a black overcoat and hat who arrived on the scene by automobile to investigate the incident. We were never told, but it was rumoured that Old Shatterhand escaped with a strongly worded reprimand.

At certain times of the year we had to help out with the harvest on the estate. These were fun times, but it was part of the official policy that our contact with Polish children and the population generally be restricted to encounters under strict supervision. The villagers seemed desperately poor, deprived of even the most basic amenities. Their existence was primitive, serf-like. Everyone worked on the farm or at the distillery. I don't think any of the kids went to school. Apart from a little family chapel on the estate, there was no church, although on Sundays people were allowed to hitch up a wagon to attend church in Oborniki, six kilometres away, the closest town of any size. The houses were primitive, some with thatched roofs and very small windows. They were built close together along a dirt road.

Compared to Forchheim, this place was behind the moon. Instead of fancy "*potchambres*" substituting for inside toilets, they used ordinary tin cans or pails that were emptied through the back window in the morning. They had no need for gardens since the estate supplied them with most of their necessities, such as flour, dairy, and garden produce. In the early spring each family was allocated a pig to feed through the summer and butcher in the fall. In the summer the pig competed for the limited open space behind the house with the chickens and the outhouse. There was no evidence of any pens or shelters for the animals, so we assumed that in the winter the chickens shared the family's sparse living quarters.

The pigs played the main role at the *Schlachtfest* in the fall. Just as in Forchheim, this was an important social event, except that vodka was the preferred beverage to lubricate the procedure. There was even more gaiety than I would have observed in the Black Forest. The festivities took place in front of each house, with all the neighbours, their kids, and dogs in attendance. Nobody seemed to be in charge, but everybody seemed to know what to do. The animal was hit on the head with an axe. An expert slice across the throat sent the blood squirting to the ground. Someone operated the hind legs just as we did the pump handle on our well, presumably to expedite the flow.

Even the town's dogs worked with great precision to liberate from the scene the entrails that had been extracted from the belly of the beast, dragging them along the dusty street. The carcass was then lifted onto a plank supported by two sawhorses, where it was cut up and allocated to its various uses. It was an all-day event, with festivities lasting well into the night.

This routine, varying only with the seasons, continued until 1945 with little news from outside. Once a month, during the afternoon study periods, we were tutored in the art of letter writing to keep our parents informed of our activities and the progress we were making with our studies. No one, I'm sure, would have had any reason to doubt that their children were well cared for and privileged to receive such special training and education. Neither would there have been cause for the students to feel neglected or deprived in any way. As time wore on, we felt progressively less need for the affection of our parents and siblings. On the whole, we were happy, content, and secure.

There were some notable events that did serve to disrupt the routine. All too frequently, in fact, we were forced to share in the sorrow and grief of our comrades as they received an unexpected visit from their family with the dire news of a father or a brother killed in action. Normally, parents were discouraged from visiting, but exceptions were made to deal with such situations.

It was my mother who came to deliver the bad news of brother Ludwig being listed as missing in action shortly after the Allied invasion in Normandy on June 6, 1944. I found her in Boronovski's office after our return from a short field trip. It was not a happy scene. Frau Herter had tried her best to console her, but my mother had already been told that taking me home with her, as she'd intended, was out of the question. She went into hysterics, losing all control over her emotions. Together with two of my classmates, I was allowed to walk her back to the train in Oborniki, but the scene there as the train pulled out of the station, with her cries of agony and despair drowning out the clatter and noise of the engine, provided me with little comfort to help deal with the news she had brought—and even less reason to feel anything more than pity for my mother. I realized, perhaps for the first time, how estranged I had become from my parents and how reliant I had become on those around me for security, comfort, and support.

Fortunately, it was only a short time afterward that Mom could write with some good news about Ludwig, even if there was bad news about Lina and Erich. They had received word through the Red Cross that Ludwig, seriously wounded early in the action, had been taken prisoner by the British. As it turned out, he not only received the very best of medical attention, but spent the rest of the war in relative serenity on a farm in the English countryside. In the meantime, both Lina and Erich, who was only 16 at the time, had been called up to serve as part of what Josef Goebbels, Hitler's propaganda minister, called the Total War that would result in our total victory.

There were two memorable occasions when we were visited by an army messenger on a motorcycle. The first was on July 20, 1944, when I was 12. It was the first motorized vehicle we had seen in a long time, and our curiosity interfered with an important soccer game, the outcome of which remained undecided. His message, addressed to Old Shatterhand, informed us of the assassination attempt on the Führer.

Had the news been of injury to our parents, we could not have been more devastated. What a cowardly act! For days we talked about nothing else. We took up a collection of what little money we each had to send to the Red Cross to speed up his recovery. I, as the only one to ever meet the Führer in person, was allowed to tell of the experience in front of the assembly.

Of course, we were totally unaware that the war had taken a turn for the worse. We had no idea that a million Allied soldiers had crossed the English Channel in the last three weeks of June. In late August of that year, Paris was liberated by the Allied forces of the United States, Britain, and France. In Belgium, the Battle of the Bulge went General Eisenhower's way and the Allied march on the Rhine began. Of far more concern to us, if we'd known about it, was the collapse of the eastern front and the advantage the Soviet army had gained.

When, for the second time, a motorcycle trailing a big cloud of dust raced into the village, it was to deliver much more ominous news. It was January 14, 1945. We were halfway through clearing the tables and washing the dinner dishes when we were given 10 minutes to assemble in full uniform in the classroom. There Lieutenant Boronovski, his demeanour reflecting the gravity of the situation, told us that the Russian army had advanced to the outskirts of Poznań and that the fall of the city was imminent. We had been ordered to abandon the school without delay and to assist in the evacuation of the baron's family back to Germany.

There was no immediate news regarding the fate of any of our parents.

Most of us had come to the school as 11-year-olds. We had been there for just over two years, yet it was enough time to be conditioned to absorb such news without display of emotion or shedding tears. When I recall the event, which even today remains deeply etched in my mind, that fact seems to me perhaps the most remarkable of all.

My friend Joachim and I had a very special reason for finding this news difficult to accept. Just two days earlier it had been our turn to make the regular biweekly trip to Oborniki, the closest town with a post office, to pick up and deliver the mail and run some other errands. It was always something we looked forward to because it meant skipping school for a whole day, and the trip was considered a privilege and a reward for some academic or other meritorious achievement. We left right after breakfast in the morning and stayed in town to collect the mail late in the afternoon.

Hoping to perhaps catch a ride on one of the farm vehicles part of the way, we had stayed close to the road, but on the way back we took our usual shortcut through the woods. It had been late and getting dark when we left Oborniki, and there was a blanket of new snow on the ground. As I soon learned, our decision was the wrong one.

Frau Herter seemed to be most agitated as she ushered us into the kitchen, closing the door behind her. She was a kindly lady who for some unknown reason ended up with us from Heidelberg, which was only 50 kilometres from Forchheim. Because she and I spoke much the same German dialect, for which we were incessantly teased, I could always count on just a little extra attention from her. However, on this particular evening she had something other than a treat for me. First, she made us promise never to reveal the source of what she was about to tell us.

My parents, aware of the impending disaster and the turn the war was taking, had made plans to once again abandon their home and flee westward from Poznań. I was included in their plan. Dad had managed to commandeer a vehicle and driver from the factory to pick me up. They had arrived shortly after lunch, to be told by Lieutenant Boronovski that I was away for the day and that, even after my return, he would not be able to release me. There were heated arguments that Frau Herter had overheard. Mom simply repeated that she would not leave without me. She became more belligerent and inconsolable as time went on. But the car had to be back at the factory that night, and Dad finally had to drag her from the scene, literally kicking and screaming. As a final blow, I learned that they had left no more than half an hour before we arrived. Had Joachim and I chosen to walk the road on our way back, we could not have missed them.

Next, several of my friends came into the kitchen to tell me that I was to present myself to Old Shatterhand's quarters immediately. He had a small private office, which I had visited on only one other occasion. My voice was quivering as I entered the room. "Heil Hitler, Herr Lieutenant," I said.

He invited me to sit down. He must have suspected that I had been briefed on his encounter with my parents, but he spared me from having to break my promise to Frau Herter. He basically repeated what I already knew. Then he reminded me of our creed and the responsibility to my comrades: "One for all and all for one." He told me that the time had now come for us to prove ourselves and to put to the test what we had learned and trained for.

"I ask you now, would you desert your comrades at such a critical time?"

"Nein, Herr Lieutenant." But my voice was getting shaky again.

"I am very proud of you," he said, and then he did something neither he nor anyone else had done to me in a very long time. He stood up and pulled me close to him, stroking my head.

"I know that your brother Ludwig is all right in England," he said, "and I am sure that your parents got back to Poznań unharmed and that you will be reunited with them very soon." As I found out later, he wasn't sure about my parents' safety at all. In fact, he was convinced of the opposite and that was the reason he had refused to let me go.

Drowning in a wave of emotion, I managed to sneak up to our dormitory, forgetting all about Frau Herter's promise of a special supper. My whole body convulsed until I finally could let go of my tears. It was no longer anger. It wasn't homesickness or loneliness, but a deep sorrow for my mother. I could feel her pain and share in her utter despair, knowing that all her children would be without her love and protection as the dark descended in a most uncertain future.

If I only had a way to tell her that I was all right, that I was proud to stand by my comrades and trusted our leaders, that I had found a new home. But how could any mother possibly understand how her child could be conditioned at such a tender age to embrace an entirely new set of ideals, substituting them for the love and protection of his mother and father?

In any case, it was too late to worry about such things now. We were faced with the test of which the lieutenant had spoken. The order, we were told, came directly from the Führer's headquarters. We were given an hour to pack and prepare for departure. Our route would take us in a southwesterly direction back to the Fatherland, perhaps on the theory that the Russian army, hoping to beat the Western armies to the capital, would prefer a more direct route to Berlin.

We were to take only what we could get into our rucksacks, on top of which we would strap the three blankets each of us had. We were to double up on our underwear and would be allowed to wear our overcoats, which were not part of the uniform.

It was a sombre lot that turned up for the assembly. The night was bitterly cold, without a cloud in the sky, allowing the moon to dispel some of the darkness. Old Shatterhand spelled out the marching orders. Since we would have to march through the village to reach the estate, it would be important not to display any sign of weakness or defeat as we passed by the Polish houses. So we marched out singing and in proper formation. Our song was the obvious choice. It was the one that had spread anxiety and fear throughout the world with its lyrics asserting ownership of Germany and our determination to own the world: "*Denn Heute gehört uns Deutschland und Morgen die ganze Welt*" ["Because today we own Germany—tomorrow the whole world"]. Our neighbours had gathered in small groups, keeping to the shadows of their houses or peeking through their windows. We had given them no cause to feel hostile toward us; we had been taught to be respectful, polite, and courteous toward them. I doubt, however, that the same could be said for the baron and his family, who appeared to have kept their workers on a very short leash indeed. Their souls belonged to the estate. They were a depressed and conquered people, and it was only natural for them to hasten the hour of our departure and to celebrate their liberation.

Later that night, encamped at the estate, we discovered that in our haste we had forgotten to lower our flag at the school, which would have been an important symbolic gesture in the decommissioning of our domain. Naturally we were honour-bound to correct that oversight.

Very reluctantly, Boronovski gave his permission for a small group of six volunteers to undertake the mission. Everyone immediately looked at Albert and Thomas, who were the two tallest and burliest among us. Thomas was perhaps not as tough as Albert, but was even bigger. Another few hands went up, but then everyone looked at me because of my special talent and claim to fame: the ability to shinny up the flagpole every time the rope came off the top pulley, which happened frequently. This was no time to be a coward, but I did wish I could change my mind after the lieutenant took us into the mansion to give us his instructions.

We were to keep out of sight, finding our way behind the houses to the school and back. He was obviously worried that the Poles would take advantage of the situation to show some heroism of their own. Then he went to another room and came back with two guns. One was his own rifle, which we had learned to take apart and reassemble a hundred times, but had never been allowed to actually discharge. At the school we had only had air rifles for target practice. The other gun was one of the baron's shotguns. Boronovski loaded both and instructed Albert and Thomas, who were the only ones big enough to carry them, not to use them unless threatened, and then only to shoot into the air.

We thought we had made it to the school undetected, but we no sooner started to lower the flag than a crowd of people showed up on the street in front of the building. If we weren't scared before, we were scared now. I had my hand on the rope, hoping and praying that it would stay on the pulley, when Albert, facing the crowd, rifle in hand, began to sing our customary flag-lowering song: "*Ein Jungvolk Junge hält treu die Lager Wacht*" ["Dutifully a Jungvolk boy stands on guard"]. We were shaking with fear but had no choice but to chime in.

The flag came down without incident. One of the other fellows and I started to fold it, but Albert, who displayed his heroism several times more over the next few weeks, decided that we would carry it unfolded right down the middle of the street. Four of us led the parade, holding one corner each, with Albert and Thomas, brandishing the guns, following behind. We didn't know any other way to march but in step, and we headed right for the group of our neighbours blocking access to the road. Miraculously, they parted to let us through to march back to the farm without another incident.

In retrospect, I have nothing but the highest regard for those people whose good sense and judgement saved us, and perhaps themselves, from serious harm. For myself, it turned out to be the last time I ever marched in any formation or to anyone else's tune.

Back in the courtyard of the baron's chateau, our friends had built a huge bonfire, using straw and a pile of long poles for which the family would no longer have any use. The place was a beehive of activity. People, not all that keen to assist, were ordered around by the shrill voices of the baroness and her daughter-in-law. Boronovski, his cane in one hand, another of the baron's guns in the other, stood by to reinforce the orders.

We knew little of the family we had been ordered to protect. Once or twice a year we had been invited to their place for an outdoor picnic, but in general they were very distant and, as is typical of Prussian aristocracy, stiff and aloof. There were six draft horses available, which limited us to three wagons to be hitched up and loaded with everything imaginable. At first the family even brought furniture and paintings out of the mansion, but it was soon apparent that there would be little room for anything other than food for the horses and ourselves, clothes and bedding, and perhaps a few valuables the family could not bring themselves to leave behind.

One group, under the supervision of the Polish caretaker, was busy butchering about a dozen pigs. They were simply gutted, sliced in half and thrown into the bottom of each wagon. A pile of large pails filled with lard and jam, which came out of the mansion basement, was added to the load. On top of that were sacks filled with oats for the horses and with flour. Whatever space was left was simply filled with hay and straw for us to sleep on—and later to be fed to the animals.

It was early in the morning before we were ready to leave. There was a long delay as the crew to drive and tend the horses had to literally be recruited at gunpoint. The final act was bringing the elderly aunt out of the house and lifting her onto the wagon set aside for the family.

As the Polish workers mounted the wagons and the lieutenant began urging her to do likewise, even the baroness lost some of her composure. She would have known no other life. Her son and her grandchildren were born in this place, which had sustained their most privileged life. Embracing her grandchildren, who were crying uncontrollably, she stood for a time facing the stately mansion for one last look. Her fierce pride did not allow for tears, but her face nevertheless reflected the agony and pain with which she suppressed them. Then she turned, raised her head defiantly and walked away without so as much as a glance toward the people who had served her all their lives and now stood and watched in stunned silence. No one, among the adults at least, was under any illusion that they could ever return.

CHAPTER 4

The Great Trek

As long as war is regarded as wicked, it will always have its fascination.
When it is looked upon as vulgar, it will cease to be popular.

—Oscar Wilde, Irish dramatist, novelist, and poet

Some did wave gingerly, but there were very few tears from the throng of people who had gathered to watch us leave. For these Polish villagers it was a final goodbye to people who personified the system that had dominated their lives from cradle to grave—system to which they were completely subservient and on which they had been utterly dependent. A system that had spawned a poverty not only in the material sense, but also of the spirit. Rather than euphoria, however, what their faces reflected was the fear and anxiety of an uncertain future.

After all Poland, throughout half of its history, had been dominated by its powerful neighbours. Some left their mark with attempts at cultural assimilation, but the Mongols in the 10th century and the Russians in the 17th century came only to exploit and subjugate a once proud people. The Germans, who had reasserted their claim to major parts of the country, were only the latest of the invaders. Those familiar with the history of their country found it difficult to regard the Russians as liberators or even the lesser of two evils. The fear of what was to come appeared to be as strong as the instinct to punish the now departing tormentors.

Not everyone was as fortunate as we were to escape the wrath of those who remained. The baron's family asserted their complete dominance to the very last minute. People in most other places were not nearly as lucky. In some cases, as the Russian counteroffensive crossed the Polish border in January 1945 and the beleaguered Polish people became convinced of yet another reversal of fortune, they started celebrating their liberation by exacting revenge on the departing German families. There was widespread looting and killing on both the country estates and in the cities, including Poznań. Later, when we joined the Great Trek winding its way westward, we encountered a steady stream of refugees with stories of horrifying experiences. Some had fallen victim to physical abuse and torture by their Polish workers. One family claimed to have found their neighbours in the dining room of their mansion with their tongues nailed to the table.

It was a great relief to see an end to the frantic activity of the night as the wagon train finally got assembled and underway. Apart from having to cross the Warta River near Oborniki, we had no precise plan for our route, as far as I knew. Progress was very slow as the horses tried to find their footing and adjust to the dark. The only sound was that of the hooves and the crunching of snow under the heavily burdened wheels. I had huddled under a pile of loose hay and straw in the last wagon. Lieutenant Boronovski positioned himself immediately behind the drivers to keep an eye on the caravan in front. Frau Herter took charge of the wagon in the middle. The rest of the crew sat crowded together for warmth, divided between the two wagons assigned to us. Die Hexe had managed to arrange it so she could avoid her responsibility to help with the dramatic events unfolding. She had been away in the city on an errand and simply failed to return, for whatever reason. No one seemed to miss her much. There was no talk as each was occupied with his own thoughts. Dead tired and hungry, we even managed some sleep.

But the relative peace and tranquility didn't last long. We awoke to the cursing and swearing of the drivers, who were desperately trying to control the horses slithering along the icy road, threatening to crash into the lead wagon. There was a commotion up front where shadowy figures could be seen among the horses, taking hold of their reins to bring them around to head in the direction from which we had just come. The baroness's voice pierced the darkness, and once our eyes had adjusted to the scene we could see her defending her position with the help of a whip she had appropriated from the driver. Everything had come to a standstill in a mass of confusion by the time Old Shatterhand, whom we had trouble arousing from sleep, came to life to survey the situation. Judging from what we could see of the terrain, we were close to the Warta River, on the outskirts of Oborniki.

We were confronted by a commando unit of German soldiers with orders to take charge of the village and, with our help, keep control of the

Polish population to allow the orderly retreat of German forces to a new line of defence, one closer to the border between Poland and Germany. At first Boronovski tried to reason with them, pointing to his own orders and the fact that a bunch of 13-year-old kids and an officer with only one leg would hardly be of much assistance. However, the sergeant in command was obviously as interested in the provisions we carried in the wagon train as he was in the human cargo. He ordered the Polish drivers to turn around.

Lieutenant Boronovski, rifle in hand, immediately jumped off the wagon. He opened his heavy overcoat, revealing his uniform decorated with the Iron Cross. "You will have to proceed over my dead body, Herr *Unteroffizier*," he said.

"That," the under-officer replied, "can be arranged."

It was a tense standoff, but some of the obviously seasoned soldiers in the unit expressed doubts about being able to carry out their orders while running a kindergarten. One even told the sergeant that he would have to rely on himself alone to carry out the sentence should he decide on a firing squad to assassinate a German officer. In the end, reason prevailed and we were allowed to continue on our road.

Our wagon was now in the lead, and it was not very long before we reached the next obstacle. This time we were stopped by a roadblock manned by two German soldiers with orders to halt or reroute all traffic. We had reached the Warta River and they were about to destroy the bridge. We would have to make a detour of many kilometres to find another crossing, without any guarantee that it would still be intact.

Again Boronovski took charge. He simply grabbed the reins from the Polish driver and took the whip to the horses. The other wagons followed.

"You'll get yourself blown up," shouted one of the soldiers, but the lieutenant could still see some activity on the bridge. He got the horses to shift to a fast trot, slithering and sliding as they tried to find footing on the icy surface of the road, while the others followed at a slower pace.

"You've got no more than five minutes to get off this bridge," shouted the officer in charge of the demolition crew as we went by. We were barely a kilometre away when we heard the explosion, but the time was all we'd needed. For the moment we were safe.

It was just getting to be daylight as we approached a small stand of trees, now in unfamiliar territory. It would provide some shelter from the wind and an opportunity to rest the horses. It was a relief to get off the wagons and stretch our legs, and we discovered that we had all the provisions to make breakfast and prepare meals. We had to rely on an open fire to boil water and fry eggs, but breakfast had never tasted as good. With the warmth of the fire, the world started to look much more hospitable.

There was an almost jovial mood around the campfire. No one would ever again refer to Lieutenant Boronovski by his nickname unless it was with great respect. His stature was now bigger than life. Where in the past we had been trained to find comfort and security from within the collective and to build on its strength with our individual efforts, we now began to realize how utterly dependent we would be for our survival on the singular heroism and strength of our leader.

The cold was almost unbearable as we set out on our first day of the "Great Trek," a term borrowed perhaps from the history of the Boers' epic journey into the interior of their new colony in South Africa. As we began to converge with some of the arterial routes, we became part of the huge column of refugees who were fleeing from their German settlements in the Ukraine and other regions of western Russia and Poland ahead of the retreating German army. The conglomeration of vehicles of every description stretched for hundreds of kilometres, a steady stream of desperate old men, women, and children, dispossessed, haggard people making their way west to the safety of the Fatherland.

We burrowed deep into the hay and straw and huddled close to find warmth and shelter, but it never seemed enough to be comfortable. Furthermore, there was always something to impede progress. One of the horses would slip and fall. Some of the leather rigging would break, and our Polish drivers appeared in no hurry to make repairs. We had made very little progress by the time we stopped for our first night on the road at a farm outside a small village, not unlike the one from which we had come. The place appeared to be totally abandoned, with no sign of life other than the livestock in some of the barns where we found shelter for our own horses.

No one, it seemed, had cared for the milk cows in some time. They had been neither fed nor milked that day and were making their discomfort known. It might have been the only warm place within miles, but to sleep in it would have been impossible. The noise the cows made was deafening. The baroness and her daughter-in-law joined our Polish workers and set out to relieve some of the poor beasts' swollen udders, saving part of the milk into containers we found and simply spilling the rest on the ground. There was no electricity, and the only light came from some rather primitive oil lamps that would constantly flame out, turning the scene into one from a horror movie. The Polish drivers bedded down with their horses in one of the other barns, while the rest of us opted for our wagons as a place to try to get some sleep.

But there was to be little rest that night. From others on the trail we had picked up stories of looting and attacks from marauding groups of Poles seeking out isolated wagons as their prey. As well, we could sense that the Polish people who had worked the farm were hiding nearby, perhaps waiting for an opportunity to attack us. Boronovski ordered us to build a fire in the yard and to organize ourselves into groups of six, each of which would guard our encampment on an hourly rotation. He himself, perhaps most worried that our Polish drivers would make an escape, stayed up all night, rifle at the ready. The watch detail became the standard procedure for the rest of the trip, but apart from the fear and anxiety associated with it, we never suffered any harm.

The following morning we managed to find an old stove in one of the sheds to cook breakfast on, but when we went to the horse barn to invite our drivers to join us, we discovered that despite our vigilance, they had made their own plans during the night. Even though their prospects could hardly be much brighter in Poland, they had understandably chosen to face the future with their own families in the village. We were now on our own.

Again, we could sense that the people of the village were all around us. There was an eerie silence, interrupted only by the urgent bellowing of the still unfed cows. As we all huddled to assess our situation, it became painfully obvious how desperate it was.

At first we debated whether we should continue on foot, but that was quickly rejected because Boronovski would not be able to walk any distance with his prosthesis. As it was, he had great difficulty getting around, and the cold did not help his condition. Furthermore, we would have had to abandon the women and children we were charged to protect. The old lady was unable to walk and, to this point, had not been assisted off the wagon.

We also considered commandeering replacements from among the local men, but that would be fraught with danger and would likely again be only temporary. Then the baroness took charge. We had clearly formed the wrong impression of her and her daughter-in-law. Obviously they had not always overseen the management of their estate from the comfort of their mansion. They felt at ease around the horses and set to work getting them rigged and hitched to the wagons, shouting orders and giving instructions as they went about their business.

After giving us a brief course in driving the horses, the baroness mounted her wagon and steered it onto the road without looking back to see if anyone was following. Albert and Thomas were the first to practise our new-found skills, but in the end we all competed to take our turn. We were surprised at how well everything went. Other than the exposure to the cold, it was a fun experience.

During the day there was only a brief stop by a small creek, where we fed and watered the horses without unhitching them, and by evening we had made excellent progress. Even the weather had moderated somewhat to improve our spirits.

We began to settle into a sort of regular routine. It seemed that no one had any clear idea as to the route we should follow, nor do I recall the names of any of the sparsely populated towns we passed through. We had become part of the refugee flood, an unbroken chain winding its way in a southwesterly direction as far as the eye could see. Progress was slow in that the movement was restricted to the daylight hours and was frequently interrupted by mishaps or breakdowns of some of the wagons preceding us. Such interludes were not only welcome for the animals, but for us as well since they provided the opportunity to meet with other people and share in their experiences.

Some of the traffic continued during the night, but like us, most groups pulled into an open field or an abandoned farmyard to spend the night. We still had an ample supply of feed for the horses, and Frau Herter was very resourceful, making the best out of what she had available as she cooked over an open fire. With the help of the baroness, her daughter, and our own kitchen detail, she managed to provide us with a regular meal during the evening and a hot breakfast in the morning.

There were even one or two occasions when, after we had cared for the horses, we found sufficient fuel for a campfire that provided enough warmth and comfort to inspire some gaiety and singing, in which we were joined by some of our fellow travellers. During the day we chose periodically to walk along with the horses to stay warm. At night we often joined other groups with whom we shared watch detail. It wasn't long, however, before we were starkly reminded of the urgency of our mission.

It was during the early morning hours of my night watch. The world around us was still shrouded in darkness, the sky overcast with a thin layer of clouds. All of a sudden, one of my comrades pointed to a thunderstorm lighting up the eastern horizon—except that it was midwinter and I had never known of thunder and lightning at this time of the year. We decided to wake Boronovski, who quickly provided a much more ominous explanation for the red glow and the occasional rumble we could now hear. Distant as the sounds still were, they were our first introduction to the raw fear that was to become our constant companion for the rest of the trip. The war was catching up to us for real.

In no time, everybody was awake. Boronovski's orders were short and crisp. A detail was appointed to help Frau Herter prepare a light breakfast. The rest of us would feed the horses and hitch them to the wagons. We were off even before the light of a new day had a chance to erase the glow in the eastern sky.

There was now a sense of urgency. Our fellow travellers were competing more aggressively for their space on the road, attempting to pass slower vehicles and causing disturbances among the horses and altercations with those left behind. Having been on the road for several weeks, some people were in desperate circumstances, running short of food and provisions for their livestock. Others had tied cows to the back of their wagons to enable them to trade milk for other commodities, which slowed their progress.

We started to make periodic stops at larger farms—even those requiring a detour of several kilometres—to replenish our own supply of feed for the horses and fresh milk. The reception was never friendly, and on several occasions we had to make threatening gestures with our guns to press our case.

This of course slowed our progress even further. One week turned into two and we had no idea how much farther it would be to reach the point where our safety could be assured. To make matters worse, the weather started to deteriorate again. It snowed for several days, making the roads treacherous. At the same time, the temperature dropped to the point where even a short exposure resulted in frostbitten ears or fingers. Then, just as we thought things couldn't possibly get worse, disaster struck again.

It was early in the afternoon when our second wagon, going around a curve that was slightly banked, slid sideways into the ditch, breaking the rear wheel and causing the wagon to tip over. Miraculously, everyone managed to jump to safety and no one was hurt, but the cargo—dozens of large pails of preserves, pickled hams in wooden containers, and pails of lard—had all burst open, spilling its precious contents and creating a colourful contrast with the snow. Boronovski came running as fast as he could.

"God," he said, "if You are still with us, You have a strange way of giving us reassurance."

Fortunately, the two horses survived the mishap without injury. Had we been able to foretell later events, it might have been wiser to abandon the wreck, salvaging whatever we could. Instead, Boronovski asked for volunteers to lead the team back to a farm we had passed a short time earlier to commandeer a replacement.

By now, Albert, Thomas, and I had become a standing committee. Albert and Thomas, the two guns we had previously used over their shoulders, three others, and I volunteered for the task. We straightened out the mess the horses had got themselves into, wrapped ourselves in blankets and, with our feet covered with bits of canvas and clothing to stave off the worst of the cold, set out on the mission.

It seemed like many hours, but was of course much less than that, before we reached our destination, which was some distance off the road. They saw us coming. The only way into the place was through an open archway bridging buildings on both sides. There were about a dozen Polish workers, some of them with clubs in their hands, forming the reception committee. From a distance our group must have looked like a couple of horses on the loose, dragging some rubbish behind them. They must have wondered, when we got closer, what could have occasioned the visit of six ragged boys, the tallest of us perhaps just over five feet, just bundles of blankets and rags tumbling along behind the beasts.

I was the first to venture the suggestion that we should turn around. Albert never even slowed down. He let his gun slip off his shoulder and, with a motion that suggested he knew what he was doing, levered a shell into the barrel. Thomas was not far behind in loading the baron's shotgun. As we passed the reception committee, Thomas turned to walk with his back toward us, while Albert covered the front.

At the back end of the large courtyard we found what we had come for. There were several wagons. The problem was that they had to be pushed back by hand and then turned around to hitch up the horses—and a bunch of snow had drifted against them. Albert and Thomas were otherwise engaged and someone had to hang on to the horses, which left too few of us to dislodge the wagon and manoeuvre it to a position where we could hitch the horses. Albert was only a year older than the rest of us, making him a ripe 13, but he acted like a grown-up who was not about to lose his cool. He waved his gun barrel, gesturing to some of our hosts to lend a hand. Nobody moved.

What happened next made my blood curdle and my heart jump to my throat. Albert raised the gun and pulled the trigger. The bullet hit the side of a building, splitting the frigid air with its whining sound as it ricocheted into the void. He then lifted the gun to his shoulder, taking aim at the men still grouped at the entrance. Thomas followed his lead, making his barrel move between the wagon and Albert's target to reinforce our demands.

This time they got the message. Several dropped their clubs and put their hands in the air as they made their way behind one of the wagons to put their shoulders to the wheels. Shaking with fear, I was hanging onto the horses when, to my surprise, two of the men offered to take the reins and attach the rigging to the wagon. I was even more surprised when one of them walked into a nearby shed to fetch a long leather strap to replace one that we had roughly knotted together after it had broken a couple of days earlier.

This inspired Albert to make his own visit to the shed, dragging out as much of the gear as he could and loading it on the wagon. "Who knows," he said later, "when we might need it for ourselves." Meanwhile, Thomas nervously kept his shotgun raised at the ready.

It was now time to make our exit. Thomas marched ahead and Albert brought up the rear. The rest of us had climbed up on the wagon, using the whip to get the horses to overcome their reluctance to exchange the warmth and comfort of a nearby barn, which they could undoubtedly smell, for the open road. When they finally moved, it was in a fast trot, leaving our two sharpshooters to catch us on the fly.

Just as after our flag-retrieving trip, there was a hero's welcome awaiting us when we got back, but we were much more interested in the small fire they had built to stay warm. In later years I would be caught many times in critical situations—for example, when I had to brave -40°F temperatures in northern British Columbia—but I don't think I ever came as close to freezing to death as I did that day.

Incidentally, Lieutenant Boronovski took Albert aside to point out to him that he had failed to discharge the empty shell from the rifle, meaning that he could not have fired a second round without reloading. I doubt that Thomas would have mustered enough courage to pull the trigger on his shotgun. At the time we attributed our safe departure to the cowardliness of the workers, but as with the baron's villagers, it was undoubtedly their good sense, and perhaps their charity and sympathy, that helped us escape the scene unscathed.

Incidents like this tended to reinforce our confidence and courage as long as we stayed together as a group and could depend on our leader. We did not have access to news of how the war was progressing in the west, while people on the road from the east told us of being attacked by low-flying aircraft and of the unspeakable horrors to which they had been subjected by the Russian liberators. Both these factors helped us to stay focused and to deal with some of the adversity that made our journey increasingly difficult from day to day and made our mission ever more urgent.

We were driving the horses until they were totally exhausted. Their coats covered in a thick layer of frost, foam dripping from their mouths, their eyes showing panic and confusion, they dragged themselves along, giving us the last ounce of their great energy. The roads were very narrow in places, making it almost impossible to pass slower traffic. There were constant arguments and fights as the urgent rush of man and beast made unavoidable contact.

It was on such an occasion that we had to abandon the replacement wagon we had risked our lives to find just two days earlier. We were passing a group that had stopped in front of us on the side of the road when one of our horses suddenly halted to reach for straw being fed to the other horses. The horse to its right lost its footing and fell, sliding under one of the parked wagons.

It took us the rest of the day to untangle the mess. In the end, we had to destroy two of the horses, including one of our own. It meant abandoning a critical part of our cargo that could not be accommodated within the remaining two wagons. The family had to make the painful decision of parting with some more of the belongings that were not essential to our survival.

We made camp close by for the night, but none of us got much sleep. We had now been on the road for 10 days, and by all calculations we should have been near the Neise River, the last obstacle between us and Germany. The old lady was seriously ill. She had not been off the wagon for several days, and the baroness and her daughter-in-law were hard to console. All our senses were now tuned to the sounds of the battle lighting up the eastern sky, adding to our fear and anxiety. No one spoke of it, but it seemed clear that we were losing the race against time.

We were not alone in our misery. Everywhere along the road we found abandoned vehicles, even some tractors that had exhausted their supply of fuel. Dead animals, their bellies bloated, cluttered the landscape. Slowly our morale started to wane, and panic began to set in. When, two days later, cold, hungry, and utterly exhausted, we entered a small town near the border, our spirits were at their lowest ebb ever.

The place was crowded with refugees. Some of the men among them were obvious deserters, but they helped to give the place some semblance of organization. The town square served as a feeding station. The smell of hot stew filled our nostrils. Open spits were used to cook meat, and the baroness generously contributed several sides of the pork we had slept on throughout the trip.

The place was rife with rumours. Some said that the Western Allies had offered to cease hostilities in the west and join a revitalized German army to fight against the Russians. Another "reliable" source claimed there was a counteroffensive well underway. The plan was to lure the Russians into

As the German troops fought a last-ditch battle against the French forces flooding across the Rhine, the roads were clogged with refugees like these from Mörsch and Forchheim.

a trap, allow them to penetrate deep into Poland and then close off their supply routes from behind. That naturally had to be the reason why the Russians had been allowed to advance so far. How could we have been so blind as to doubt that the Führer had a plan?

It was certainly tempting to find comfort in these rumours and to rest, fill our bellies, get some sleep. But rumour also had it that plans were afoot to blow up the railway line, which was about 20 kilometres away across the border, with the last train being allowed to leave for the west that very night. If our leader ever totally trusted the Führer's judgement, he now chose to ignore any rumours and rely on his own experience and intuition. He opted to put as much distance between us and the enemy as possible. If there was a train that could take us closer to Germany's heartland, he would make sure that his boys were on it.

However, the baroness had made a different choice. Her daughter-in-law had family in the area who would surely take them in until the danger had passed and it was safe to return. With her old aunt in very critical condition, she had made up her mind to go no farther.

Boronovski tried without success to talk her into letting us use one of the wagons. None of us were too unhappy with that, since it meant seeing the last of the beasts we had tormented, and been tormented by, for so long. Besides, considering their condition, it was doubtful that they could be relied upon to take us much farther.

"We'll carry on on foot," the lieutenant announced. "We have not come this far to give up now." Already he had cast his eye on a nearby lumberyard from which to appropriate the materials to nail together a couple of rough sleighs on which to pile our rucksacks. Generously, the baroness did offer to supply us with a pail of jam and one filled with lard to sustain us on the trip, making sure, however, that we picked ones that had suffered damage during our mishap.

Except for Frau Herter, the rest of us set out on our own. She decided to take her chances with the baroness. To her and the other women it meant an end to the indignity of having to relieve themselves on the open road, in full view of 37 12- and 13-year-old boys, and to the stress and worry of having to feed us. Apart from a very emotional farewell with Frau Herter, our goodbyes to the baron's family, despite what we had been through together, were brief and without much feeling. There was not a word of thanks or any good wishes from the baroness, who had not suffered the loss of her arrogance. Only the little girls cried and waved goodbye as we set out in the early afternoon.

It was a bitterly cold day, with a dense ice-fog shrouding the scene and the eerie silence pierced by the snow being crunched under the runners of the makeshift sleighs and our boots. We knew time was of the essence. We started out by running as far as we could, with Boronovski sitting on top of the lard pail on one of the sleighs. From time to time he would get off to lighten the load and walk for whatever distance it took to help us catch our breath. Surprisingly, the lumber slid easily on the hard-packed surface of the frozen road. Every half-hour or so we would stop to dip into the pails. To this day I feel my stomach turn when I think about swallowing a spoonful of lard with jam.

Two hours or so into the trip, we had to abandon the sleigh on which Boronovski had been riding. It had come apart, with its various component parts and cargo scattered across the road. Without the means or the time to patch it back together, we carried on as best we could. However, the problem was compounded by the fact that one of our comrades, Peter Landau, who had been complaining for some time of being ill, was no longer able to carry on. He had allowed himself to be dragged along by hanging onto the sleigh when, from sheer exhaustion, his legs gave out beneath him. For most of the rest of the epic journey, we carried our rucksacks to make room for both Peter and Boronovski on the remaining sleigh. Without the enormous courage of our leader, who stumbled alongside with us as often as his own condition permitted and constantly urged us on, it is doubtful that we could have gone as far as we did. When finally, after what seemed an eternity, we arrived at our destination, all of us collapsed in a heap, having depleted the last reservoirs of our endurance.

In all, we might have come just over 200 kilometres. It had taken us less than four hours to cover the last stretch, no doubt making much better time than we would have if we'd stayed with the horses.

The scene at the tiny railway station, located in a nondescript little village, was chaotic. People were crowding into the place from all directions. The train had been delayed for several hours while attempts were made to attach additional cars to accommodate the mass of humanity. The train crew, to whom punctuality was a religion, were horrified, but their delay was our good fortune. There was a military contingent at the station, and its commanding officer was trying to convince people that another train was being organized for the following day, but he did so without conviction. I overheard him tell Boronovski: "If you want to get these boys out, this is your last chance."

Having surveyed the situation, the lieutenant issued his orders. "It's every man for himself," he said. "We have come too far to be stopped now. If we are not able to stay together, I make every one of you responsible to get himself on this train in any way you can. It will stop in Görlitz about two hours away. I will see you there."

We didn't need to be told twice. In some places we had to crawl between people's legs to fight for a space. We found out later that Peter had been a problem. The four hours on the road had been too much for him. He was now seriously ill, with a very high fever and a bad cough. Boronovski and Albert took charge of him, and with the help of the military personnel they ended up on the locomotive, the best seat on the train. The rest of us, some minus our rucksacks that got lost in the shuffle, were packed together like sardines, having to wait for at least another hour in the station before we finally got underway. Most of the boys, born and raised in East and West Prussia or the Baltic States, had never been to the heartland of Germany. Unlike me, they could not see the train as a means of transport on a route that would eventually take them home to a grandfather and an extended family. But none of us had any energy to spare to think about what the future might hold beyond finding shelter from the cold and relief from the pain of hunger.

CHAPTER 5

Dresden

Whoever fights monsters should see to it that in the process he does not become a monster.

—Friedrich Nietzsche, German philosopher

A single death is a tragedy, a million deaths is a statistic.

—Josef Stalin, Soviet dictator

The trip to Görlitz was not a long one, perhaps only a hundred kilometres, but it was a stop-and-go affair lasting more than six hours. It was six hours I will never forget.

Joachim and I were together, but the only place we had managed to secure was on the platform bridging two of the cars. Dozens of people crammed together: old men, women trying to console crying babies, and children pushing and shoving to improve the space around themselves. There was one woman I noticed in particular, standing right next to me with a baby clutched tightly to her breast. There was not a sound out of the child, but the woman was relentless in her whining, interrupting it periodically to make an animal-like guttural sound as she rocked her baby in rhythm with the moving train. It became more and more irritating as time went on.

I heard an old man standing behind me whisper to his wife, "That baby is dead." After that, I felt goosebumps on my back every time the motion of the train made me come in contact with her and the child. As time wore on, people tried to console her. Her whine only got louder.

"Can I hold your baby for a while?" one woman offered, but that only made her hold it closer as she turned away from the intruder. We tried to make space for her to sit down, but she was inconsolable.

Then, during one of the stops, she simply pushed herself to the exit steps and slowly climbed down. Without stopping she walked off the track and out into a field with the snow high above her ankles.

"Hey you, get back on that train if you don't want to be left behind," shouted an authoritative voice from the outside. But she just kept on walking, making her strange noise. She just kept on walking until she was swallowed by the night, and no one made a move to bring her back.

The train started to move and there was no attempt to stop it. Even today I can still hear her lament, and I can still see her walk into the night, unwilling to abandon her child on its journey to a better world.

We arrived in Görlitz in the middle of the night. Somewhere during the six hours we had crossed the border. The mass of humanity spilled into the station. There was no place else to go. We soon found each other and gathered on the platform. Like everyone else, we were too hungry to sleep and too exhausted to forage for food.

The next morning the Red Cross managed to set up a soup kitchen, but we were taken to a youth hostel outside the city before we got to eat. There, a number of local women did everything possible to make us comfortable and to shower us with their kindness and charity. How we all wished that this could be the end of our journey. After all, we were now back home in the Fatherland. Surely the Führer would be able to look after us here. And, for a short period of time, the lieutenant got us back to an almost normal school routine at the hostel, except for a shortened school day and more time for outings in the surrounding hills.

Our newly found happiness and contentment was short-lived. On February 13, right after breakfast, we were given some good and some bad news. There would be no school that day, but we were once again ordered to move. This time, however, we would travel by train to a permanent home farther to the west. The school had been allocated the use of a youth hostel in Lengenfeld near the city of Zwickau in Sachsen. The place would still be 500 kilometres from my relatives in Forchheim, but aside from my curiosity about the whereabouts of my parents and siblings, this was less of a factor for me now that we were back to a relatively orderly existence. To get to our destination we would have to change trains in Dresden, our first stop.

We had very little time to get ready. Not that we had much to pack— most of us had abandoned or lost our meagre belongings in the struggle to board the train—but there was the question of what to do with our friend Peter, whose condition had worsened. He was in no shape to travel. An army doctor, who had been consulted, ordered him hospitalized, but the closest hospital, hopelessly overcrowded, had refused to admit him. Besides, there were no doctors to care for him there.

The local people did offer to find Peter a home and look after him, but he pleaded with us not to be left behind. Boronovski tried to tell him that he would arrange to have Peter catch up with us as soon as his health improved, but Peter was not convinced. As usual, it was left to his comrades to decide. Based on the dictum "One for all and all for one," we would not abandon him. We could either stay or take him with us. We took him with us.

It was a sorry-looking group that trotted off to meet the train taking us to our new home. Peter was bundled up on a stretcher, and Boronovski, having developed trouble with his prosthesis, was back on crutches. However, there was a marked improvement at the station over the last time we were there. We were even issued tickets to board the train, which left right on time. (Trains in Germany are always on time.)

Dresden was famous for its architecture, its cultural infrastructure, and its amenities. Apart from the railway marshalling yards, the city was not of any military significance, but it was the catch basin for tens of thousands of refugees from the east and the Berlin area in the north: women, children, and old men, whom we were about to join. Little did any of us know that we were on our way to a rendezvous with hell, a savage attack that would be remembered in the annals of history as one of the war's most indefensible acts of vengeance and brutality.

There was no warning for the Dresden fire-bombing of February 13, 1945. The attack was planned with great precision and calculated to achieve maximum impact in the form of human casualties and collateral damage. The best estimates have the number of casualties ranging from 35,000 to 135,000 deaths. They were mostly women and children, and many were refugees from parts of Germany and the east that had suffered the worst of the Nazi atrocities, making the attack doubly callous. Nobody ever took count of the hundreds of thousands who were injured, maimed or crippled for life during these terrifying hours.

There were two more attacks on Dresden the next day. In total, over 1,400 bombers were involved, dropping more than 4,000 tonnes of mostly incendiary bombs, creating a firestorm comparable in size and ferocity to those generated by the atomic strikes on Hiroshima and Nagasaki. Nothing was spared. The Frauenkirche, one of the city's great landmarks, the palace, the opera house, the cathedral, and the Zwinger Museum, a priceless cultural icon in Germany, were all reduced to rubble.

Today historians tend to trace Winston Churchill's decision to order the attack back to the Yalta Conference, which preceded it by just a few days. At the conference, the leaders of the Allies, Churchill, Roosevelt, and Stalin, agreed on the manner in which the final stage of the war was to be prosecuted and how the spoils were to be divided. Historians, noting that Churchill was quoted after the war as saying, "We have butchered the wrong pig," speculate that the Western leaders were not inclined to leave many industrial installations or cultural amenities to Russia, the "pig" which was to receive eastern Germany, including Dresden, as part of its bounty.

It was still daylight when we approached the great city. Our train came to a sudden stop some distance from the station. The air outside was bursting with the thunderous noise of hundreds of aircraft engines and the percussion of bombs raining down. It was only the first of four waves of concentrated attacks, but the phosphorous bombs had done their work and we could already see fires reaching high into the sky. Fearing that the train would become a target, Boronovski ordered us off, while the train crew suggested the safest place would be between the tracks under the railcars. A mad scramble followed as hundreds of passengers struggled for shelter there.

Dresden was not equipped with any air defences, and the depleted Luftwaffe, unprepared for the attack and by that time short on fuel and ammunition anyway, could offer no resistance. Apparently this left the fighter squadrons supporting the bombers with little to do but invent their own sport of finding interesting surface targets away from the centre of the main attack. Our train was an obvious one. Three or four fighters took several strafing runs at us, adding to the terror. At one point someone shouted, "Peter is hit, he is bleeding," but the source of the blood that covered Peter's stretcher and blankets was not a bullet wound. He was choking on the blood discharging from his lungs.

None of us would remember how long the ordeal lasted, but after what seemed hours, the noise mercifully started fading and people began crawling from beneath the railcars. Everyone scrambled back inside the train for some warmth. Miraculously, not a single person on the train seemed to have suffered any injury and there was surprisingly little damage, at least not to our car. Even the locomotive remained intact.

It was pitch-dark as we finally pulled into the railway station in Dresden. Again to everyone's surprise, there was no visible damage there either, but the city in the distance appeared to be a ball of fire. The loud wail of the air-raid sirens announced the end of the attack. And we were now desperate to find help for Peter. Once again our usual commando group of six set out in the direction of the city in search of medical facilities.

It was a chaotic scene. People fleeing the city, others rushing toward the centre looking for loved ones or hoping to aid in rescue operations and firefighting. We were only desperate to find someone to help our friend, who was in obvious pain and slipping in and out of consciousness. Four of us carried the stretcher, the other two ran alongside holding Peter's hands. We were cold, hungry, and terrorized by what went on around us. Even though the danger had passed, we ran blindly, down one street and up another, shouting at people for directions without ever getting a response. Like wild animals fleeing from predators snapping at their heels, everyone was running in one direction or another. This was not a time to worry about the problems of others. It was everyone for himself.

It seems as if it's part of our human condition to filter out certain of life's most horrifying experiences, registering them only in a subliminal way, so that, even today, my mind produces flashbacks of certain unimaginable scenes without putting them in any order or sequence of events. I remember, for example, how we found ourselves rushing toward the flashing lights of an ambulance parked in front of a building that looked more like a school or some kind of administration centre than a hospital. Bodies were being unloaded and carried inside. We followed along blindly to become part of an indescribable pandemonium. There were bodies everywhere and people screaming with pain, some with grotesquely disfigured features. No one seemed to be in charge. We stepped over people who had just been deposited on the floor, their skin obscenely blistered by the inferno from which they had managed to flee. We just walked from room to room until at last, stumbling into what served as an operating theatre, we got the attention of a Red Cross nurse, who shoved us back out and ordered us to leave the stretcher on one of the benches parked along a wall. After what seemed hours, we finally managed to grab a doctor with whom we pleaded for attention.

It took him no more than 30 seconds to render his prognosis. When we asked him how long he thought Peter would have to stay, pointing out that we had a train to catch, he just looked at us sadly. "You have done all you can for your friend. He is on the last train he'll ever catch. Get out of here while you can."

I never knew that one could say so much with just one's eyes. Peter was unable to speak, but he regained consciousness long enough to plead with us not to leave him there alone. We stayed until another nurse came and ordered us to leave, telling us that Peter was now in good hands. We desperately wanted to believe it. And it was a relief to get away from the screams of agony and the nauseating smell of burned flesh that had assaulted our senses and would stay with us for days afterward.

Some time later Boronovski made inquiries to determine Peter's fate, but without success. We had to assume that our dear friend was among the tens of thousands who perished in Dresden that night. Innocent, helpless people who were consumed by the firestorm and the lust for revenge without regard to identity or guilt. They perished without a trace. There is no grave or any other mark to identify the victims or give an indication that they ever lived.

CHAPTER 6

The End of the War

It is always easy to begin a war, but very difficult to stop one, since its beginning and end are not under the control of the same man.
—Gaius Sallustius Crispus, Roman historian

The Dresden fire-bombing started again the next day, and we might well have been among those victims had it not been for the infamous German maxim that the trains must run on time, under any circumstances. Soon after we left the hospital and rejoined our group, the train left punctually for Zwickau and our new home in Lengenfeld, another 120 kilometres to the west.

We were put up at a relatively comfortable youth hostel, which gave us a brief respite before the final end of the war and its aftermath. There was still sufficient local authority to order farmers in the surrounding countryside to supply our kitchen in return for our help once work started in the fields after the long winter. Some local women were hired to manage the kitchen, and Boronovski even filled our spare time with some school instruction. The war was going badly, of course, but for the moment we were safe and still totally convinced that it was just a matter of time before Germany would triumph, thanks to the Führer's much-touted secret weapon.

At times during the long evenings we were allowed to listen to a radio that had been installed in the hall that served as both classroom and dining room. At first Hitler's propaganda machine lost little of the bombast that characterized the reporting from the two fronts, but as time wore on, attempts to disguise the reality of the situation appeared ever more pitiful, even to us. Boronovski, who was usually in attendance at these sessions, had a hard time disguising his real feelings.

I doubt that the lieutenant was ever a true believer in the Nazi doctrine. He was both a gifted teacher and a Prussian army officer in the finest tradition. His was not to question why; his was just to do or die. I am sure he would not have been in sympathy with the high-ranking officers in the military establishment who, with their attempt to assassinate its leader, plotted to overthrow the Nazi regime. But, at the end, that must have made it that much harder for him to reconcile his principles with the crimes that had been committed.

The Western Allies were getting close to crossing the Rhine, throwing everything behind the final thrust of their offensive. They were worried about Hitler's secret weapon, and with reason. Albert Einstein had warned U.S. president Roosevelt as far back as 1939 that Hitler had given German scientists free rein to pursue the concept of nuclear fission as a means to develop a super-bomb. Scientists, stripped by the Nazis of position and citizenship for being Jewish, had fled to the United States and were working feverishly to beat their former colleagues to the punch. Such eminent people as Einstein, Leo Szilard, Niels Bohr, and, of course, Robert Oppenheimer, who had either studied in Germany or actually helped on the project, were all too familiar with the work going on there.

But time was running out for Hitler and his new secret weaponry. Hundreds of Allied bombers flying overhead in broad daylight, unencumbered by resistance from the Luftwaffe or anti-aircraft guns, removed any doubt that the end was near. Only rarely were we treated to the spectacle of a dogfight, which we observed from the roof of our youth hostel. They were one-sided affairs. German Messerschmitts were no match for the jet aircraft—the first of their kind—that the Americans were now using.

One attack we witnessed showed just how much the American and British fighters were given their own way. From the vantage point of the top of the roof of our building we watched the fighter pilots doing their target practice on a poor farmer and his team of horses in the valley below. Their approach to the target could not have been more than a couple of hundred feet directly over our heads. There were three of them, their jets screaming as they descended to line up on their target. It took three tries to kill the horses and then, for good measure, they made a fourth run to target the farmer, who was running for cover in a nearby forest. Their aim had got better. He never made it.

It was not the end of this heroic venture. Our own presence on the roof of the building, which was decorated with the German eagle sitting on top of the swastika, was too much to resist. The next salvo was aimed at us. Before we knew it, bullets were flying, spraying the clay tiles all around us. My buddies and I had barely enough time to jump off the building and run the length of our soccer field into an adjacent pine forest before they were lined up again. Guns blazing, they came again and again. I remember someone screaming at me, "Get down! Get down!" as I ran like a wild animal to escape the terror.

Miraculously, apart from some nasty cuts and bruises, none of us were seriously hurt. However, not far away we could hear a woman's inhuman, blood-curdling scream. When the flyboys, having lost sight of any moving targets, finally got bored and moved off, the screaming didn't stop. It took us some time to find the courage to investigate. When we did, we found a woman, her whole body drenched in blood, clinging to a bundle of tissue and flesh—the decapitated body of a small child.

"Help me, help me," she screamed as we came on the scene. "Her head, her head—I can't find it." The arrival of some adults who urged us to leave came as a great relief, but the image of it still lingers today. As I remember it, I can't help thinking that surely there must be ways other than such heroic acts as these to liberate a people from a regime that had run amok. God help us all if He ever intends to punish the crimes that are committed by all sides of such conflicts.

For our little band, the incident began to shake our faith in the Führer and added to the desperation of our situation. It deprived us of any hope for mercy if the monsters who had just tormented us from the air ever got at us on the ground.

Added to this fear of the unknown, hunger was once again a constant pain. Even the townspeople now seemed to abandon us. There was no longer any help in the kitchen or with the maintenance of the facility. By the spring of 1945, Lengenfeld's people had their own children to worry about, and food was short. Farmers in the valley no longer ventured out to prepare fields for new crops, opting instead to hoard whatever food and essentials they had in the hope of hanging on as long as possible. Toward the end, we spent our days scouring the countryside and begging for scraps of food or foraging for such edible greenery as watercress in the ditch of a small creek running through the fields below the hostel. But our nightly forays into the neighbouring farmyards, their root cellars and chicken coops, proved much more productive, if not less risky.

Through all this, Boronovski, the only adult among us now, became ever more submissive and resigned. He often forgot to shave and became careless in the way he dressed. Perhaps it was the sinking of his spirits, his reluctant acceptance of defeat, that contributed to his failing health. He spent most of his day in his private quarters, showing little interest in what was happening around him. By and large the 36 of us 13-year-olds were now left entirely to our own devices.

In anticipation of the inevitable, our leader pleaded with the local authorities, such as there were, to take on the responsibility of caring for us until we could be reunited with our parents. The response was not overwhelming, not surprising given the notoriety we had earned with our nightly missions and the townspeople's own adjustment to the rules of the jungle. Finally, after a visit of some local party officials, it was decided that we would be split up and placed in homes throughout the region.

Our first reaction was to defy the order. If we could no longer occupy the hostel, we would simply continue living off the land. After all, what could be worse than the winter we had just lived through? Whatever the future held, we were determined to face it together.

In the end, however, we were persuaded by one last promise Boronovski made us on behalf of the Führer. (Just think, there was our great leader, the eastern front collapsing, western enemies pouring across the Rhine, such bosom friends and advisers as Martin Bormann and Heinrich Himmler making arrangements to flee to South America, yet apparently he could still spare the time to worry about Lieutenant Boronovski and his band of hapless children. Perhaps he remembered that nice bouquet of flowers I had given him during his visit to Poznań.) There seemed to be no conviction in Boronovski's voice as he told us that the Führer had done us the honour of decreeing that our school, as soon as the situation was brought back under control, would be reassembled and converted to an Adolf Hitler School, the admission to which was normally restricted to the brightest and most promising of German youth.

"I was able," Boronovski told us, "to convince the leadership that we had the necessary academic credentials, and through our heroic efforts during retreat from Poland, we had earned the right to be accredited with this honour."

The announcement was made during one last assembly. We were given a couple of days to prepare for it. Everyone was to make the very best effort to present himself in full uniform—upon our arrival in Lengenfeld we had been supplied with new shirts and pants, although they were below standard. Our once proud, austere leader, by now a mere shadow of himself, had managed to get his own uniform refurbished, his decorations polished.

It became a very emotional scene. With a shaky voice, the lieutenant informed us that despite the fact we were underage, he was also authorized, in accordance with recommendations he had made, to elevate us to the status of Hitler Youth. Somehow, somewhere, he had managed to acquire for each of us the appropriate pins and the knife that was the symbol of the organization. Brimming with pride and with shining eyes, we accepted his handshake and his congratulations.

In retrospect, I have often wondered how he felt. How painful it must have been for him as he contemplated the uncertainty in which our future was shrouded and as he was forced to accept the ugly and now undeniable truth of the lunacy of Hitler's dream, which would be a scar on the souls of all future generations of the German people. Hardest of all for him must have been the knowledge that he had failed in his promise to keep us safe until we could be reunited with our natural parents. No doubt he now realized that after what we had endured during our flight, and considering the privations to come, it would have been much more prudent to dissolve the school before our evacuation back to Germany became necessary.

The first group of our friends was picked up the very next day for billeting with individual families in a nearby town. My turn came a few days later.

Joachim and I were called into Boronovski's room. Looking pale and dispirited, he informed us that he was preparing to go to a hospital in Zwickau, some distance away, but the only place with a doctor. Before he left, he felt it was his duty to tell Joachim that his parents had been killed before they could leave Poznań, where they had owned a prosperous market-gardening business that the family had built over several generations and which they had been reluctant to abandon. Boronovski had obviously known of their fate for some time. I remember being much too afraid to inquire about the status of my own parents.

Boronovski knew that my prospects of being reunited with family were much better than those of most of the others who came from Poland, Silesia, the Baltic States, or Germany's eastern provinces, now overrun by the Russians. Knowing that Joachim and I were close friends, he hoped Joachim's fortunes could be tied to my own, so arrangements had now been made for both of us to be billeted with a family in town. They were about to pick us up.

Joachim was shattered. "Why wasn't I told?" he shouted as he stormed from the room. It took some time for me to catch up with him, sitting on a log in the pine forest, his whole body shaking as he tried to suppress his tears. He refused to be comforted.

"What will I do, where will I go?" he asked. We spent the rest of the day wandering aimlessly through the countryside. Hungry, miserable, and dispirited, but with a strengthened bond of friendship, we snuck back to the hostel. There the mood of the half dozen of our friends still left did little to cheer us up.

We had a last visit with Boronovski when he came into the dormitory where we were huddled together, hungry, scared, and utterly confused. At first I didn't recognize him. Boronovski was in civilian clothes. With his face pale and distorted and his meagre frame failing to fill out the clothes he had chosen for the occasion, he seemed like a total stranger to us. His voice and demeanour invited no response or argument as he gave us his final instructions. Joachim and I were given directions to a place in town where we would have a temporary home with a woman who had tried to collect us the day before. A priest and some members of his congregation in a neighbouring town had agreed to pick up the rest of the group later in the day.

Boronovski was moving with the aid of his crutches and appeared to be in great pain. Just before his arrival, we had seen a military vehicle pull up in front of the place. Now the driver, perhaps impatient to get underway, interrupted the pregnant silence in the room and tried to assist his passenger out.

"Wait outside," the lieutenant ordered him in an agitated tone. "I will manage on my own."

Finally, he told us: "In accordance with what you have been taught, I expect you to be respectful and obedient to the people to whom you have been assigned. I am very proud of you all and wish that things could have turned out better for us." This time there was no reference to either the Führer or any prospect of being reunited with us in the future. Then, as a final gesture, he extended his hand, and as each of us stepped up to him with our customary salute, rather than returning it he reached out and briefly hugged us to his body. After that, he turned and, without looking back, hobbled away to the car that was to take him to the medical facility in Zwickau. Through the window, we saw his expressionless face looking at us from the back seat as the driver pulled away.

Of the eight of us left for this final encounter with Lieutenant Boronovski, whom none of us would ever forget, only Joachim was missing. As we turned to face the room, which suddenly seemed strangely empty, and looked to each other for support, we saw him crouching behind one of the beds, tears streaming down his face. He was the first of us to confront the stark reality. We had been severed from our last tie to a source of order and stability. There would be no one to comfort us in facing the reality of the loss of our parents and whatever comfort and security the school environment and our comradeship had provided. We were set adrift in a sea of utter chaos, confusion, and despair. Finally, we succumbed to what might be considered a natural reaction for 13-year-old children in such a situation. We no longer felt shame in shedding our own tears.

In Lengenfeld our hosts, Frau Ebert and her 10-year-old daughter, did their best to make Joachim and me feel welcome, but apart from a comfortable bed in an upper-class apartment, they had little else to share. Her husband, a major in the SS, had been home for only brief visits since the beginning of the war. He had been reported missing in action some time earlier, but his wife had enough spunk, fanaticism, hatred, and revenge-inspired energy to fight for both of them. Her preferred honorific was Frau Major. In retrospect, I realize she fit the profile of a typical Nazi. It wasn't charity, but patriotic duty that inspired her to take us in and look after us.

It was a precarious life of near-starvation. Dodging low-flying aircraft, we spent our days searching the countryside for food, although thanks to Frau Ebert's zeal, we did it with freshly washed and ironed uniform shirts and pants. We dug over fields, looking for potatoes or kernels of corn left over from the harvest the previous fall. Frau Ebert was very resourceful, as she had to be. She had no friends or neighbours who showed any sympathy or compassion for her. To her, they had been and were Jewish pigs, traitors, or cowards. She spent her time waiting for the day of reckoning, still totally convinced of the Führer's cause and ultimate triumph.

Meanwhile, U.S. forces marched closer and closer. My 13th birthday on March 24 coincided with the day that General Patton had his picture taken urinating into the Rhine. (They haven't caught an edible fish there since.) President Roosevelt's death on April 12, 1945, did little to slow the momentum the war in the west had by now accumulated.

Frau Ebert baked one of her potato-peel cakes for my birthday, but our current existence was hardly conducive to a mood of celebration. During bombing raids she refused to go to the bomb shelter with all the "cowards and traitors," so we spent most of the day in the basement of her three-storey house. The air-raid sirens and the deafening sound of hundreds of aircraft overhead kept us in a constant state of fear.

Finally, early in April, we were told of the possibility of a tank attack. The warning would be an uninterrupted high-pitched siren until the attack actually commenced. People were instructed to stock their bomb shelters with sufficient supplies to last for several days. In our case, there was little to hoard. It had been much too risky the last few days to venture outside in daylight to scrounge for scraps of food. All we could hope for was that the end would be quick and less painful than starving to death. This time there was no talk of escape. There was no place else to run.

When the attack came, it was almost a relief. Having lived with the fear of it for so long, our minds were conditioned to accept the final act with a sense of calm resignation. When, at mid-morning, the sirens started, Frau Major simply reached into one of her husband's closets and pulled out some shirts for us to hide our uniforms. I remember her walking calmly through the apartment, pausing in front of her husband's picture, resting her hand on the desk he had occupied for the years they had lived there together. Then she embraced her daughter, who was still much too young to understand and accept that the only way she would ever see her father again was to join him in another dimension.

We debated whether it would be wise to build a fire in the basement stove, which had been installed to offer some comfort during our nights of refuge there, but we decided against it for fear that the smoke would give away our position. Instead, we buried our Hitler Youth knives in the ash bin and resigned ourselves to our fate.

It seemed a lifetime. The slightest noise made everyone jump, mother and daughter clinging together tighter and tighter. Someone ventured to suggest it might have been a false alarm, but the sirens kept on wailing. To our surprise, there was no shooting. At first there was only the vibration of the building above us, followed by the rumble of the heavy tanks passing outside. There must have been 20 or 30 of them charging toward the centre of the city. Silence again. Then a single blast of a cannon somewhere in the distance, followed by more traffic on the road. This time it sounded like it was going in the reverse direction. The sirens were still grinding away at our nerves, but soon we heard the more familiar sound of airplanes and bombs shattering the air.

We learned later that the tanks had pulled up in front of the city hall to wait for some signal or sign of surrender when someone—no doubt one of Frau Ebert's friends, who preferred to die fighting—fired a *Panzerfaust* [an anti-tank missile] at one of them. It didn't cause much damage, but it was enough to convince the tanks to retreat and let the bombers take over. The subsequent attack was another of those senseless acts of utter cruelty and revenge. It lasted long enough to destroy much of the town, which up to then had been spared the worst effects of the war.

Our own house was heavily damaged. There was no direct hit, but nearby explosions had shattered every window and cleared the roof of all its clay shingles.

Hitler and Goebbels had once again fulfilled one of their promises: most of the German workers fortunate to have survived the war could certainly be assured of finding their houses "sunny and airy." In Frau Ebert's case, the sun was shining right into the living room of her apartment, which was cooled by a strong breeze flowing through the shattered windows.

The bombing raid must have lasted no more than half an hour. Mercifully the sirens had been stilled, and we were now huddled together again in eerie silence.

After what seemed an eternity, we once again heard the rumble of the tanks on the street outside. Next, a voice came over a loudspeaker. The message in German proclaimed that a new military command had been established and urged people to co-operate, stressing that any further resistance would result in swift retaliation. All residents were to present themselves in front of their houses immediately. Every house had to display a white object signalling surrender. Anyone in possession of weapons was to deposit them on the sidewalk.

Slowly we made our way up to street level, Frau Ebert perhaps as curious to see what was left of her house as she was about the fate that awaited us outside.

The scene was not unlike those in the newsreels we had seen showing victorious German soldiers marching into Paris, Warsaw, or Brussels, except that these weren't German soldiers. To my surprise, the soldiers' faces looked just like ours. We couldn't see their belt buckles or any other detail of their uniform to determine whether God was with them as well. People were lining the street, which was piled with mountains of rubble from collapsed buildings. Big plumes of smoke and flames engulfing half the town were billowing toward the bright afternoon sky.

The strangest sight of all was the reaction of the people themselves. Perhaps it was triggered by fear and, certainly for some, relief, but to Frau Ebert nothing could justify the behaviour: children's faces paralyzed with fear; old men with arms stretched above their heads; women, some on their knees praying, others cheering, even throwing flowers at the armoured vehicles and jeeps with mounted machine guns pointed at them.

"Whores, sluts, traitors!" Frau Major was shouting, literally frothing at the mouth. Her daughter pleaded with her to stop, but she went on until a jeep came screeching to a stop just inches away from us. Out jumped what must have been an officer, who was attracted by the strange behaviour. As other vehicles stopped to attend the commotion, he grabbed Frau Ebert by the scruff of her neck and dragged her, kicking and screaming, inside the house, with her daughter clinging to her skirt. Joachim and I had no choice but to follow. In one of the bedrooms the officer ripped a sheet, torn by some of the fallen glass, off the bed, ordering her to hang it outside the window. But before she did, she stuck her foot into one of the holes, ripping it apart as a final act of defiance. With an undignified kick in the rear, she was escorted back to join the confusion in the street.

After a while, we could see specially equipped vehicles carrying large coils of telephone wire and other supplies catching up to the armoured column ahead. We stood for what seemed hours until people simply started to drift back into their damaged homes, sweeping up the broken glass, starting to bring some order to the chaos and destruction, but above all relieved that it was over and that our lives had been spared.

I remember the next few days only by the hunger and the cold we had to endure as a result of the latest order that confined the population to their houses. When we were allowed to venture outside once more, it was to register at what was left of city hall, bringing with us any form of identification with any unit of the military or party affiliation, including the Hitler Youth.

Joachim and I only had our knives, which we had retrieved from the basement. As we made our way toward town, we encountered a long lineup of people pushing toward a corner in the market square, where the soldiers had set up a field kitchen. In defiance of their orders not to fraternize with the local population, they handed out bread and dished out some goulash. One of the soldiers picked us out of the lineup and escorted us to the front, obviously touched by the haggard figures we had become. Not having a receptacle for the stew, he simply pulled off his helmet and filled it with the first decent meal Joachim and I had had in several weeks. It was also the kindest thing anyone had done for us in a long time.

Joachim ran back to the house to invite Frau Ebert to the banquet, but she declined, allowing only her daughter to accept the charity.

When we finally reached the registration centre, our spirits were markedly improved. It was a large room with several tables set up, each manned by two former town officials and an officer of the new military authority. When it was our turn to step up to the table, our training took over. In unison, both of us clicked our heels, raised our arms and shouted "Heil Hitler." The room, full of people, fell deathly silent, every eye shifting between us and the American officers sitting at the table. The silence in the room was deafening. We didn't need it explained to us what a fatal error we had committed. This would surely be the end. But to everyone's relief, the officer at the table next to ours broke the silence by jumping up, clicking his heels and also shouting "Heil Hitler." Joachim and I just stood, our faces drained of blood, as everyone else broke up in laughter.

There could be no doubt now that the war was lost. There were conflicting reports about Hitler's fate. We learned only much later that he and some of the top echelon of the party had taken their own lives. But none of that was of any concern to us, nor were Hitler's former promises. Hunger had reduced us to a subhuman state with only a single obsession: the search for food.

We were mostly fortunate to be under American rule. The civilian population was treated with decency and respect. One would assume that the British and the French operated under similar rules of engagement. To everyone's relief and surprise, it didn't take any time at all for the situation to normalize and improve. In just days the military command had re-established a civilian authority invested with powers to appropriate whatever food farmers had cached or merchants had hoarded and organize it for rationing among the population. Families fortunate enough to find their homes in livable condition were required to share space with those less fortunate.

Joachim and I spent most of our time on the street, picking up small pieces of wood for Frau Ebert's kitchen stove and foraging for scraps of food to supplement our entitlement and stave off the worst of the famine. Any, even the tiniest, evidence of a new order being restored gave the locals cause for celebration and hope for the future. There was a tight curfew in place, and even in daylight hours people were forbidden to gather in any numbers, but this could not prevent the tearful reunions of family and friends. They were meeting each other again for the first time, hoping to share information about the fate of their husbands, fathers, and sons or simply to celebrate being alive.

Part of the population of Lengenfeld consisted of several hundred Poles who had volunteered to work in German factories throughout the war. They had been confined to a compound at the outskirts of town until they were liberated by the Americans, and then, for several days, they roamed through town, raping, pillaging, and plundering whatever was not nailed down.

This did not endear them to the American military personnel, nor did their behaviour when they eventually left to be repatriated in a convoy of trucks destined for the Polish border. As a final act to show their appreciation for being allowed to spend the war years in relative comfort and security, they deposited their ample stock of American-supplied food in a large cesspool at the end of the compound's sanitary system.

Word got out quickly, and Joachim and I were among the throng of people fishing out whatever could be salvaged. Whole cases of canned goods were among the bounty, together with sacks of sugar and flour. We secured much more than our share, arriving back with a wheelbarrow loaded with the smelly but precious cargo. The sugar packaged in paper sacks suffered little dilution. The flour sacks were slit open, and once the outer core, which had been penetrated by the sewage, had been removed, they yielded a quality of flour Frau Major had not seen in years.

The story ends with a bit of poetic justice. The Poles, expecting to be greeted as conquering heroes on their arrival at the border, suffered the most brutal beatings by their fellow countrymen, who considered them traitors instead. The Americans had no choice but to load them back on the trucks and bring them back to their Lengenfeld camp. They were a subdued and dejected crew as they marched back into the compound. To add to their misery, their liberators locked the gates behind them and pointed to the sewage pit as a source for food.

They were still at the camp when Joachim and I left Lengenfeld on the final leg of our journey.

There had been rumours right from the beginning that the American troops would eventually be replaced by far less kindly conquerors: the barbarians from the east whose exploits of senseless cruelty and torture had come to our ears on the road. As part of the agreement reached between the Allies at Yalta, the Americans began preparations for the surrender of Sachsen province to the Russians in exchange for part of Berlin.

To her credit, Frau Major Ebert, even though her situation would no doubt worsen without our contribution to the food supply, urged us to throw ourselves on the mercy of what she considered the lesser of the two evils. And I had not given up hope that my parents might have survived and found their way back to Forchheim. Failing that, I was sure Grandpa Leibold and all the relatives would be there to look after us. The time had come for Joachim and me to hit the road again.

CHAPTER 7

Living Off the Land

Man is the only [animal] to whom the torture and death of his fellow creatures is amusing in itself.

—James A. Froude, English historian

It wasn't until May 7 in 1945 that the war finally came to an end in Germany, but there was no longer any doubt about the outcome when Joachim and I set out on our adventure to once again escape the Russian invaders from the east. Forchheim and Grandfather were 500 kilometres away, and this time we would be entirely on our own and would have to rely on our feet alone to get us there.

It was toward the end of April, and Mother Nature had once again refused to be "subdued and conquered," despite the unbridled lunacy of, and attempts by, her most highly developed species to disrupt the natural order and to lay devastation and destruction over the landscape. Spring was in the air, giving new hope to a people who had been deprived of it for so long.

Joachim and I set out with little else but Frau Ebert's best wishes and the ragged clothes she had somehow stitched together for us to complement what could be salvaged from our uniforms. We had learned that the sun sets in the west, so that was to be the general direction for us to follow. We carried with us a list of city names along the route: Hof, Bamberg, Schweinfurt, Würzburg, and Heidelberg. These became targets for us to aim at along the way.

But throughout most of the journey, the hunt for food was our principal obsession, one that would challenge all our ingenuity and senses. Like me, Joachim was now just barely 13 years old, and most people we encountered in the early days of our adventure were still far too concerned with normalizing their own situations to offer charity to others. We would have to survive on our own.

Our progress was very slow, but as time wore on we found ever more ingenious ways to stave off hunger and cheat death. We discovered that our prospects of finding food were much improved by hunting in packs. We often tagged on to groups of marauders. They were mostly soldiers—some with girlfriends—who had avoided or escaped prison camps or had deserted before the cause became too hopeless. That meant sticking to the back country for fear of being caught or worse. The main targets were isolated farms, whose inhabitants could be persuaded to contribute, willingly or otherwise, to our culinary needs.

In return for the benefits we gained from joining such groups, Joachim and I would try our luck whenever we were near a main road, positioning ourselves so as to catch the attention of the drivers and crews of the seemingly endless columns of army convoys hauling supplies in both directions. The drivers were almost without exception black Americans. They were a curiosity to us. The only black person I had ever seen before was part of a small circus troupe that had visited Forchheim before the war.

At first they took great delight in scaring the living daylights out of us, but with time we got to know them as the most friendly and charitable of any of the foreign army personnel we encountered. We could always count on a generous bounty of army rations and even some fruit, like bananas or oranges, that hadn't been seen in stores since before the war. Even then they were unfamiliar to me because such luxuries would find their way onto Mom's shopping list only on very special occasions, such as birthdays or perhaps Christmas.

There was another luxury the American personnel could provide, one that finally crystallized my experiences of the last two years into disillusionment. With the rest of the gang having to stay away from any main roads, it was part of my and Joachim's duty to satisfy their smoking requirements by collecting any cigarette butts flipped out on the road by the crews. To some in the group, that part of the bounty was prized even more highly than the food, and it earned us particularly high praise and endearment.

On one such occasion, Joachim and I foraged for butts along the highway while a large convoy of trucks approached from the distance. Among our band of marauders at the time was a highly decorated Luftwaffe pilot who had run out of fuel on his last mission and ended up ditching his plane. He and the others were hiding some distance away in a clump of bushes and trees, waiting for the convoy to pass. It was a particularly charitable crew of drivers, and by the time the last truck had disappeared in the distance, there was a bounty of provisions and a mad scramble from the bush to help us collect it.

Suddenly, out of nowhere, an army jeep came bouncing over the field with guns blazing. The occupants had observed the band rushing toward Joachim and me and, thinking that we were about to be robbed, had come to our rescue. Everybody was rounded up at gunpoint with no way to escape, and there were some tense moments before we could explain that we were part of the assembly. Our Luftwaffe hero was soon engaged in a lively exchange of bartering, including the offer of his *Ritterkreutz* [Knight's Cross] as payment for a package of Camel cigarettes. I couldn't believe my eyes.

That was it for me! Here was one of our idols begging his enemies to spare his miserable life and offering up one of his country's highest decorations of valour, for which he had put his life at risk on many occasions. It may explain why the Luftwaffe offered its pilots ample supplies of cigarettes as part of their daily rations. They might otherwise have sold their aircraft to the enemy to satisfy their cravings. To me, it was contrary to everything Lieutenant Boronovski had tried to instill in us during our time under his tutelage.

Not until that moment had it occurred to me that all the pain—the agony, the suffering we had endured, all the blood that our parents and brothers had spilled for the Fatherland—was in vain. I had never felt more humiliated and betrayed, more alone and dejected, than I did at that moment. It's hard to explain why, but even the news on April 30 of Hitler's death and on May 7 of the official unconditional surrender of the German army had less of an effect on me. It was at this precise moment, watching the Luftwaffe pilot get his cigarettes, that I began to realize the magnitude of what had happened, the trickery and deception that had been perpetrated on the German people, the brainwashing to which we had been subjected. It was the final straw.

It's this event, perhaps more than any other, that instilled in me the cynicism and skepticism that have shaped my lifelong obsession for independence and self-reliance. I felt abandoned by my parents, even though they had no choice in the matter. The system to which we had transferred our loyalty turned out to be a fraud. The people we looked up to with veneration and entrusted with our faith and love were now identified as criminals.

I swore then that never again would I surrender control over any part of my life to, place my trust in or tie my fortune to any system, ideology, or person. I even began to doubt my faith in God. If there was a god, I would have to find or invent him myself because the prayers I had been taught in Pfarrer Dorer's church were never answered.

But there remained a last glimmer of hope that pulled us along on our epic journey. Grandfather Leibold would have an explanation for it all. He would know what to do. He would know the truth and help me find my way.

Toward the end of our trek, as some normalcy returned, Joachim and I were less dependent on others to make it through the day. The Red Cross started to organize feeding stations for the thousands of homeless refugees, their ranks now swollen with soldiers who had managed to avoid being taken prisoner during the last days of the war. The American military personnel were now allowed contact with the general population, making life much easier. In most larger centres, public buildings that had survived the bombing were made available as hostels where people could camp out for the night. Some nights, after eliciting sympathy for our situation, we were even fortunate enough to be invited to private homes for a meal and bed.

At times these acts of kindness led to overindulgence, for which I paid dearly in the following days. I was suffering from dysentery and dehydration, the after-effects of which stayed with me for years, causing constant pain and discomfort and making it at times almost impossible to control my bowels. Privations like the ones we and many others endured during these dreadful times are never fully recovered from, and the legacy of them carried on long into my adult life.

Finally, late in May, Joachim and I reached Heidelberg, only 50 kilometres from Karlsruhe. The great historic city on the Neckar River was like an oasis in a desert of chaos, destruction, and devastation. We arrived there late in the afternoon after a long day's walk. The city, by design, had been spared any of the effects of the war. Like Baden-Baden, 90 kilometres to the south, it had been designated off-limits to the bomber squadrons.

Why these two cities and not Dresden? Well, for one thing, one might cynically say that the West felt the Russians shouldn't be allowed anywhere near them to desecrate their historic beauty and splendour. For another, the elite of the civilized world, who might have studied at the 500-year-old University of Heidelberg or had occasion to visit the old spas and casinos in Baden-Baden, would soon be in need of a civilized place to stay and rest during their stressful visits to Germany after the war to observe their handiwork. In any event, the Heidelbergers weren't complaining. The American high command was well established by the time we got there, helping to restore some order and civility to the place. In fact, the army command kept most of the riff-raff wandering the streets away from the city, so the two of us, covered in rags and wearing shoes with the calluses on our feet acting as the soles, looked almost out of place.

A kindly old couple invited us to stay with them for a time. Their daughter and their two grandchildren—about our age, judging from the pictures we were shown—had perished during one of the air raids over Mannheim. They shared what little food they had, and the woman even managed to scrounge a few pieces of clothing for us.

In spite of this kindness, we were eager to complete the last leg of our journey. We were told that the French were occupying the region of the Black Forest, and there were reports of the worst kind of atrocities being inflicted on the local population. We were urged to wait for some improvement in the situation, but new energy, spawned by what might have been homesickness, forced us back on the road for the last part of our journey home.

Following the advice we received, we kept well away from main roads that would have brought us in contact with the French. This slowed progress considerably, but we did manage to cover the last 50 kilometres to Karlsruhe in two days without further incident.

Coming from the north, our first stop would have to be Onkel Anton's place in Daxlanden. I was unsure about how to find my way there, since I'd only visited there once or twice as a young child, but I knew it to be a suburb of Karlsruhe. The city would be my best tool for orienting myself.

After hiding out in a forest for the night, we entered the city early in the morning to come upon indescribable scenes of devastation. The entire city was in ruins. Ghost-like figures climbed over the rubble of what used to be their homes, hoping perhaps to recover a picture or just a small memento to keep alive the memory of someone who may have perished under the debris or would not return from the war. Only grudgingly did they accept our intrusion into their thoughts, pointing out directions without returning a greeting, their faces void of expression, interest, or curiosity. After the first few encounters I felt panic-stricken, fearing that Forchheim and my relatives there could well have suffered the same fate. All of a sudden there was an urgency in our steps as we put the last two kilometres behind us.

Leibold siblings, for whatever reasons, were never known to have any great affection for one another. They came together only on such special occasions as weddings and funerals. As my brother Ludwig tells it, Onkel Anton visited our house only once, and before my time. The family was at the supper table when the kitchen door opened just wide enough for Anton to reveal his face. (None of the houses had locks on the front doors in those "good old times.")

"If you want to see Grandmother alive once more," he told his sister and her family, "you better get there soon. She will not make it through the night." With that he was gone.

My only recollection of him was that he had lost one of his legs in an industrial accident. I remembered him coaxing me to touch his prosthesis to satisfy my curiosity, but I felt kind of queasy about it.

I knew he and his wife Frieda lived in Daxlanden, on the edge of Grandpa's forest. We didn't have difficulty finding the place since Uncle Anton was well known and respected in the area, but it took some considerable time, and Joachim's urging, for me to muster enough courage to knock on the door. Afraid, perhaps, of being confronted with bad news about Mom and Dad or the rest of the family, I was almost hoping that no one was home when my aunt answered the door. My heart was racing a mile a minute as I looked for a sign of recognition, but I was as much a stranger to her as she was to me.

"Who are you and what do you want?" she sternly demanded to know.

"It's me, Franz—Franz Oberle," I stammered.

"O, Jesus, no—Jesus, no," was all she uttered before she ran past us to the back of the house, calling for Onkel Anton. "It's Rösel's youngest, Franz," she shouted at him as he came around the corner toward us as fast as his wooden leg would carry him.

"Oh my God," he said as his eyes surveyed the two pitiful creatures framed by the doorway. "Are you alone? Where are your parents?" Of course he didn't realize that by asking this question he shattered any hope I still had that they'd survived the aftermath of the war and preceded me home.

Karlsruhe in the summer of 1945.

Still no sign of life—Karlsruhe city centre 1946/47.

"I thought they would be here," I said, close to tears.

"I am sure they won't be far behind," Anton tried to reassure me, but I was not at all convinced. There was good news to cushion the pain: Erich had come back some time ago and was staying with Grandpa and Tante Johanna.

"In God's name, Frieda," Anton pleaded with my aunt, "find something to eat before these two boys starve to death right on our doorstep." She didn't need to be prompted, but I had lost much of my appetite. All I was interested in now was covering the last three kilometres home, anxious to meet up with my brother, Tante Johanna, and, of course, Grandpa. Nevertheless, Onkel Anton insisted that we eat something and offered to chauffeur us the rest of the way on his bicycle.

Onkel Anton must have guessed how reluctant Tante Johanna would be to take us in and what kind of reception Joachim and I could expect. He told us what a pity it was that Grandma had died at such an early age. She would have been the right person to deal with such a crisis.

I regret not having known Grandma Eufrosina Leibold. She must have been an angel. I mean, she had to be, raising the five kids and running the farm while Grandpa was away in the First World War and later balancing his other full-time duties as the town's forester with the mountain of manure piling up at home. In fact, from all accounts she was a kind and generous soul with the voice of a nightingale that could be heard throughout the neighbourhood.

The story goes that, entranced by her singing while being milked, each of her cows gave an extra four litres of milk every day. The barn bordered on the road leading to the forest, where the woodcutters on their way to work long before daybreak found their inspiration for the day listening to Grandma sing. I wonder what it would have been like had she still been there to preside over the homecoming of one of her lost grandchildren.

However, that was now up to Tante Johanna—moreover, it was her Christian duty to take us in. Because she had inherited the ancestral home, property, and farming enterprise instead of one of the older siblings, as would have been the custom, it naturally fell on Johanna's shoulders to care for her aging parents—now just Grandpa—and assume whatever obligation they would, both legally and morally, have to the extended family. Everyone, certainly Onkel Anton, took it for granted that this obligation would naturally extend to the situation Erich and I found ourselves in.

There was never any doubt in my mind where I belonged. In fact, it was the certain knowledge that if I failed to meet up with my parents, I would live with and be cared for by my grandfather and Tante Johanna that sustained me throughout and gave me the energy and courage when at times, out of sheer desperation, it seemed senseless to carry on. I had some uncertainty about Joachim and how he might be received, but as Onkel Anton strained the muscles in his good leg to pedal his bicycle the last few metres from the forest's edge and across the little creek that had once been my favourite playground, I knew that I was finally home.

I could recognize Tante Johanna from a distance. She was out on the street talking to one of the neighbours, and not being aware of any scheduled wedding or funeral, she instinctively sensed what other major event could possibly have occasioned a visit from her brother.

My heart was in my throat as Anton struggled to balance the bike and lift me off the crossbar. Tante Johanna had no trouble recognizing me, but she just stood there, clapped her hands above her head and shouted unpleasantly, "My God, here comes another one."

It was much easier to detect the pleasure Anton harvested from his sister's distress, as he reached behind him to produce yet another half-starved skeletal body from the package carrier on the back of his bicycle, than to discern anything other than horror in Johanna's face. However, Anton did not linger to enjoy it.

"Come and visit us any time," he said to me as he departed the scene without exchanging any words with his sister or so much as a glance in the direction of Grandpa, who was watching the proceedings from the front door to the house. As I eagerly made my way up the stairs to greet him, my four cousins exploded onto the scene from all directions, everyone talking at once.

Had Joachim landed in some remote village in China, he could hardly have been more confounded or confused. The German dialect spoken in Forchheim at that time might just as well have been Chinese. No one paid any attention to him as he stood in the middle of the yard, confused and unable to reconcile the impressions he had gleaned from me with the reality unfolding before his eyes.

I was pushing my way toward Grandpa until finally I stood to face him. I remembered him to be taller, certainly younger than he appeared to me now. He seemed disinterested and resigned, offering no embrace but for a handshake to indicate any warmth or emotion. Without inquiring about any news I might have brought of my parents or my other siblings, my great idol, after mumbling something I could not understand, just left me standing there and retreated to his quarters.

Johanna's reception came as an even greater shock. She wasn't interested either in what I might have to say about my travels or in how I'd managed to find my way back. Instead, she delivered herself of a tirade about my parents' frivolous lifestyle and what an imposition it was on her to have their starving children dumped at her doorstep. Was it her fault that they were so irresponsible, first to leave home, and then to abandon their children in a strange land? It was hard to believe my mother was her sister. She told me in no uncertain terms that some other accommodation would have to be found, at least for Joachim. Even before I was finished introducing him to my four cousins, Johanna had not only settled on a plan, but was ready to execute it.

Erich had managed to finish his apprenticeship in a business school before being drafted in late 1944. He had been sent to the eastern front, but before he could be assigned to any particular unit or action, he was caught up in the chaos and confusion of an army in total disarray. Like me, he simply struck out on his own and made his way home to Forchheim. His reception when he first arrived was no more hospitable. In fact, shortly after his arrival near the end of the war, Johanna found a farmer about 20 kilometres up the Rhine who was in need of an extra hand and willing to offer room and board to a suitable applicant. Erich, as I was now to find out, chose to strike out on his own instead and to throw in his lot with Berta Kistner, Hanna's mother, and her three children. Johanna, never one to procrastinate on difficult decisions, quickly made up her mind to offer Joachim to the farmer as a substitute.

It all happened so quickly. I thought surely there would be some time to reflect and to allow Grandfather to have a say. In any event, I was mostly interested in learning from the girls where Erich was to be found and therefore slow in registering what was happening. Before I could comprehend her intentions, Johanna had Joachim's spindly body on the back of her bicycle and was heading up the road. We never even had a chance to say goodbye.

I ran after them for a short distance, tears streaming down my face, but it was no contest. The eyes of a starving child don't shrink in proportion to the rest of the body. Disappearing into the distance, Joachim's eyes, looking at me from the back of the bicycle, reflected his utter confusion, his fear, and his despair as Johanna's strong legs pedalled up the hill, increasing the void between us.

We never saw each other again, but those eyes would pierce my inner conscience for the rest of my days. After being inseparable throughout the long ordeal we had suffered together, we had formed a bond so strong that losing him felt for a long time like part of myself had died.

Johanna, when she returned, complained of how hard it had been to hold the farmer to his word.

"What am I to do with this bale of bones? He's just a child," he had complained to her. He was about to chase her off his property when apparently his wife, having no children of her own, intervened and took pity on the miserable creature that was dumped on her doorstep.

It was more than a year before I finally had the strength and the opportunity to start looking for my friend. Johanna was charitable enough to tell me where she had left him, but my reception there was no less hostile than the one she had received.

"How are we to know where the vagabond ended up? We haven't seen him since he ran away," was the farmer's response to my inquiry. Allegedly, he ran away a few days after his arrival, and as far as they were concerned, good riddance.

The woman, hiding behind a wagon being unloaded in the yard, looked mysteriously frightened to me and acted oddly. It's possible that Joachim might have lost Grandfather's address, or he might not have wanted to get in touch with me ever again after his disappointment with my relatives, but I've always had a lingering suspicion that my friend came to harm. In the immediate aftermath of the war there would have been no one to turn to. There was no authority or agency to which one might appeal for help, no postal service to deliver a letter—not that it mattered much in Joachim's case since, even though he knew the address of his parents' place in Poznań, there was no one left there interested in what he might write. My only friend, brother, and soulmate just vanished from the face of the earth like so many millions of others, victims of a time during which the civilized world took a step back to the past to revisit the caves whence it had come.

CHAPTER 8

Home at Last

I cannot sing the old songs I sang long years ago
For heart and voice would fail me and foolish tears would flow.
—Charlotte Alington Barnard or "Claribel," English songwriter

Spring had turned into summer, the war was now history, and people began to take stock of what they had left to rebuild their lives with. Forchheim had been spared direct bombing raids of the sort that destroyed most of the cities. Whatever damage there was to property resulted from the artillery bombardment aimed at the town during the final days of the war.

But there was one incident that did leave its mark when a particularly vicious attack on Karlsruhe missed its intended target. Toward the end, no longer encumbered by any German defences, Allied bombers would arrive by the hundreds. Two or three of the aircraft would fly in advance of the main column to identify the area to be hit on any given night. They would drop a "Christmas tree," some flares similar to modern fireworks that would stay suspended over the intended target, marking it for the main strike force. One night there was a strong wind, which carried the marker in the direction of Forchheim.

Fortunately, the hundreds of tonnes of explosives fell on fields just outside the town, but the location included a flak battery manned by about two dozen, mostly teenaged soldiers. All of them gave their lives to the Fatherland that night. When the townspeople arrived on the scene the following morning, they found most of the bodies decapitated. The chinstraps on their helmets had proven strong enough to withstand the concussion.

As I learned later, toward the end of the war Forchheim got more of its share of the blessings that came from artillery bombardments. The assault started around the middle of December 1944 with an intermittent barrage

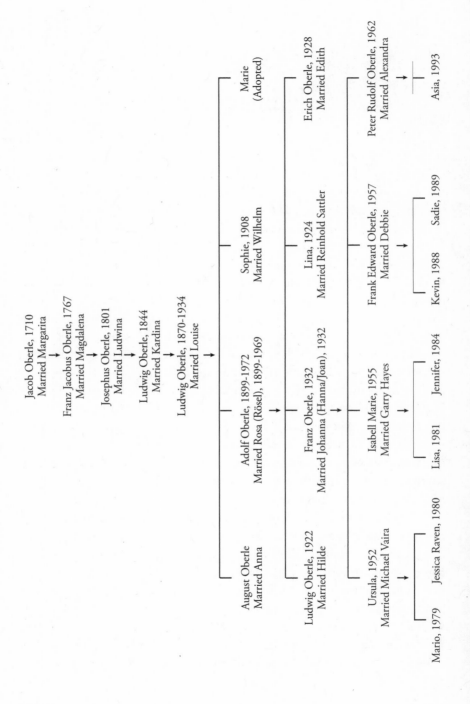

By the time American troops reached Karlsruhe, a typical street looked like this. The graffiti mocks the Volkswagen, "the People's Car" that was promised to every German.

of artillery fire and constant assaults by low-flying aircraft, forcing everyone to turn their basements into permanent living quarters. Several people were killed venturing outside just long enough to replenish whatever food and drink could be scrounged to feed the livestock. The villages of Forchheim and Mörsch had to endure this torture until the end of April 1945.

This type of warfare, much like that visited upon the people of London by Hitler's V-1 and V-2 rockets, is accompanied by its own very special kind of terror. The fear is multiplied as the subconscious mind registers the seconds between the discharge and the detonation of the explosives. The fact that most people survived this with their sanity intact is a miracle in itself.

Just around the time that Joachim and I left Lengenfeld on our journey west, the French under General de Gaulle, after crossing the Rhine just north of Karlsruhe, began working their way south. They encountered little resistance until they got to Mörsch, where a contingent of the SS made its presence felt. The SS was fighting on two fronts, one against the advancing French army and the other against the local population, who had adorned their homes with white bedsheets, signalling to anyone who cared that they'd had enough of war and were no longer in the mood to assist in the defence of their town. After being driven farther up the Rhine, the SS rewarded Mörsch with its own artillery bombardment.

The Germans did issue warnings in advance of the attack, ordering the citizens of Mörsch to gather in or near their church, which they promised would be spared. The French, to their credit, ordered both Mörsch and Forchheim to be evacuated instead. With a few little hand-drawn wagons and some hitched to cows as their only means of transport, the inhabitants took whatever they could, leaving their livestock behind to find refuge in Daxlanden or nearer to Karlsruhe.

The ordeal was brief, but their return home brought more misery. With a keen memory of the SS directive, the people of Mörsch headed for their church and found it and the immediate area around it in ruins. The bells that for generations had called them to worship, chimed during their wedding celebrations and honoured them at their funerals had fallen eerily silent. The French forces had done their work as well. Not a single domestic animal was spared from the vengeful orgy of death and destruction in which the "liberators" had indulged. The chickens, pigs, and cows of Forchheim and Mörsch, having been taught a lesson, would never again conspire to start a war.

The initial French fighting force was soon succeeded by a different contingent altogether. De Gaulle's occupation force was made up of a company of Moroccan servicemen who, together with their French comrades, apparently were much better trained in the use of what was dangling between their legs than what was slung over their shoulders. Stories of their atrocities were legion. Any girl from 12 to 60 was fair game. They raped and pillaged to their hearts' content. Most of the young girls in the community spent weeks on end hidden away in cow barns, under haystacks, or in basements. Old men who refused to give them away or, worse, attempted to protect them were beaten to a pulp.

The brutality touched my own family. Onkel Otto Leibold and Tante Gretel told me how they had made the crucial mistake of not removing Hitler's picture from the print shop of their elaborate business establishment, which included the store and their living quarters. There was no consideration of the fact that it was obligatory for businesses of that sort to display the Führer's image in a prominent place. The family was forcibly invited out on the street to be entertained as their life's work was put to the torch. Friends and neighbours stood helplessly by, weeping and sharing their sorrow. The cruelty of such an experience is indescribable.

The SS promised to spare Mörsch's church, but shelled it along with the rest of the town.

The French liberators were still there when I arrived back home. However their exploits, after coming to the attention of some of the more civilized officers in the French army, had been stopped. The Moroccans were confined to their barracks. Any of them caught roaming the streets or pestering civilians were hunted down and horsewhipped back to their confines.

The war had robbed my little hometown of its innocence. It destroyed the myths that had stabilized those unwritten laws to which everyone was obedient. Not a single family had been spared the sacrifices of human life the war demanded. The Treiber family, who owned one of the local bakeries, had six sons, all of them drafted and serving the Fatherland. Only two returned from the war. Four of the Rastetter family's sons, as well, were among the 233 of the 2,800 residents of Forchheim at the beginning of the war who were killed in action or remained listed as missing. To this day, people recall their fear and anxiety every time the town's mayor was spotted in the company of an official of the Nazi party or a ranking military officer, making their way through the streets to deliver the Führer's gratitude for the ultimate sacrifice another native son, husband, brother, or father had made for the glory of the Fatherland. Only death itself can bring an end to the pain and restore the peace, which those who were left behind would be deprived of for the rest of their natural life.

Once demarcation of the various occupied sectors was complete, the French retreated as far as Rastatt, 30 kilometres south of Forchheim. Their pillaging continued in another form and lasted as long as it took to clear-cut most of the stately trees in the Black Forest and ship them across the Rhine.

Karlsruhe and its surroundings were brought under the authority of the American armed forces. From what I was told by my relatives and friends, they were greeted as liberators, not so much from the Nazis as from the French. Soup kitchens were set up to stave off the worst of the famine, and some prominent citizens were given authority to begin the process of rebuilding local government to act under the auspices of the new occupation force. Fortunately, most of the new interim civic administrators in Karlsruhe, and all of those in Forchheim, served with distinction under the most difficult conditions. Within a very short period of time they managed to re-establish some of the most essential public services. By mid-year even some limited rail service was re-established.

People started to gather whatever was left of their belongings and their shattered lives. Nature, the only remaining constant, had not abandoned her rhythm. The balm of spring began to dispel the smell of death and destruction. People ventured out into the fields, planting and seeding whatever was available. In Karlsruhe, a network of small-track railroads was constructed to remove the rubble that covered the streets. Outside the city, huge mountains of debris attracted scavengers looking to salvage bricks and bits of other materials needed to repair and rebuild.

During all this, I was too ill to be interested in anything besides getting reacquainted with my relatives and some of my old classmates and friends. Aside from Onkel Otto Leibold, none of my relatives in Forchheim had suffered any serious damage to their homes and businesses. The Oberles in Mörsch were not so lucky. Onkel August and Tante Anna's home and barn were spared, but Tante Sofie and Onkel Wilhelm lost everything during the artillery bombardment. I found them and my two cousins, Lothar and Hans, living in a little shed, perhaps the size of a one-car garage, which one of their friends had made available to them. Meanwhile, aside from the love and friendship offered to me by my four cousins at the Albecker household, my life there was no less awkward and difficult than the first reception had been.

I was assigned Grandma's old bed next to Grandpa, but sleep was out of the question. First, I had not slept in a bed so soft and warm for as long as I could remember. I was terrified that if I fell asleep, I might not wake up to get to the toilet in time. I still had little or no control of my bowels. The toilet, such as it was, was outside, over the manure pile across the yard. Once or twice I managed to sneak out, but Grandpa was usually awake when I got back. He had it fixed in his mind that I was sleepwalking, and for the rest of the night, every time I got up, he would chase me back to bed. Needless to say, neither of us had much sleep, and things were in a horrible mess next morning.

Even before breakfast after the first night, Grandpa decided to cure my diarrhea. His remedy was swift and simple. A raw egg sucked right out of the shell and a diet of dry bread. Try as I might, I could not bring myself to suck on the egg. Grandpa, slapping me across the face to subdue my resistance and putting me in a chokehold, finally administered the slimy mess. My stomach was convulsing, squeezing out the little it had taken in. I was delirious for days, clinging to life. One of the nuns was summoned for help, but I am not aware that any medicine was administered.

Deathly ill, tormented by the lingering doubt that I would ever see my parents again, unloved and rejected by my grandfather, I had reached the low point of my miserable existence. Had I been able to convince myself—I was often burdened by the thought—that putting an end to my life would in some way punish or evoke remorse among my tormentors, I might have found the courage to do it.

In the end, it was Erich and his friends who inspired new hope in me and the will to live. He was never far away, showing up at the most critical moments to show his concern, his genuine love, and affection. Still a teenager himself, but matured by his own frightful experiences, he acted in a manner far beyond his years. I will never forget our first reunion after my arrival.

He was the first person I visited, just an hour later. He had discovered an oasis of relative comfort and security to which I myself was introduced when cousin Lore escorted me to the other end of town. Erich, Tante Johanna explained, had found refuge with "Wagner Jörg's Berta" because she was in need of a "man" in the house. There were only unconfirmed reports that Emil, Berta's husband was still alive in a Siberian prisoner of war camp—and she was struggling to pay off a mortgage on the house and raise her own three children. It was an unlikely place for a couple of starving children to find a home.

Despite the many strange sights they'd seen in the war, people in Forchheim must have wondered who that bundle of rags was with one of the Albecker girls, dodging from house to house to avoid attention. I could sense we were being observed from behind windows, some still without glass. As we approached the Kistners, I could feel my emotions welling up in me. Would Erich be able to shed some light on the whereabouts of our parents and other siblings?

Ludwig's situation, of course, was known. He was a prisoner of war with the British. He had not been drafted until late 1944, after D-Day and the Allied landing in Normandy, when, in desperation, the Nazis resorted to enlisting retirees and teenagers to be part of the Total War. Ludwig was 22 at the time. After just a brief engagement at the front, he was lucky to fall into the hands of the British. Unlike the Russians, the Western Allies not only treated their prisoners with respect and dignity, but also lived up to their obligations under the Geneva Convention and informed families, through the German authorities, of their status and whereabouts.

But, I wondered, what about Lina? Had anyone heard from her?

The Kistners were all there, in the garden behind the house, picking gooseberries—Erich, Berta, and the children: Cilli, who was Erich's own age, Rudi, and Hanna. Only Hanna saw us coming through the gate and crossing the front yard. She got Erich's attention, perhaps sensing that because I looked as starved as Erich himself did, we might have something in common. It was a far different welcome from the one I had received an hour earlier. As soon as the first obvious and urgent questions were out of the way, Berta, seeing no need to ask whether or not I was hungry, ran into the house to scrounge up something to eat.

Somehow, the harsh reality that nothing had been heard about my family was cushioned by the genuine concern and warmth of these friendly people. We talked for hours. Hanna just kept looking at me with those inquisitive eyes, as if she already knew that she would share her destiny with

Frank, at about age 14, holds hands with Hanna during a family picture. Next to the couple is her brother, Rudi, and in the back row (from right) are Hanna's sister, Cilli, Hanna's mother, Berta, and family friends Leo and Berta Licht.

me. Berta promised to find some way to replace what was left of my clothes. It was hard, at Lore's urging, to go back to my grandfather's.

The Kistner household became a haven for me, partly because Hanna had ignited a spark of interest in me on that bright summer day in the garden behind the house, although neither of us realized just how fateful our third encounter was to be. I also got along well with my four cousins. They thought it was great to have a boy around the place, someone to tease, share the chores with, and share some of the mean spirits of our intolerant grandfather and their overworked and stressed parents.

At Grandfather's, Tante Johanna finally decided on her own remedy to cure my illness by ordering the girls to include me in their daily prayer ritual. Formal prayers were delivered five times a day: in the morning before getting up; at noon lunchtime, before and after the meal; at suppertime; and before going to bed. This presumably got my name on God's agenda at least 20, perhaps even 30, times every day, depending on whether Johanna, her husband—Onkel Otto Albecker—and Grandpa also participated. Since some of the prayers were directed exclusively at Mother Mary, it remains uncertain who deserved most of the credit for the gradual improvement of my condition.

In any case, thanks to God and Mary I was on the mend. My first outing, on the back of Johanna's bicycle, was to the Oberle relatives at Mörsch. Onkel August, Dad's older brother, was nursing his wife, who was on her deathbed. Nevertheless, Johanna subjected them to a lament about how she, a pious servant of God, had been burdened not only with the duty of serving her own family, God-fearing as they all were, but also the care of her parents and one of Grandpa's half brothers, Clemens. He had died some time earlier but had spent his adult life under her roof. The fact that the trade-off was the inheritance of the family estate did not enter the conversation.

To top that off, Johanna lamented, she was now being tested by her own wayward sister, who had abandoned her duty to God, the community, and even her own children. Would it be too much to ask—with the likelihood fading that Rösel and Adolf had survived the war—for some of the other relatives to assume responsibility for the children they had left behind?

Onkel August, a kind and generous man, was out of the question as a benefactor, but Tante Sofie, without hesitation, put her arms around me and declared that there was always room for one more. Eyeing the sparse surroundings, I couldn't quite figure out where that room would be, but reminded myself that I had been in much worse situations, none of which radiated the warmth and kindness I felt here. Cousin Lothar even offered to come with us to help fetch my things. How could he know that there were no "things"? All my worldly possessions were the rags hanging on my skeleton.

It might have been just a tiny twinge of conscience that prompted Johanna's decision to first discuss the matter with her husband and Grandfather Leibold, who naturally had a say in the matter. So I returned with her to Forchheim once more and, as it finally turned out, ended up with the Kistners instead.

Erich had been offered a real job at a larger farm in Durlach Aue, on the other side of Karlsruhe, and had left Berta. So instead of emigrating to Mörsch, which would have been Johanna's preference, I accepted Berta's offer to take Erich's place, moving only half the distance to the Forchheimer *Oberdorf* [upper Forchheim] to share what little she was able to scrape and scrounge together to keep her own children from starving. It was this third encounter between Hanna and me that would blossom into friendship and bond us together for the rest of our lives.

The Kistners had not been spared the ravages of the war. True, the house suffered only minor damage, but Emil, Hanna's father, after he was drafted in 1939, had been sent to march into Poland and Russia. His children, Cilli, Hanna, and Rudi, were 10, 7 and 3 years old, respectively, when he left. Emil had been reported missing in action two years earlier, leaving Berta to fend for herself and the children. With some help from her family, who were prosperous farmers, she somehow managed to survive. Her sister Anna, who operated a small corner grocery store, adopted Hanna at the tender age of nine to live with her for the duration of the war or until things normalized.

Hanna may have had enough to eat, but it was no bargain. She was assigned considerable chores as a member of a household operating a busy store and caring for Anna's chronically ill husband. At first there was Cousin Edward, Tante Anna's only child, to share the chores, and he earned Hanna's love and affection, becoming like a brother to her. But he was drafted into Hitler's Children's Army and gave his life for the Fatherland on the very last day of the war. Our own son Frank's middle name honours his memory.

Hanna's story was no less traumatic than my own, her emotional scars no less deep. She contributed her childhood to the arrangement. She would not be able to recall even one hour wasted in what normal children call playtime. She never had a single toy that would have warranted wasting idle time on anyway. Her work schedule started long before the rooster in the backyard announced the day and ended long after the chickens had retired for the night. Her only remuneration might have been some innovative accounting of the ration stamps Berta cashed at the store during the worst periods of food shortages.

Among her regular duties, after attending the 6 a.m. daily mass, was to act as the purchasing and delivery agent for the store's merchandise. This meant regular 14-kilometre round trips on foot to Karlsruhe pulling a hand wagon and under constant fear of being attacked by low-flying aircraft.

Tante Anna was a devout Catholic who followed the faith slavishly. Like all mothers, she knew her son to be very special, but in her case God had confirmed that. Why else did He call him home so young? Obviously, he had been chosen for a higher calling in another world. Tante Anna expected that like Holy Mother Mary herself, she would be rewarded in heaven for having borne and raised this prodigy. In the meantime, she expected everyone to follow her example, living the faith according to God's very own representative, Pfarrer Dorer, who guided her and absolved her in the confessional from any minor diversion from the path of righteousness.

Berta, too, took strength from her faith in coping with the particular burden God had placed on her shoulders. She chose to give her son to God as well, although in less dramatic fashion. Rudi was being groomed for the priesthood, and nothing, not even Rudi, who was much too young at the time to have an opinion on the matter, would stand in her way. One might point to ignorance as the basis for such blind faith, but without it, how could these people have survived the savagery they experienced? These women were entirely on their own. Their faith allowed them to accept what would otherwise have been humanly impossible to absorb.

Late in 1945 one of Emil's returning comrades reported seeing him at a railway station in East Germany on his way home. It's hard to describe the excitement this news caused. Even before the fall of Berlin and the final surrender, some soldiers from other war zones had started to drift back to live in hiding until a general amnesty was declared, but husbands, brothers, and fathers who had been deployed on the eastern front were not heard from for months or even years. Emil had only been home on furlough two or three times before he was reported missing in action in 1944.

Despite this news, it was another three years before Emil finally did make it back, a human wreck. Even his own wife and children could barely recognize him as he walked through the front gate. His solid athletic body had shrunk to 95 pounds of skin and bone, and his toothless face was marred by exposure to the elements, pain, the abuse he had suffered, and the loneliness and despair he had endured. He had been declared unfit for work at the POW camp in Siberia and ordered released, only to be imprisoned again. The cattle train he was on was travelling west when it met an eastbound train carrying a cargo of more able-bodied prisoners. Some of them escaped, creating a problem for their guards, who had to account for any of the missing. The solution was simple: since none of the POWs had identity papers or tags, the vacancies were filled with passengers of the westbound train. Emil, too weak to protest or escape himself, was among them.

His final homecoming in 1948 was traumatic in itself. It took many months for him to regain enough strength to begin living a normal life. Not all his compatriots even had this small good fortune. Of the few who did return, most were marred for life. Perhaps the saddest case was that of one of Emil's comrades from a neighbouring town who had summoned his last ounce of strength to make it to the front gate of his home, the gate through which he had walked on his way to war seven years earlier. It was the middle of the night and his wife, who had pined for his love and prayed for his return all the time he was gone, looked out a window to inquire who was there. "*Ich bins der Anton*" was all he could mutter before his voice failed him and the emotion of the moment snuffed out what little life he had left.

He became one of the tens of millions of soldiers and civilians who lost their lives during the Second World War. His wife and children are among the hundreds of millions who will carry their physical and emotional scars to their graves.

In retrospect, it's amazing that people did eventually manage to achieve some semblance of normal life. It's nothing short of miraculous that they managed to carry on after such harrowing experiences. Even more astounding is how quickly it all happened. By the end of 1945, school had started again. Hanna and I were in Grade 8, together with 66 other students and one teacher, who had the job of trying to impose some discipline and re-establish customary decorum.

By then I was back with Tante Johanna, Onkel Otto, and Grandfather Leibold. What had happened was this. Hanna and I returned from a trip to the French sector, where we scrounged for fruit and fresh vegetables, to hear from Berta that Grandfather had developed some form of homesickness for me and was demanding that I return to live with him again. The real reason was that rumours were circulating about my relationship with my maternal family. Who knows, Tante Johanna might also have experienced a rare moment of compassion, perhaps while in close proximity to God in Pfarrer Dorer's confessional. All I know is that the priest delivered an exposé of my situation, without mentioning any names of course, during his Sunday sermon.

At first I refused to accept the invitation. I even contemplated striking out on my own again, but Berta persuaded me to accept my fate. Fortunately, I did not have to spend too much time at Tante Johanna's house. Always resourceful, she managed to find me a job at the large government-owned tobacco research farm outside town for the rest of the summer.

Once school resumed in the fall, things started to settle down. Onkel Otto Albecker was back at his job in the city during the day, and Tante Johanna was glad of the extra hand in the fields during harvest. I assume that I was credited with earning my keep, but was still reminded at every meal that they had never seen anyone who could eat as much as I did. Perhaps I should have been thankful for the good care and the concern that was shown in monitoring my diet.

Erich still made his regular visits on weekends to check on me. Once we were in the company of Grandfather on our way to church when Erich boldly asked him if there was nothing he could do to make sure I got enough to eat. Could he not see that I was starving to death?

Grandfather was never much of a talker. He simply replied that he had enough trouble looking after himself. He and the Albeckers lived through the war relatively unscathed. Onkel Otto, for whatever reason, had been excused from serving in the military. They had managed to keep their livestock, usually two cows, a calf, one or two pigs, chickens, and other assorted farm animals. They farmed enough acreage to provide plenty of feed for the animals and themselves. True, they were required to deliver a certain quota to the market for redistribution, but there was always some flexibility and even enough to spare to supply Pfarrer Dorer with his daily stipend of milk and the odd half-metre of sausage.

Otto, before the war, even managed to save enough money to afford the luxury of owning a motorcycle. It was his pride and joy. Riding around town with his Baron von Richthofen leather helmet and gloves elevated him to a much higher social stratum than he was otherwise entitled to. However, toward the end of the war, with fuel in short supply, and fearing that the green monster might be confiscated by either the Germans or the liberators, he decommissioned it. Not even the girls knew where it was hidden, something that ended up putting me in jail.

CHAPTER 9

A New Law and Order

I do not feel obliged to believe that the same god who has endowed us with sense, reason, and intellect has intended us to forgo their use.
—Galileo Galilei, Italian astronomer and physicist

The Americans, soon after their arrival, decided that their authority should be backed up with some civilian police presence. There were few guidelines set out for the one-man detachment in Forchheim. Ernst Meier, the person chosen for the job, used a lot of ingenuity and his lively imagination to develop his own operational policy. It must be assumed that Ernst had some previous experience that qualified him for the job. Not being an original Forchheimer, however, he could expect it to take some time for him to earn respect in the community. And when it came to me, it was perhaps his misfortune to be the first person to try to reacquaint me with order and authority after the collapse of the old institutions. I certainly was not ready to once again respect and trust anyone who, just like his predecessors during the Nazi period, threatened innocent people with the most severe consequences should they fail to submit to the new rules.

Meier, dazzled by the prospect of becoming a motorized force, had developed an interest in Otto Albecker's 125-cc motorcycle and decided to empower himself with the authority to commandeer it for his exclusive use. Grandfather was home alone, and I was just getting back from a milk delivery, when he arrived to expropriate what he had been told was Otto's most prized possession. Grandfather pleaded ignorance. As far as he was concerned, he had never seen nor heard of a motorcycle around the place. Assessing his options, Ernst quickly determined me to be the softer target against which to press his case. Surely a boy my age would be curious to know where Onkel Otto was hiding his precious motorcycle. I, of course, took my cue from

Grandpa. If he could tell such a blatant lie, so could I. Ernst warned me that refusing to co-operate with him would land me in a prison for incorrigible Nazi boys. I told him that I doubted I would be any worse off than I was in my present situation.

Since he didn't yet have handcuffs, he picked up a piece of rope, wrapped it around my wrists, and escorted me to city hall for further interrogation. Once there, in a tone not unlike that Lieutenant Boronovski might have used in such a situation, he tried to reason with me, explaining the importance of his mission and the authority backing it. I told him of a particular place, somewhere between his legs, where he could stick his authority.

The jail in Forchheim was never intended for dangerous prisoners. It was about an eight-foot-square room in the basement of the Rathaus with a small window, near the ceiling, looking out the back of the building. I have the distinction of being among the very few people who ever occupied the place. No one would have spent more than a night there. In my case, it was perhaps half an hour before I was taken before the interim *Bürgermeister* to learn my fate. Fortunately, he was a man who knew my dad well from the time they sang in the local choir together, and he shared my dad's sympathies for the Social Democrats. He obviously had great sympathy for me and told his chief of police not to be so stupid and let me go on my way.

The story didn't end there. Several days later, Ernst showed up at the Albeckers' again. This time we were all sitting around the kitchen table for lunch. He entered with a hearty and cheerful "*Grüss Gott*" ["God's greetings"]. To Johanna's invitation to share a piece of bread and cottage cheese with us, he responded with a convincing "*Vergelts Gott*" ["May God reward you"]. How could such a pious man come with any bad intent?

Ernst then started to explain how much he regretted military command's orders that he should appropriate transportation for himself to carry out his thankless task. Fortunately, he explained, Otto would receive adequate compensation for the short time his motorcycle would be required, and Ernst would see to it himself that Otto received the proper licence to put it back in service as soon as it was returned. That promise netted him a second piece of bread and a trip to the hayloft, where the hidden treasure was surrendered. Ernst even insisted Otto take it for a quick spin through town before he took possession of it.

Sadly, the story does not have a happy ending. A short time later, Otto received an official letter from the headquarters of the newly formed civilian police commission in Karlsruhe informing him that his motorcycle had been stolen from a repair garage where it had been taken to be painted. The only compensation he ever got was the satisfaction of seeing Ernst pursue his "thankless task" on foot.

With the help of some of my new-found friends in school, to whom my jail experience was a badge of honour, I got my revenge as well. Every time we met Ernst on the road, we would crouch down on our imaginary motorcycles, extend our arms toward the imaginary handlebars, and rev up the imaginary engine with a powerful *vrooom, vrooom*. His complaints to our teacher fell on deaf ears. Compared to the war he was waging against the unruly mob he had to tame, this ranked as a very minor skirmish.

Clearly I was not alone in my loss of respect for authority. Others of my age group had had experiences equally as traumatic as mine during the war. All had taken on adult responsibilities. Since they grew up without fathers or older brothers, their mothers, no matter how resourceful, often had to depend on them to make ends meet.

I myself felt abandoned by my parents. Why had they not waited for me on that fateful day back in Luckland? But there were many people around town who pitied me as an orphan and encouraged me to hope that my parents had somehow survived and would eventually return home. I tried to convince myself that there was a logical explanation why Mom and Dad had been delayed. Yet with every passing day my hope faded, leaving little on which to sustain any optimism. I felt betrayed by the system for which I had been forced to trade the love of my parents. Even though I was not yet able to understand the full extent of the crimes and atrocities that had been committed in the name of the Führer, it was nevertheless clear to me that the guilt for what happened would eventually have to be shared by the German people collectively.

Worse, I felt betrayed by my idols. Even Lieutenant Boronovski had to be part of the conspiracy. Grandfather, my childhood hero, called me a *Strassen Raüber und ein Taschendieb* [a street robber and pickpocket] and treated me as such. He never even attempted to lift a hand in protest against my arrest by Ernst Meier.

My faith too was shaken. If God, as Johanna and Pfarrer Dorer would have me believe, was the source of our suffering, why was I singled out for most of it? Only a community as solidly anchored, as slavish, to the church could accept such reasoning. I felt no attachment to such moorings. Certainly Pfarrer Dorer, who regularly made me a target of his temper tantrums and the physical abuse he liked to dispense, set me adrift even further, adding to the uncertainty and doubt about the faith in which I was raised.

Millions of children, the real victims of war, were permanently scarred by experiences similar to mine. Some undoubtedly spent much of the rest of their lives unable to commit to any loving relationship, seeking instead every opportunity to get revenge for the torture and pain they had unjustly suffered. For my part, as my hometown got on with rebuilding, I found it hard to share in the excitement, new hope, and joy.

Forchheim was undergoing big changes. Despite the carnage the war had inflicted on the male population, there was all of a sudden no shortage of people. The town was obliged to absorb and provide shelter for hundreds of ethnic German refugees who had flooded into the west from Poland, East Germany, and Czechoslovakia. Officials of the newly appointed municipal government went from house to house, appraising the value, assessing the damage and, in accordance with a formula that had been worked out, designating any space that was surplus to the immediate needs of the occupants for the use of the newcomers. The Kistners, for example, had to take in a family of five to share their living space.

In addition, properties that had survived unscathed or suffered only minor damage were assessed an equalization tax, which was added to the mortgage. Naturally, none of this happened without a lot of complaint. But considering the plight of those who had nothing left at all, it was deemed an acceptable sacrifice. There was always much arguing and shouting any time a new transport of people arrived with nothing but the clothes on their backs. However, I always greeted them in the faint hope that Mom and Dad would be among them.

In subsequent years people began to speak of the positive impact the influx of new blood had on the community. The immigrants proved themselves to be most industrious, offering eager hands to help with rebuilding, and contributing to the local economy with demands for shelter of their own and other needs. While some old-timers refer to the newcomers as *Flüchtlinge* [refugees] even today, it was just a generic nickname. Better to be called a refugee than a pickpocket. Apart from the language barrier, I cannot recall any serious problems, not even at the school, in assimilating the people and the culture they brought with them.

From time to time I still found an excuse to visit the Forchheimer Oberdorf and to drop in on Berta and the kids. The *Schlachtfest*, Forchheim-style, was one such occasion.

Berta had managed to raise a pig to the appropriate size (at least 200 pounds) for slaughtering. The preparations leading up to the day were as complex and elaborate as the main event.

Our very good friend Kneisel—his nickname—was hired as the director of operations. His reputation and credentials as a butcher were legendary. He would have torn his hair out if he'd seen the villagers' method of slaughtering pigs back on the baron's estate in Luckland. For one thing, the blood was one of the main ingredients for his art. It had to be stirred for hours before it was mixed with a variety of other components and spices to produce some of mankind's finest delicacies. As well, he didn't waste an

Kneisel displays two hams from the Schlachtfest, Forchheim-style. Rudi, Berta's son, squats in front, while Berta is on the right with the author. On the left are Frau Fuchs and her son visiting from the city.

inch of the precious intestines, which were meticulously cleaned to act as envelopes for his sausages.

Kneisel had been drafted and served in the army, but God, no doubt persuaded by the desperate pleas of Forchheim's starving flock, found a way to call him home. Not to heaven, of course—that would have required giving his life for the Fatherland—but home to Forchheim, which only required the loss of one of his legs. I often wonder where all the legs lost on the eastern front were buried.

Well over six feet tall, Kneisel was a big man who presented an imposing figure. Even without his leg, he must have weighed as much as the fattest pig the Forchheimers had managed to hide from the marauding armies. His thumb was bigger than my forearm, and only the great esteem in which the locals held him matched the size of his heart and cheerful demeanour. His skills and the manner in which he applied them ranked him near the top of the social order, especially during the last desperate months of the war.

Accepting the role of director of operations at a Schlachtfest imposed on him the burden of dealing with the authorities, who, given the desperate food-supply situation, were ruthless in discharging their mandate. Before a licence for slaughter could be issued, the animal had to be inspected. The inspector had to appraise not only the amount of *Schinken* [ham], *Wurst* [sausage], and all-important *Schweineschmaltz* [lard] the animal would yield, but also the size of the household to which these delectable commodities would accrue. Then he would determine how much of the harvest was to be delivered to local stores for distribution and, in addition, how long the family's ration cards would be suspended. Needless to say, this inspection was critical. One could assume that the inspector himself might be grateful for a small donation in return for a lenient appraisal, but this approach was always fraught with danger.

However, Kneisel had his own innovative ways of handling this situation. He opted to use an understudy during the inspection. He would borrow from another farmer some scrawny 125-pounder to stand in for the star of the show. After the inspector had gone, the rightful candidate would be restored to play his intended part. Kneisel—his sleeves rolled up, his arms in the *Wurstkessel* [a huge tub containing all the ingredients for the various types of sausages] up to his elbows—would delight in describing his encounters with the officials.

On one occasion, the inspector was curious to know from which poor orphanage this scrawny little pig had been acquired. Kneisel volunteered the information that it had lost all its weight being chased up and down the Rhine by the French army, who couldn't shoot straight enough to kill it. On another, the inspector was puzzled by how such a small pig could produce such an ample manure pile.

"Can you show me the asshole which produced these fat turds?" he wanted to know. Kneisel, never at a loss for words, simply lifted the critter by its tail and, pointing to the appropriate place, explained, "This being a female pig, it's the second hole from the bottom."

Just like spending time in Ernst Meier's jail, it was a badge of honour to be on the butt end of one of Kneisel's practical jokes. During Berta's Schlachtfest, I had worked up a sweat stirring the blood and keeping the water in which the animal was submerged hot enough to allow the skin to be scraped clean of hair. Kneisel seemed to become increasingly frustrated as he tried, unsuccessfully, to scrape all the hair from the crevices and wrinkles the pig had acquired around its jowls and head.

"This beast has more wrinkles in its face than Pfarrer Dorer has on his scrotum," he declared, and with that he cut the whole head off, strapped it on the back of my bicycle, and ordered me to take it to the barber to have it professionally treated.

At first I thought it might be the proper thing to do, but I did have some doubts as I carried the bulky object with its bulging eyes into the shop. Anton the barber was busy with one of his customers, and there were several others waiting. I was sitting in the only vacant chair, the pig's head in my lap facing toward the room, when Anton turned to greet his new customer. I don't know what must have been funnier to the others in the room: me sitting there, perfectly serious, with the pig head, or the sight of Anton, his eyes at least as big as the pig's and his mouth, which he had opened a bit too wide, snapping desperately at his false teeth as they tried to escape. I felt the blood drain from my face as Anton came for me, his straight razor still in hand. He waved it in front of my eyes as he escorted me out of his shop with a message for Kneisel: "You tell him, the next time I see him, I'll use this to make him look just like this pig and he'll never need a barber again."

Despite this humiliation, I was grateful for the friendship and special affection Kneisel showed me. There was always a word of encouragement or a sausage end for me when we met on the street. To the townspeople he was truly a godsend. With so few able-bodied men around, everyone called on him to help with the chores, like killing a few chickens or castrating the odd pig, that were just too onerous for some of the women to do. I am not aware of the origin of his nickname, but given that one of our classmates, a cousin, also carried the handle, I assume that it was inherited. Had it not been the rule in Forchheim that a nickname must somehow be derogatory, he would have been called "The Friendly Giant," for that he truly was.

Kneisel's career blossomed after the war. Together with his industrious wife, he established one of the finest restaurants and inns in the area, where the service and the food were legendary. Our friendship continued even after my emigration to Canada and lasted until his untimely death. Knowing how homesick I was in a foreign country for some good wholesome sausage, he always made sure, whenever Joan and I came for a visit, that Berta was stocked with sufficient quantities of his hams, sausages, and other delicacies.

While life began to be more bearable in the rural areas, it took much longer for people in the cities to focus on anything other than finding the next meal. The more industrious city folk scoured the countryside, seeking to trade whatever possessions they had salvaged from the ruins of their homes for food. Money had little value, mostly because there was not much to buy. Farmers who had managed to hide a few chickens, some milk, or even some meat were paid with fine silverware, Persian rugs, even furniture. The large department stores in the cities were geared to do business strictly on the barter system. One was able to trade fine china for an overcoat or a dress for a handbag.

More important items, such as bicycle tires or spare parts for machinery, required visiting a more sophisticated but very open black market. Here a pair of nylon stockings, a novelty at that time, might fetch a few litres of gasoline or a 10-pound Black Forest ham, which in turn could be traded for a 100-pound bag of *Ami Mehl*—flour supplied by the American military.

Erich was among the first to find a real and permanent job in his vocation. Recognizing a need, the military authority appointed people with the right credentials to begin publishing a regional newspaper, and Erich was hired as an advertising clerk. He managed to make the best of his position, which put him in the centre of some of the black-market activities. Visiting him in his office, I could always count on a handful of chocolate bars or a helpful hint on how to improve my situation.

The newspaper, *Badishe Neuesten Nachrichten* [Latest News], grew into one of Germany's major regional tabloids, and Erich ended up spending his entire working career there, retiring as a senior executive.

By the end of 1945 my tobacco farm job had ended, and I continued on at school. Apart from Hanna, I hardly remembered the classmates from my first school days in 1938. Nor did I have very much in common with them at first. However, once I had reacquainted myself with the local dialect, I quickly earned their friendship and respect.

Conforming to the new discipline was quite another matter. Our teacher, Herr Becht, had little time for, and perhaps less interest in, the advanced methods of teaching to which I had been accustomed at the residential school under Lieutenant Boronovski. Becht and his colleagues were of the old school. Discipline was enforced with the strap and by humiliating students in front of their peers. Pfarrer Dorer, who was the only other regular teacher, took a particular interest in me. His reasoning, I suppose, was that since I had no parents, I must be deprived of any regular corporal punishment, which he felt was an essential part of a proper upbringing. He made up for the deficiency, and fighting back only made the situation worse.

Frank is about age 14 in this photograph.

My new classmates and I openly rebelled against being treated like children who had grown up under normal conditions. In the years after the war we formed strong bonds of friendship that have lasted a lifetime. As I write this, several of my classmates have passed on, but those who remain still get together on a regular basis. A group of 28 visited us in Canada in 1987, and every time Joan and I return to Germany for a visit, a reunion with our friends is among the highlights of our trip. During our reunions we celebrate our intimate relationship and our individual accomplishments against all odds. None of us had an opportunity to pursue an academic career—the only formal training we received after graduation from grade school was some occupational instruction—but even so, many of my classmates have excelled in their own businesses or achieved high-ranking positions in some of Germany's largest corporations.

On the national scene, life also began to follow a relatively normal routine. Even though it wasn't until 1949 that a new national government was re-established in Germany, the occupation forces agreed to the reorganization of semi-autonomous local and regional authorities. The country was divided into four sectors controlled by the respective military commands of the United States, the Soviet Union, Britain, and France. Right from the beginning it was clear that the Soviet Union would never agree to the development of a new government based on the principles of democracy and a free-market economy. Stalin interpreted his victory over Germany as a licence to expand his sphere of dominance throughout eastern Europe, including such countries as Hungary, Bulgaria, Romania, Czechoslovakia, Poland, and the Baltic States. While the Western Allies agreed as early as 1946 to join their jurisdictions and engage future German statesmen in planning a new constitution, the Soviets insisted on a divided Germany.

In Karlsruhe the French had recruited German nationals to help them re-establish some semblance of law and order. As police commissioner they installed Georg Kaenemund, to whom Ernst Meier reported.

It is reported in Karlsruhe's city archives that Kaenemund had left Germany for France in 1933 and joined the French Foreign Legion in 1939. His qualifications for the post of police commissioner were further solidified by the fact that the Gestapo had arrested him in 1941 and kept him in prison for most of the war. Among his first recorded recommendations were the immediate establishment of a number of brothels, for the convenience of the French military, and the establishment of two concentration camps, one for juvenile males aged 12 to 17 and one for female detainees of the same age group. This, he told his French masters, was necessary to insure the isolation of residual Nazi sentiments and the reorientation of youth who might be hostile to any new order.

The French, to their credit, accepted only one of his recommendations: As one of his first duties, Kaenemund was ordered to select and expropriate suitable premises for the brothels. The prisons for young Nazis, which Ernst Meier undoubtedly had in mind for my re-education, were wisely rejected.

Unlike Ernst Meier, who eventually did earn the respect of the community and distinguish himself as an officer of the law, Commissioner Kaenemund soon discovered that the French Foreign Legion was a poor training ground for a civilian career in law enforcement. His exploits were too much even for the French occupation force. Three months after his appointment he was arrested and sent to jail himself.

CHAPTER 10

A Family Reunion

You gain strength, courage and confidence by every experience in which you really stop to look fear in the face. You are able to say to yourself, "I have lived through this horror. I can take the next thing that comes along."

—Eleanor Roosevelt, American First Lady, diplomat, and humanitarian

The post office in Forchheim began to accept mail in late fall of 1945. I remember my pulse quickening every time I saw the postman making his rounds. If Mom and Dad were detained somewhere, they would surely write and let me know. Once I even visited the post office to let them know that I was expecting some very important mail from my parents or my sister Lina. The postmaster gave me new hope, pointing out that the service was not yet functioning in the sector occupied by the Russians. Would it not be reasonable to assume, he said, that if Mom and Dad were held up somewhere, it would be in the east?

It also occurred to me that they might not be as eager as I had been to return home and resume the life they had left behind. I was much too young at the time to understand, but I could recall Mom and Dad talking about how shabbily her relatives treated them. Maybe they had found a new place to settle and re-establish themselves, shedding the encumbrances of past miseries. And once they were able to travel, they would arrange to have us all reunited.

The answer came early in the new year. We had just come in from the barn after finishing the chores and were seated around the kitchen table when Grandpa came in and announced that there was some commotion at the front gate. He and Otto went out to investigate. The rest of us peered into the darkness and cold through the front door and Grandpa's front window. We could hear the men talk and then a woman's voice choked by tears. I was down the front steps of the house in one leap and into the arms of my mother in another.

My parents were alive, and they had come home at last. I could not believe it. Not even Dad, who never allowed himself to show much emotion, made any attempt to hide his tears. We just stood there for the longest time embracing each other, touching and crying, trying to find our voices and compose our feelings.

Finally Grandpa insisted we go inside before we all froze to death. Mom just kept repeating that I was the last person she had expected to find at home. I remember the shock of seeing my mother in the dim light of the low-wattage light bulb dangling over the kitchen table. I recognized only her voice and her demeanour. Her face was beaming with happiness but distorted by the after-effects of a serious illness that had also claimed all of her hair. Dad, having shed a lot of his weight, looked very tired, very old. We talked for what must have been hours until Dad remembered the belongings they had brought with them, loaded on a little wagon they had pulled by hand all along the same 500-kilometre route I had walked with my friend 10 months earlier. What with all the excitement, it was still parked outside the gate.

After I had left my parents in Poznań, Dad told me, Lina had been drafted to work with the Red Cross, ending up in Denmark at war's end. As I knew, Erich and Ludwig had been drafted into the army, leaving Mom and Dad alone when the Russians crossed the border into Poland and the Polish people started exacting their revenge on the Germans. Some of our Poznań neighbours did not escape the rampage. But Mom and Dad, aided by some of their Polish friends, managed to escape with nothing but their lives on one of the last trains leaving the city for the west.

It happens to people all over the world even today, but it is still hard to imagine what it must have been like for them to walk away from a lifetime of hard work and frugal living with only memories, and without even an album of family photos to sustain them. Apart from a few papers and documents, they had not been able to salvage the smallest memento or personal item to help us preserve the memory of our happy home in Poznań. There was no hope of ever retrieving what was left behind.

Apart from Joan and me, none of the family ever visited the place again. Travelling in an official capacity in East Germany, we went to Poznań for a nostalgic visit 45 years later—against the advice of my siblings. The city itself showed the signs of neglect and disorder customary under Communist rule, but, to our surprise, people were making attempts to adorn their houses and apartments in the city with flowers, disguising the ugly grey of facades that had not been touched by a paintbrush in all the time we were gone. It appeared to us that, unlike the people in East Germany, the Poles managed to live through the period of Soviet domination with much more of their dignity and self-respect intact. It was a pleasant surprise to see the well-tended garden and buildings in our former neighbourhood.

In 1946 Frank was finally reunited with his parents, Rösel and Adolf.

As I stopped in front of our old house to take some pictures, it must have been obvious to the residents that we had a special interest in the place, perhaps dating back to the war. They showed no hostility, but no friendliness either. I only hope that some of them, regardless of how they got custody of the place, were among those we knew as friends, who, perhaps at great risk to their own safety, gave us back our parents by allowing them to escape with their lives.

After fleeing Poznań, Dad had found temporary work dismantling a textile factory, which was to be shipped to Russia. As it turned out, without knowing, we had lived not more than 30 kilometres apart in the same region of Sachsen. After that, my mother's illness had prevented them from leaving the area in advance of the Russian occupation.

They said little about what it had been like. Dad's pay consisted of scraps of food and as much as the little wagon could carry of the finest pre-war textiles the factory had produced and hidden in its warehouses. The cargo was worth a fortune. For the moment it was to be stored in the barn, but Mom insisted on digging out some small presents they had brought for the Albecker girls.

During the discussions about sleeping arrangements for the night, it was made clear that even a temporary stay at Mom's ancestral home would be out of the question. Dad's polite suggestion that a corner of the barn be fitted for temporary quarters met with firm resistance. For the night Grandpa offered to surrender his room for our use, but tomorrow we would have to find some other solution.

"They are finding proper living quarters for all the gypsies and other riff-raff flooding the town—surely they can find something for you," Johanna suggested.

I spent a miserable night. Mom, lying in the very bed she was born in and in which her mother had died, was overcome by her emotions and quietly sobbed, clutching me to her body. Having been deprived of this kind of affection for so long, I found it most discomfiting. A mixture of sorrow, anger, and frustration brought on a flood of tears of my own. I felt as much sorrow for myself as I did for my mother. But I was angry and disappointed as well. My mother had been thoughtful enough to think of my four cousins and to greet them with some small presents, but not me. My parents had clearly abandoned any hope of finding me alive.

A visit the following day with the *Bürgermeister* did not solve the need for living quarters. However, later in the day, Mom came back with the news that she had run into a former neighbour, Frau Berrie, who would be more than pleased to take us in rather than having to accommodate total strangers.

"But they are Protestants," one of the Albecker girls exclaimed, and even Johanna expressed some reservations about our accepting such an offer.

It needs to be explained that there were only two Protestant families in Forchheim before the war. They were both well-to-do, but were looked upon as heathens. Not being baptized in the Catholic faith, they were of course destined to stoke the fires in hell for all eternity. As children, we always found it curious that the Berries, being such nice and friendly neighbours, never showed any outward sign of despair over their hopeless situation.

Dad just pointed out that perhaps Protestants in Forchheim would understand the feeling of being rejected by their community, making it easier for them to have some sympathy for people like us.

The move next day was simplified by the fact that a good portion of the cargo from Mom and Dad's little wagon was left behind. Not that Johanna needed or wanted anything for herself, but Otto hadn't had a new suit since long before the war, and some of the cloth could be fashioned into new clothes for the girls. When Erich found out, he was furious and related the story of our treatment, but it only unleashed another flood of tears from Mom, who could not bring herself to believe what she was being told.

It was to the Berries' house that Lina found her way back not too long after we had settled there. She arrived, relatively healthy and unscathed, late in January 1946 in a military Jeep. Thanks to her station with the Red Cross in Denmark, her experiences during and after the war, relative to the rest of the family, were mercifully mild and much less traumatic.

We had been allocated a more suitable apartment in Karlsruhe by the time Ludwig returned from England. Erich was still working on the farm at Durlach Aue, and it was on one of his regular missions of mercy to us, with a rucksack full of potatoes on his back and assorted other edibles strapped to his bike, that he discovered Ludwig sitting on the front steps leading to our apartment on Am Zirkel. Ludwig had reason to be grateful to the British, not only for saving his leg and foot—badly mangled after he was run over by a piece of heavy armoured equipment—but also for his assignment as a farm labourer once he had recuperated from his injuries. He too, apart from his permanent disability, had been spared the worst of the hunger and deprivation the rest of us had had to endure.

Ludwig found us all keeping busy. Dad had already been called back to work and was helping out with the rebuilding of his old factory. Mom was rising very early in the mornings to get to Forchheim in time to help her relatives—once again—with their field work. Sister Lina had found a job in one of the large department stores in the city. Ludwig looked for work too, and he surprised everyone by choosing his acting hobby as his first career. He appeared as Judas in a Passion play that was performed in several different locations throughout the country. As for me, I was facing the question of what to do next. It was time for me to think about my future and to select a trade.

There was some talk that my age group, because of the prolonged interruptions and interference caused by the war, should have an additional year added to the traditional eight-year basic education. However, because of an acute shortage of teachers and classroom space, this idea was rejected. So, in the summer of 1946, I graduated from school.

It was customary to dedicate a special church service to celebrate these events and send the graduates into the world with the church's special blessing, but Pfarrer Dorer chose to ignore this custom in our case. Instead, he dedicated his Sunday sermon to berating the congregation for raising such a mob of hooligans and asked for special prayers to invoke God's mercy on our souls. Given what had happened to the poor souls who had been given Pfarrer Dorer's blessing on the way to war, I counselled my classmates to consider it an advantage not to be burdened with such special privilege. It is still astonishing to me how little understanding the church, and almost everyone else, had of what we had been through.

My first shot at a career was unsuccessful. Onkel Anton offered to use his influence with a friend who operated a tinsmithing and plumbing shop near his place in Daxlanden. With the prospect of having a central water and sanitary sewer system installed in Forchheim over time, this seemed like a job that showed a lot of promise. Onkel Anton arranged to have me introduced to his friend who, regarding my pitiful posture, expressed some skepticism, but as a favour to Anton granted me a trial period during which everyone was sure I would prove myself to be a worthy candidate for the job.

As much as I liked the people with whom I worked, my starving, underdeveloped body was ill-suited to the task. It didn't help that moving to the city compounded the chronic food shortages. Potatoes were the only staple, supplemented by little else than what Mom brought home from her relatives. I was simply unable to live up to everyone's expectations.

One morning on my way to work, after about two months on the job, I passed out on a streetcar. It was decided that I should be placed in a food-services apprenticeship that would provide me with room and board. Thus, after a short period of convalescence, I signed up for a three-year program with *Bäckermeister* [master baker] Benz in Karlsruhe to become a baker and pastry cook.

I was still only 14 years old when I started my apprenticeship. By today's standards it would be considered nothing less than child slavery, but for my parents and me it was a wise decision since it satisfied our overriding concern—

Frank sits in the driver's seat of the bakery van while a co-worker, Bernard, leans against it.

that I would get enough to eat. While the trade proved little use to me later in life, the apprenticeship at Benz's bakery did turn out to have a supplementary benefit in that it offered an advanced curriculum in sex education.

My workday started at 4:30 in the morning. By 6:30 I was delivering fresh buns to those customers in the neighbourhood who had the means and necessary connections to afford them. Except for one day a week, during which I attended school to supplement the practical training Bäckermeister Benz was administering, I worked until about four in the afternoon, then had two hours of rest before spending another hour after supper preparing for the next day's operation. On Saturdays I worked until lunchtime. The weekend, which was the only free time allowed, ended at six o'clock on Sunday evening, at which time I had to report back to work.

Any remuneration, apart from room and board, was at the discretion of the *meister*, who in my case deemed five *Reichsmarks* a week to be appropriate. In fairness, apart from the living accommodations, which were above the bakery itself and therefore stifling hot at all times, I was well fed and treated as a member of the family.

The morning bakery delivery was the most stimulating part of my job. It led me to become acquainted with many female clients whose motherly instincts netted me the benefit of their kindness and pity. Suffering from another type of starvation, some could also be expected to let their housecoats slip open accidentally, offering revealing glimpses on which to base some comparisons with what my mind's eye had registered during the encounters with "Snow White" in Luckland. Much to my clients' disappointment and added frustration, I am sure, I usually fled such encounters to allow my blood, which had rushed to my face in its entirety, to resume its normal equilibrium.

But this was not the only supplement to my education. Mr. and Mrs. Benz had three sons. The oldest worked in a pharmacy, where he had earned himself some notoriety for his black-market activities in dispensing drugs. Franz, their second son, did not return from the war, while Hans, now 17, had just finished serving his own bakery apprenticeship. The latter had a severely overdeveloped sexual appetite, which frequently required him to appropriate my room above the bakery for his clients, as he called them. His sexual prowess was legendary, attracting women ranging in age from 15 to 50. Depending on the severity of the case, his *Sprechstunden*—his office hours—were often arranged at short notice and could be held in mid-afternoon or at any time during the night. It was not unusual for him to be still busy with a client at the time when it was customary for Mr. Benz to get things organized in the *Backstube* [bakery] below.

On such occasions it became my duty to smuggle his rosy-cheeked companions from the premises while Hans found some pretence to divert his father's attention away from the escape route. I also had an additional duty. His clients, deprived of the companionship of their husbands and sweethearts by the war, would no doubt have been grateful for the service alone. However, Hans always insisted on paying for the pleasure he himself derived from the enterprise with a 10-pound bag of flour. This gift I had to appropriate from the storeroom.

Needless to say, these forays tended to deprive me of a lot of my much-needed sleep. There being only a light partition between my bed and the storeroom, to which I was assigned during *Sprechstunden*, I couldn't help it that my own curiosity and awakening sense of sexual adventure were aroused and entertained.

Mr. Benz, my employer, was very strict with me, but no more so than he was with his own sons. I recall only two occasions when his temper got the best of him and he actually administered a beating. It was my chore to make

The apprentice.

One of the baker's sons, Hans, taught Frank more than just the bakery trade.

the daily deliveries to the hospital, quite a distance away. On Saturdays, when the load was heavier than normal, I needed the assistance of one of the nuns in charge of the kitchen to help carry the baskets laden with bread and buns to the basement for storage. There was one nun in particular who was always very eager to lend a hand, and on occasion, in the dark of the storeroom, that hand would accidentally slip to make contact with certain delicate parts of my anatomy. Sometimes parts of her body competed for the space where my hands happened to be busy, arousing both curiosity and perhaps embryonic tender feelings of pleasure.

I had grown quite fond of Sister Ann, and I was grateful for her help as well, since there was heavy lifting involved in getting my merchandise stored in the proper place. However, on this particular day, Sister Ann was nowhere to be seen and, when after repeated requests, nobody made any move to assist, I simply pulled the big ugly cart with its steel-rimmed wooden wheels through a freshly washed and waxed corridor to the top of the stairs. From there, I pulled the heavy baskets off the cart and down the freshly washed and waxed stairs to the storeroom. Just as I was coming up for the last of about seven or eight baskets, I saw first the white shoes and stockings and then, as I slowly raised my head, the rest of the enormous figure of Mother Superior staring down at me from the top of the stairs. She was breathing fire, furious at the damage I had caused to the freshly scrubbed and waxed floors. After delivering a string of words that I thought strange coming from the mouth of a bride of God, she simply instructed me to tell the Herr Bäckermeister Benz that, as of the following Monday, the hospital would make new arrangements for the supply of bakery products.

Knowing how important this particular client was to Benz's business, I contemplated delaying the delivery of the message until the following Monday. I thought I might well have reached the end of my short career in the bakery trade. Without the hospital as a client, Benz's bakery business would be marginal indeed. In the end, however, I decided to face the music at once. Benz couldn't believe what he was hearing. His mouth frothing with rage, he started for me, hands and fists flailing. Had it not been for Mrs. Benz's intervention, the damage to my delicate body would no doubt have been much worse. Nevertheless, as anticipated, I was told to pack my things and not bother coming back until my father had been consulted.

I did have another plan for employment, but first I had to face the music at home. My family was now back in Forchheim, where we had been allocated one of a number of small houses built hastily to accommodate the ever-increasing influx of refugees from the east. When I got there, I was actually very surprised by Dad's reaction to my dilemma.

Sporting a black eye and some healthy bruises, I explained that I would rather go hungry again than go back to that hellhole. Dad agreed, but insisted that we delay a final decision until he'd had a little talk with Mr. Benz. I was instructed to meet Dad in the city after work on Monday evening. I had never seen him so angry. On the way to the bakery he confessed to his feelings of guilt and the agony that Mom and he felt after abandoning me in Poland and being unable to protect me from the suffering I'd had to endure on my own over the last two years. This time, he said, he would not shirk his duty as my father.

At first we were told by Mrs. Benz that her husband was away on an errand and would not be able to deal with my situation that night. Unfortunately, I had seen the good *meister* out of the corner of my eye, heading for the bakery across the courtyard behind the house. Dad informed her that we would not move until he'd said his piece to the monster who had mutilated his son and had heard his side of the story of what prompted him to administer such a barbaric punishment on a child not even his own.

Mrs. Benz pleaded with Dad to let her explain what had taken place and to allow her to apologize for her husband, particularly since the punishment now appeared to have been unnecessary. She had been able to get Mother Superior to rescind her decision. Apparently Mrs. Benz herself had paid a visit to the hospital, where she found Mother Superior in the presence of Sister Ann, who was giving testimony in my defence. Sister Ann had explained that she routinely made it her business to assist me with the delivery and proper storage of the merchandise, but being busy at the time, she had given me instructions to do exactly what I ended up doing. This, of course, was a blatant lie, but I had no doubt at all that God would forgive Sister Ann, if for no other reason than that it brought the matter to a most amicable settlement. Mother Superior apologized for her ill-considered condemnation, while Mrs. Benz promised that I would be given help to make any future deliveries to the hospital.

Mr. Benz also apologized and offered to rescind my dismissal. "What can I say, Herr Oberle," he said as he entered the room, "other than to tell you how sorry I am for what has happened."

Dad wasn't taken in by this schmooze. I was never more proud of him than for the way he laid on his lecture and the threat that if anything like this ever happened again, Benz would have him to reckon with. The only regret I have over the affair is that I never again found the opportunity to work at close quarters with Sister Ann or even to thank her for deliberately blemishing her soul and adding at least a millennium to her time in purgatory just to save my skin.

My other employment plan involved my good buddy Rolf Beller, and perhaps this would be a good time to introduce him. He was a former classmate who had chosen the same career path, probably for the same reason. He lived in similar circumstances to mine, spending only one night of the week at home in Forchheim with his mother and grandmother. His father had left the family shortly after Rolf's birth, without leaving a forwarding address. A handsome-looking specimen with a scar cutting across his left cheek that made him appear much older than he actually was, Rolf had an unbridled enthusiasm for adventure, the riskier and the shadier the better.

His employer was located right smack in the middle of the red-light district, a much expanded version of the one first established by Police Commissioner Kaenemund. It was now catering to a wider clientele, including a new class of black marketeers. As one might imagine, the ladies of the night and their support staff were no more inclined than the owners of the largest department stores to sell their wares to customers offering to pay with *Reichsmarks*. Even though it was the currency Hitler had used to finance his war, it had lost much of its attraction to currency traders around the world. In the cities, people reportedly paid 150 marks for 20 cigarettes, 550 marks for one pound of coffee, 150 marks for six eggs, and 10 marks for a small box of matches. Who knows what the going rate for 10 minutes of fleshly pleasures would have been.

Rolf and his friends seized this opportunity to establish a currency exchange, trading marks for flour appropriated from the storeroom of his employer's bakery. In no time flat he had developed a steady clientele, providing him with an income many times the amount of the stipend his *meister* paid him by the week.

Now that the fear and pain of hunger was dispelled, we wasted little time in exploiting the freedom offered by our respective positions to the fullest. Neither of us at the time was encumbered by any lack of inspiration or money to design and pursue some of the most harebrained adventures and schemes.

Once, I remember, we set off on a weekend excursion to the wine region across the Rhine, which of course was occupied by the French, to procure some samples of the new harvest. We had learned that children shopping for food were allowed to travel unmolested by the French. By early Saturday evening we were busy helping a farmer and his crew stir several large vats filled to the brim with wine, half fermented and tasting deliciously sweet. The next thing we both remembered was waking up in the middle of a cornfield to find the sun high in the sky and ourselves violently sick with a mild case of alcohol poisoning. It was not until Tuesday morning, after a kindly farmer's wife had nursed us back to health, that we could embark on our return journey. This time Mr. Benz and my parents had consulted one another, and Dad found out from Rolf's mother what we had been up to. Needless to say, the homecoming was not a pleasant experience.

It was Rolf, therefore, whom I contacted first with the news that I had been fired from the bakery and that I was considering striking out on my own. The idea appealed to him as well, but it was decided that by working from his base of "business," we would first try to accumulate the necessary finances to support any plans we might hatch.

This stage of my life closed with one more memorable event. In 1947 Mom and Dad celebrated their 25th wedding anniversary. To find an appropriate gift that would commemorate not only that event, but also the reunification of the family, became a major preoccupation. I was charged with supplying a cake and, using my various connections, with scrounging up the ingredients for a three- or four-course pre-war meal. Lina made the list, which I first discussed with Hanna in the hope that she might tap her resources. Tante Anna's store was an obvious source, but whatever we might expect from there would have to be liberated without her consent.

Mrs. Benz offered to help in any way possible. She even made some valuable suggestions for sprucing up the menu, but apart from some spices she had been hoarding over the years, she could not contribute much more. Mr. Benz even showed some enthusiasm for getting involved with the wedding cake, but as he pointed out, the only cakes the bakery had produced during the last two or three years were by special order, and the customer had supplied such main ingredients as eggs, butter, and sugar—none of which he had in sufficient quantities to contribute to the enterprise.

Hanna became my main source of supply. Berta had a talk with Kneisel, who produced a roast. Rolf Beller and Erich used some of their black-market connections to make up any shortfall. Lina managed to assemble some of the finest china and silverware, borrowed from friends and relatives.

Later in life I had occasion to attend dinners with kings and queens, sheiks, prime ministers, and potentates, but none was more memorable than this feast. The occasion celebrated not only my parents' anniversary but also life itself—the fact that against the most impossible odds we had all managed to survive and be reunited as a family. Sure, things would never be the same. Each of us had accumulated memories and experiences that would reshape and alter our personalities and characters. But this was not the time to relive those experiences, some too horrifying and cruel to be spoken of anyway. This was a time to speak of hopes for a new beginning, for a life with dignity, free of hunger and despair. It was a time to share each other's dreams of a better tomorrow. It was a tearful day for Mom; some tears were of sorrow for what we had lost, but mostly they were tears of joy, the taste of which had only been a distant memory.

CHAPTER 11

A New Beginning

But love is blind and lovers cannot see
The pretty follies that themselves commit
For if they could, Cupid himself would blush
To see me thus transformed to a boy.

—William Shakespeare, English playwright

In one sense I found comfort in following the path my life was now taking. There were regular mealtimes, regular hours of work and school, but the more structured my daily routine became, the more restless I felt. I sensed myself being drawn into a dependency on an authority that I instinctively distrusted. The more the society around me progressed toward its former order and rigidity, the less secure and confident I felt about realizing my aspirations for the future.

I chose to invest my trust and loyalty in people my own age, friends in circumstances similar to mine. Not too unusual, of course, for any young person's progress toward adulthood. But my choice represented something much more than just the loss of innocence or the belief in Santa Claus or the Easter Bunny. Our generation turned to each other because we had been betrayed, not just by the individuals in whose care we had grown up, but by society as a whole. We had come out of the war years with strong feelings of independence and, to back them up, powerful instincts of confidence and self-reliance.

Rolf Beller we have already met. He was my closest friend who shared my thirst for adventure. Neither of us was short of ideas or the capacity to concoct new ideas for adding spice and excitement to our miserable lives. The French Foreign Legion was our first choice for a career abroad. Taking Rolf's mother into our confidence brought us into contact with one of her friends, who offered to tutor us in French in return for a steady supply of flour. We actually got off to a good start, but with the little spare time available to us, the lessons came into serious conflict with our other equally important extracurricular activities. We also discovered that the minimum age requirement was 19, which we would not meet for another three years. Unlike Rolf, I had the looks of someone two years younger than my age, so lying would be out of the question.

It didn't mean that we would give up on the venture entirely, but we had a whole range of other options to consider. Whatever we chose, we pledged we would do it together.

Things had started to take a turn for the better in 1948. On July 1 of that year, with very little advance notice, Germany had its currency replaced by the Deutschmark. Every citizen, regardless of age or status, was allowed to exchange 40 Reichsmarks for an equal number of D-Marks. Mr. Benz and I collected ours and compared our fortunes.

"You see," he said, "you're now just as rich as I am."

The Marshall Plan also came into effect that same year, unleashing a torrent of activity throughout Europe, but in Germany in particular. Historians all agree that, unlike the treaties after the First World War, this single event provided the impetus for the industrial miracle that unfolded in Germany, which in turn formed the basis of co-operation and peaceful co-existence of the European nations.

Almost overnight we could see the changes taking place in our region. Miraculously, stores and shopping centres were stocked with goods and products we had not seen since before the war. There were still some shortages of certain food items, but money once again became the only inhibiting factor to acquiring personal comfort and material wealth.

At the same time, the other huge influence in my life began to assert itself. There was someone else who started, in an ever more serious way, to compete for my attention and affection: Hanna. Toward the end of my apprenticeship with Mr. Benz in 1949, Hanna and I allowed ourselves to be drawn into a regular routine. Sustained by a strong bond of friendship and the sweetness of a budding love affair, we began making plans for a future together. We knew right from the start that whatever the future held, we would have to find our place in it on our own. Apart from some generous well-meaning advice, there was little we could expect from our parents, and, needless to say, the advice offered was of little use to us, the architects of our own castle in the sky.

Hanna was now working in Karlsruhe, where she had landed a job in a chocolate factory to supplement the income Berta needed to sustain Rudi's studies toward the priesthood. Hanna was uncomfortable with Rolf. He had started to show an interest in the female side of the species as well, and the two of us used to conduct regular forays *Ins Ausland* [abroad], meaning the pursuit of the opposite sex in Mörsch. These Saturday-night adventures were part of the ancient tradition between the two communities, and they usually ended in a street fight, with the interlopers proudly taking away a badge of honour in the form of some black eyes and nasty bruises.

Hanna put an end to these escapades, perhaps saving us from serious harm. Our relationship had begun to take a shape that made no allowance for a third partner. Eventually she confronted me with a choice: "It's either Rolf or me."

It was no contest. Reluctantly, Rolf had to rely on his own devices to satisfy his curiosity regarding the opposite sex. He opted to spend weekends close to his base in the city, where girls in the neighbourhood, all of them at least 10 years older, offered much more experienced advice and practical tutoring in the fine art of sex. Whatever mischief Rolf and I felt we needed to enhance our fortunes had to be fitted into the odd weeknight adventure.

Another bar to our relationship was Hanna's dad. Like Berta, Emil had a faith in God that helped him survive his war ordeal. But Berta, despite her faith, felt closest to God whenever she made the effort necessary to help herself. She had sufficient strength to nurse her husband back to life, but having paid off the mortgage on the house and protected her children and the property from the ravages of the war, she was not about to revert to her pre-war relationship with her husband. She simply ignored Emil's attempts to reassert himself as the head of the family. Having sacrificed love and affection to the war, she remained the dominant force in the family.

All her passions were invested in her son's career, which had now become an all-consuming obsession. She contributed generously of her time and talents to the church's women's group where, as the mother of a future priest, she commanded special status and respect.

Emil found satisfaction in tending his garden, and he invested his love in the trees that adorned it. He turned into a master horticulturist, helping family and neighbours by pruning fruit trees and even helping the town's crew restore the considerable inventory of orchards and trees held in common along the boulevards, which had been neglected during the war. However, there was one area where he fought to maintain his authority.

I was always welcome and considered the Kistner house as a second home, even after the return of my parents. Sure, there were certain rules that had to be followed. Before we were allowed out to take in a show on Saturday nights, Hanna and I might have to harvest a couple of bags of potatoes or help with some other chore. My invitation for lunch on Sundays was always conditional on my first attending mass in the morning.

After Emil's return, the relationship became more complicated and therefore more intimate. Berta tried to cover up for us as much as she could, but Emil thought it preposterous that a child of 16, his child, was allowed out of the house with a member of the opposite sex without any supervision. My first bold attempts to defy the new rules by showing up at the front gate on my bicycle were met with a barrage of rotten potatoes.

Why do parents never learn that the degree of stubbornness and determination young people show in nursing their first love increases in precise proportion to the obstacles put in their way, just as the sweetness of fruit improves when it is forbidden? Hanna and I became inseparable, and in the end Emil was no match for our ingenuity. Sure, we were much too young to make a commitment for life, but neither of us was prepared to let go of something as pure and precious as our relationship, something that was giving our miserable lives some purpose.

As my relationship with Hanna strengthened, the rest of my life became increasingly fragmented, and events in Germany as a whole heightened my unease.

In 1949 Germany became a republic, and even though the Russian blockade on Berlin—now isolated within the eastern part of Germany under their jurisdiction—had been lifted, Bonn was chosen as the new capital of West Germany. Berlin became the capital of the so-called Democratic Republic of East Germany. The new alignment of ideological adversaries exacted a heavy price from the German population who had family and relatives in both sectors and now had to contemplate the prospect of new hostilities that would have pitted them against their own relatives.

Britain's Prime Minister Churchill was among those who would have preferred to organize the Western Allies for a new military adventure against the eastern alliance, and even though cooler heads prevailed, the possibility of war remained very real. This was particularly true after 1961, when the

Soviets began construction of the Berlin Wall, which remained for 28 years as a stark reminder of the hunger on both sides for more blood, as if the 60 million dead of the Second World War hadn't been enough.

In addition, the curtain that had hidden and disguised some of the Nazi party's darkest secrets and most abhorrent policies was removed and the face of the real monster was unmasked. Now that, among other things, the Holocaust as Hitler's Final Solution to the Jewish "problem" was undeniably revealed, I divested myself of the last remnants of patriotism I still felt for the Fatherland. I decided that I had had enough war to last me for the rest of my life.

I was getting restless again. There was no future for me in these uncertain times, and Hanna made no effort to dissuade me from some of the schemes Rolf Beller and I had hatched earlier.

Naturally, much to its loss I am sure, the French Foreign Legion was now out because we couldn't figure out how Hanna could fit into that scene. Some of my friends set their sights on the great United States of America, perhaps following the dictum "If you can't beat them, join them." But I was looking for a different world, one disconnected from the past that had left me with such deep scars and disillusionment.

The adventure stories of Karl May that I had read at school came to mind again. I started to look first at South Africa and then at Canada, which, like Australia, were involved more on the periphery of the war and would not likely be major players in any future conquest. Unlike the United States and South Africa, burdened with their own crimes against their black people, Canada, from what I had learned, appeared free of any such guilt, historic or recent. Instead, people who settled there did so, in part at least, to distance themselves from the sins inherited from their fathers. Unlike Karl May, who had never been to North America, I had actually met some Canadians who perfectly resembled the characters he had invented. For a time Karlsruhe was blessed with the presence of a contingent of Canadians attached to the occupation force headquartered there. They re-enacted scenes right out of the wildest of wild west movies. During the early weeks of occupation the Americans were strictly forbidden to fraternize with the civilian population. The Canadians had no such restrictions. After the French, they were the first to acquaint themselves with the pleasures of the flesh that could be bought with army rations, cigarettes, and chocolate bars. They also brought with them a healthy appetite for the booze that was flowing freely, liberated from some of the caches in the Black Forest.

They must have been the original Crazy Canucks. Preceded and followed by hordes of children shouting, "*Die Kanadier kommen*" ["The Canadians are coming"], they could be seen on any day working their way through the streets, going from bar to bar, determined to drink each one dry. Having accomplished that, they would wreck the place and move on to the next adventure.

In the main, the only fighting they did was for sport and mostly among themselves, but on rare occasions they took on Germans who felt honour-bound to react to some of the rude, undisguised sexual advances toward their girlfriends or who objected to some of the *Frauleins* selling their flesh to feed their children. Adding somewhat of a modern touch were the American Military Police, who would attend the scene when things got out of hand. It was not an unusual sight to see them on their 1200-cc Harley-Davidsons, firing their pistols into the air, as they herded the battle-weary warriors back to their compounds.

Canada, in part at least, was still a British colony. Throughout her early history she had been a magnet and provider of refuge for many of the Motherland's less fortunate people and had emerged as the land of opportunity for those deprived of it by the rigid class system into which they had the misfortune to be born. Canada was seen as a haven for the oppressed, hungry, and persecuted from around the world, people with whom I would no doubt have a natural affinity. I could not know at the time that not even Canada was entirely pure and innocent when it came to justice, equality, and fairness. It was only much later that I found out that, particularly in dealing with her aboriginal people, even Canadian closets held skeletons.

I did continue to pursue the bakery trade my parents had chosen for me. When I graduated in 1949, after three full years of training, as a journeyman, Mr. Benz offered to keep me employed, but the business was ill-equipped to pay anywhere near the wages matching my generous assessment of my worth. For a short time I worked in two other bakeries in the city. The first I was fired from for throwing up into a bread-mixer after a late night out on the town. I considered it unfair at the time, mostly because the *Bäckermeister* never even shut off the machine or considered throwing out the specially treated batch of dough. In fact, as I was told by one of my former colleagues, at least one customer complimented the store clerk on the special flavour she had detected in her bread the previous day. The second job in Karlsruhe I left on my own initiative, taking advantage of an offer from the Kästels in Forchheim.

Fritz Kästel, a veteran of the eastern front, had just returned to take over the family bakery business. He had a lot of progressive ideas, for which he needed people willing to make a long-term commitment. The pay, even by industry standards, was marginal, but he did offer bonuses and special concessions to compensate for longer than usual working hours and extra duties related to his noodle factory, which was attached to the business.

It turned out to be a happy arrangement. As usual, being single, I was offered room and board, which in this case more than made up for the meagre pay. The kitchen was well stocked with Kneisel's sausage and other delicacies still scarce on the open market. The women who looked after the store and helped out in the bakery had been with the Kästels for years and were treated as part of an extended family. In no time at all I had them eating out of my hands.

Fritz took a liking to me right from the start. He rewarded my efforts with all kinds of special favours. He arranged for me to take driver training and put me in charge of deliveries to the city. Our clientele mainly consisted of several large factories that, as was customary in Germany, offered their workers a hot meal for lunch. On certain days, usually Fridays, when the consumption of meat in the daily diet would have invited an extended sentence in purgatory, *Zwiebelkuchen* or *Zwetchenkuchen* [onion or plum cake] provided the main course. We regularly started production in the late afternoon and worked right through until about 10 the next morning. It wouldn't be until mid-afternoon that I returned from making my rounds. On one occasion during the Christmas and New Year season we worked 32 hours without interruption, except for periodic coffee breaks. Nevertheless, I have nothing but fond memories of that time and the people with whom I shared the experience.

On the social side, I would have liked to participate in Forchheim's well-organized and lively sports activities, but my job's irregular hours did not permit it. As the people in Forchheim slowly allowed themselves to be drawn back to their pre-war social rituals, the town divided once again into two entrenched groups. The church started to shift emphasis from mourning the dead to making the best of life and embracing newcomers to the community. The Reds, somewhat slower off the mark because of the repression suffered during the Nazi period, began to reassert themselves as a counterbalance to the dominance of the church. This is not to say that the so-called Reds were less Catholic or less respectful of the church's role to guide the spirit and save the soul; they merely challenged the priest's dominance in more worldly matters.

Each of the two groups was active in sports, had its own drama clubs, choirs, and organized separate youth and children's activities. The only real competition between the two was restricted to the soccer pitch and politics: the Blacks represented the CDU (Christian Democratic Union) and the Reds, the SDP (Social Democrats). On the rare occasions when the two soccer teams met one another, the town came to a standstill. Special referees had to be imported to adjudicate the epic battles, which always produced more action among the spectators on the sidelines than among the players on the field.

Since I couldn't play soccer, which would have been my first choice, I followed my dad's lead and contributed my considerable acting talents to the Reds' drama club.

My first exposure to the stage was at the open-air theatre in Otigheim, 30 kilometres south of Forchheim, playing a Roman palace guard in *Quo Vadis*. As the summer progressed, this became a rather hazardous adventure for both the local volunteers, acting the part of enraged Roman citizens storming Emperor Nero's palace, and for us imported "guest stars," who defended it as the palace guard. The resentment stemming from the fact that we were getting the princely sum of five marks for every performance, while the locals were expected to contribute their efforts for the glory of the enterprise, engendered some discord that played itself out on stage.

I remember the production opened to rave reviews that gave particular credit to the unbridled enthusiasm of the warring parties on the palace steps. At first there were only minor cuts and bruises, but as the season progressed, the battle intensified. After several broken arms and a serious concussion suffered by one of my fellow soldiers we, in total disregard for the safety of Nero Claudius Caesar—undeserving of our loyalty as he was anyway—and the evolution of the history of the Roman Empire, decided to abandon the project.

I reached the pinnacle of my acting career in the role of Escamillo in *Carmen*. Actually it turned out to be a family affair. Brother Erich, playing the lead role of Don José, became seriously ill one week before opening night. Brother Ludwig was called to the rescue. By that time he had abandoned his acting career in favour of a more orderly family life, but his first love was still the stage. With just four days to study the complicated role, he performed it to perfection, elevating himself to hero status among the patrons of the arts in Forchheim. The fact that his contribution enticed many of his fans among the Christian Democrats to attend the Social Democrats' hall to witness the play became an added bonus.

As time progressed and his throwing arm started to tire, Emil's resolve to keep me from his daughter weakened to the point where on special occasions I was allowed to visit. The fact that he was in desperate need of some help at harvest time outweighed the stigma I carried of coming from a family whose father attended church only on Christmas and Easter. Trained in carrying 200-pound sacks of flour up the narrow stairs to the storeroom at Benz's bakery, I had little trouble packing Emil's grain sacks up the rickety ladder to the attic, something he was not yet able to do in his weakened condition. But what earned me even more of his respect was my ability to keep pace with him in quenching the thirst that such heavy labour invariably produced.

Emil's peacetime job, to which he had now been reinstated, was with one of the breweries in the city. While at the job he was accustomed to consuming copious quantities of beer to assure, no doubt, consistent quality of the product. As well, in order to keep their employees in such key positions well conditioned, the brewery supplied them, even after retirement, with all the beer they would need for their private consumption. Before diesel-powered automobiles replaced the brewery carts drawn by Belgian horses, the brew was delivered to their residences twice a week. As kids we used to watch in awe as the huge beasts made their way through town, stopping without having to be prompted at the appointed places. Their bellies, well nourished with the residue of the malting process, would from time to time produce a fart potent enough to rattle windows and shutters in the neighbourhood and a torrent of piss—with clouds of steam emanating from it—voluminous enough to fill the ditches for three blocks along the road.

I have never seen it demonstrated, but have been told by the wagoneers that holding an open carbide lamp at just the right distance from the source of the explosion will produce a torch-like flame four metres in length. In fact, so the story goes, it was an accidental explosion of exactly this kind that singed the handlebar moustache of one of Kaiser Wilhelm's corporals in charge of the horses attached to his artillery. One can only imagine how much further Hitler could have driven his cause if he had learned to harness this potent, cheap, and natural source of destructive power.

Emil took full advantage of his company's generosity. Needless to say, it was not easy to match his appetite and capacity. Indeed, there were occasions when I had to exceed the limits of moderation I had set for myself, after my wine-tasting adventure in France, to prove myself worthy of his respect.

Years later, after I had earned some acceptance from my future father-in-law, Emil chose the occasion of a major soccer match to show me off to his colleagues at the brewery that was catering the event. I remember we set off on bicycles early in the morning to assist with the erection of the brewery's tent. By noon we were well enough fortified to participate fully in the festivities around the soccer pitch and in the post-game wake or victory celebration—whatever the match's outcome might have produced. Of the game itself I remember little, and Emil even less. He had to plead ignorance to Berta's inquiry as to the final score. I do remember waiting until the thousands of bicycles in the central parking place were retrieved by their owners before we could identify our own. Neither of us had any recollection of how we found our way home, but I managed to fake sufficient stamina to keep a date with Hanna, Cilli, and Rudi at the opera. The bruises I discovered the following morning were sustained, not on the soccer field, but from Hanna poking me in the ribs to subdue my loud snores competing with Richard Wagner's melodious arias.

Meanwhile, while Emil tested my saturation point for the consumption of beer, my love and affection for his daughter became insatiable. Since Hanna was never allowed to wear a bathing suit, use lipstick, or wear nylon stockings, it follows that permission for our overnight bicycle excursions along the Rhine and the hills of the Black Forest would have been easier to obtain from the Pope than from Emil. Nevertheless, they became our favourite pastime. We used every opportunity and all our cunning to steal away from work and invented the most outlandish tales to convince Emil and Berta that their daughter would not be exposed to any temptation to taste the sweet fruits a serpent might offer along the way. We explored every nook and cranny in the Black Forest, allowing ourselves to be seduced by the natural beauty and splendour with which the region is blessed. The days were spent floating along on our bikes, singing and laughing without a care in the world. At nights we would sneak into a hay shed or seek a vantage point that offered the best panoramic view to pitch our tent.

We engaged in prolonged philosophical discussions, trying to rationalize our love and sinful behaviour against what we had been taught. What logic was there for an Almighty Creator of the natural world to show its living creatures such boundless heavenly pleasures, to give them such irresistible energy and instincts to pursue them, only to punish them with death if they did? Shouldn't those who openly challenged and disobeyed God's natural law earn His wrath instead?

In my quest for the truth, I could find little reason or logic in the church's interpretation of God's ways. It seemed to me that the church, already pronouncing itself infallible in the interpretation of God's intentions, demanded from its followers a slavish adherence and blind faith to which I was not able to submit.

Pfarrer Dorer in Forchheim would have been the last person in the world to clear up these mysteries for me. To him, sex for pleasure, even between married partners, like partaking in Holy Communion without a true confession, ranked among the deadliest of sins. I couldn't help but

Even after the war, the church continued to play a leading role in Forchheim, as this typical children's Corpus Christi day parade shows.

suspect—and there were ample rumours to substantiate it—that the good father might have been all too familiar with what he insisted on denying his flock. His own experience in the field may well have led his troubled mind to rationalize that sex is entirely too good for the more common among God's children.

There were all kinds of lesser sins that Pfarrer Dorer lectured us about, such as not attending regular church service and using the Lord's name in vain, but what I remembered most about the good father's theological expositions was that salvation in heaven could still be attained, even by the most sinful among us, as long as, at the very moment of death, the sinner had the presence of mind to beg for forgiveness and proclaim his faith. It may seem grossly unfair to those who never engaged in sexual activities other than to propagate the species and who deprived themselves of all other forbidden fruits, but it was a message of hope to me, burdened as I was with a multitude of deadly sins, but blessed with an exceptionally good sense of timing.

Neither Hanna nor I ever doubted the existence of a spiritual world beyond our understanding. But even at our age we had developed a mistrust of anyone professing to be a guide to this world. We resolved that God, rather than demanding our blood, sweat, and tears to build churches and monuments to his glory, would prefer to be discovered from within, so that each of us could judge the right path leading to an afterlife.

Of course, we also explored down-to-earth problems and opportunities. As people around us started to take our relationship seriously, they began offering advice and making suggestions regarding our future careers. Tante Anna, when Otto was still alive, always had plans to add a bakery to her business. Once Otto was gone, would it not be natural for us to be part of such plans?

What an enticing proposition this would have been for normal people under normal circumstances, but neither we nor our circumstances could be considered normal. We felt that to tie ourselves to such a scheme would not only limit the horizons on which we had set our sights, but also make us dependent on people undeserving of our trust. For all our lives I would be given credit only for marrying into the right family, and no doubt I would be reminded of that at every occasion.

"Having parents that are poor is not one's fault," a German saying goes, "but for poor in-laws one can only blame oneself."

We could not abandon our dream to seek our fortune in places far away from the memories of our tragic childhood and youth. Rolf Beller and I now began in earnest to explore our options.

The lure of the fabulous riches of Germany's former colonies in Africa, and the stories about Canada, the land of unlimited possibilities, became the focus of our pursuit. What harm was there in making some inquiries in both places to see what they had to offer? To our surprise, we discovered a Canadian consulate in Karlsruhe, while South Africa had established consular services in Munich. We boldly filled out application forms, offering our considerable talents and boundless ambition to both.

In no time at all we were contacted by the Karlsruhe office with a request for an interview. This was getting serious. Again, what harm could there be in finding out what conditions we would have to meet to be accepted as immigrants and where in Canada we would be allowed to settle?

Rolf and I met after one of my deliveries in the city and made our way to the office, rehearsing what we might offer that would enhance our chances of getting a positive response. Would our trade be a factor or were they looking, as we had been told, for people who would be willing to change their vocation to suit the needs of the labour market in Canada?

In the end, the questions turned out to be quite basic. Did we speak English or French? Would we be willing to learn? Did we have the means to pay the fare if we were accepted? Then we were given a list of documents we would have to deposit with a final application. Finally, if all requirements were satisfied we would have to undergo a medical before a visa could be issued.

We were surprised that they were only interested in our parents' status during the Nazi period, without questioning our own affiliation with the youth movement. But even though the interview had gone well, we felt that it would be unlikely that we could meet the other conditions. There were two serious roadblocks: parental consent and a police background check. We thought that, in a pinch, the parental consent form could be faked, but there was not the slightest chance of getting through a police check without Ernst Meier's involvement.

The problem was that both of us had recently clashed with the Forchheim constabulary. Rolf's latest extracurricular venture, into the scrap-metal business, had landed him in trouble over an inability to distinguish between items found in the rubble of bombed-out buildings and new material being supplied to new building sites. Copper fetched a particularly generous return, and Ernst Meier had investigated some complaints implicating Rolf. Even though nothing had been proved, the evidence could hardly be disputed.

I had narrowly escaped a second arrest by Forchheim's intrepid sleuth. It was a minor affair for which Reini, who was dating my sister Lina and eventually became my brother-in-law, should have borne most of the guilt. It started innocently enough. I had my room above Kästel Fritz's noodle factory, but decided to crash for a couple of hours at my parents' place before picking up Hanna for a show. I had just dozed off when Reini rattled my bed demanding that I help celebrate the substantial raise to his weekly pay that he had earned. Like Emil, Reini was the beneficiary of the privileges that came with a job at the brewery, so he was well lubricated even before he arrived.

The idea was to hoist a couple of pints in the *Waldfrieden,* the restaurant next to the railway station, and meet the train bringing Lina home from work. I had worked through the night and into the early afternoon so I was dead tired, but my conscience did not allow me to resist the pleas of a man dying of thirst. The train usually shook the restaurant like an earthquake, but on this particular day it must have travelled on rubber wheels, and the engineer must have forgotten to blow his whistle. Only as it was getting dark did we realize that Reini might have missed his date. If there was any doubt, Lina removed it as we got home. The two of them exchanged words, but very few of them were Reini's.

To cheer him up, I offered to take him along on my date instead, where I assured him a much more hospitable reception. Off we went on our bicycles to see Hanna, but as we came by the *Waldfrieden,* Reini felt the urge to imbibe one more pint to fortify us for the trip.

The show Hanna and I had planned to see was long over, and Emil and Berta had retired for the night when we arrived at their house. Failing to execute a proper dismount procedure, the two of us ended up in a pile of legs, arms, and bicycle parts in front of Hanna's front gate. Unlike Lina, Hanna, afraid we would wake up Emil, managed to keep the reception to a much lower key. She was dragging me toward the house as Reini attempted in a loud voice to explain the reason for our unavoidable delay. Somehow she managed to talk him into carrying on home, and the last we saw of him, he was back on his bike, wheeling across an open field.

We made it into the kitchen, where I was deposited on the chesterfield just seconds before I went to sleep. It must have been terrifying for Hanna to imagine Emil's reaction should he find me in his kitchen in my deplorable condition. Sometime during the night I regained sufficient presence of mind to realize this myself and decided to depart the scene before we were found out. I headed for my room above the noodle works.

To get there, I had to climb over a six-foot fence at the rear of the property. It was a bitterly cold night and I was wearing a heavy three-quarter-length overcoat that had originally been manufactured for the Polish army. I managed to hook the front wheel of my bike to the top of one of the sturdy pickets, intending to hoist it the rest of the way once I had elevated myself to the top. All went as planned until the rear of my overcoat draped itself over the top of one of the posts during my descent to the other side. After what must have been a prolonged struggle to extricate myself from this predicament, tired and exhausted, I fell asleep three feet off the ground, suspended by my Polish coat.

This was the scene upon which Ernst Meier made his entry, just as some faint light on the horizon began to expel the dark from a cloudless sky. At first, as he told my dad later in the day, he thought that my attempt to ride my bicycle over a six-foot fence had been fatal. Upon closer inspection, however, the intrepid sergeant managed to discern a rhythmic sound, much like a snore, emanating from my interior. His rescue effort was swift and efficient. Using one of the boards ripped off the fence, he reached up to untangle my dark blue overcoat. I awoke when I hit the frozen ground on the other side.

After a brief introduction, Ernst announced that he was placing me under arrest, but this presented an entirely new problem. One of us would have to scale the fence to facilitate the procedure. Needless to say, we were unable to agree on who it should be. Finally Ernst settled for a compromise. He confiscated my treasured bike, still equipped with Keller Herman's seat, which could only be retrieved by turning myself in for arrest. My last words to him promised dire consequences should my bike, like Otto Albecker's motorcycle, be stolen while in his custody.

Once again Dad helped out. He managed to reason with Ernst, asking him to see the humour in the situation. He even got Ernst to agree that my punishment should be decided upon and administered by Dad. But unlike the occasion involving Bäckermeister Benz, my father came as close as he ever did to assaulting not only my sensitive feelings, which had always been his preferred method of punishment, but my posterior as well. In his view, the worst part of the episode was that I had not had enough sense to come home and nurse my shame and hangover in the privacy of the family, rather than giving the townspeople a reason to consider us among the riff-raff, as some were always seeking to do. And furthermore, what would Hanna's parents think of having anybody of my type dating their daughter?

This was the background against which I was now trying to put together my application to emigrate. My prospect of getting a police certificate from Ernst Meier or a consent letter from Dad seemed dim indeed.

In the end, both these obstacles were surmounted, one with ease and the other with renewed determination. To my surprise, Rolf, who was still attached to his job in the city, encountered no trouble at all getting a clean bill of health from the police there. There was no reason to involve the Forchheim constabulary.

I attempted the same route. The officer I talked to at police headquarters in Karlsruhe didn't even know that we had a police presence in Forchheim. In any event, all the records would be in his domain, so he might as well deal with my application directly. I was flabbergasted. All the anxiety, all the worrying had been unnecessary. Now there was only one more hurdle: Dad's consent.

Some weeks went by before I found the courage and the right moment to broach the subject. As usual, I positioned my delivery van across the *Brauerstrasse* Gate to Dad's factory so as to offer him a ride home.

There are certain images observed by the mind's eye that may seem ordinary at the time, but have a lasting effect throughout a person's life. Seeing my dad, with several hundred of his fellow workers, spill out of that gate at exactly the same time, six days a week, is one of these images. Like a herd of cattle fighting their way to the trough, wearing dull, expressionless faces, none registering even the slightest bit of satisfaction at having done a good day's work, they rushed to escape the place, fighting with their elbows for enough space to mount their bicycles.

What kind of life was this? What kind of personal freedom was there in such a mind-numbing, prison-like, and rigid environment? I would rather have been dead than trapped in such an environment for the rest of my life. For most of these people, only the war had interrupted their daily routine. Was it any wonder that it was a welcome relief to be drafted into the army or to be transferred to a strange country, as Dad was, with the promise of a higher job status?

On this particular day I chose the longer route home from the factory, parts of which I knew Dad preferred from his Sunday morning strolls through the forest. Having dispensed with a few pleasantries, we rode along in silence until I decided to stop at a particular picturesque place.

Thinking of it today, it's hard to imagine how difficult it was to find the right words to approach the subject. Dad gave me puzzled looks as I began to explain my decision. He sat in silence as I, for the first time, talked to him about some of the ugly details of my life during my time away from home. I told him how difficult it was for me to conform and to adjust to the sort of life Mom and he were now getting back to, as if nothing had happened. I explained how stifling it was for me to live among my family and relatives who simply refused to speak about these issues that had so cruelly interrupted our lives, hoping that they would go away.

It pained me to look at my father sitting there in stunned silence, tired and dejected. Overcome with emotion, I was unable to suppress tears welling up in my eyes. Finally, after a long pregnant silence, he wondered with a shaky voice what Mom's reaction might be. With tears in his own eyes, he told me that even if he had wanted to, he felt lacking in the moral authority to stand in the way of any path I might choose toward happiness and fulfilment.

To my astonishment, he then confessed that he himself had made the same choice and had planned to emigrate to America at a certain stage of his young life. It was my mother and her family that held him back, something both of them regretted throughout their lives. He wanted to know whether Hanna knew about my plans and how she felt about them. In the end, he offered to approach Mom about the subject and promised that if and when the time came, I would go with his blessing.

He reminded me how hard a decision like this would be on all of us. He knew of no one who had ever returned after they left for America. Most of them lost contact with their families after just a few short years. It would be goodbye forever.

I assured him that no matter where I ended up, nothing could be worse than what my life had served up so far. I promised my dad that some day he would be proud of my having made this decision.

I filed the final application with the Canadian authorities, and a short time afterward, I received notification of an appointment for a medical. Rolf told me that he too had been notified and that he intended to keep the appointment. This was getting serious.

The family poses together before Frank's departure. Pictured (from left) are Ludwig, Frank, Erich, Rösel, Lina, and Adolf.

In about the middle of 1951, at the age of 19, I received my final approval in the form of an invitation to attend the office to discuss travel arrangements as soon as I had my passport. Dad and Hanna were still the only people who knew what I was doing, and it was time tell the others. We were sure that Emil, more so than Berta, would be relieved to see the last of me. My relationship with Hanna had become much too serious for his liking. But Kästel Fritz, my boss, would be a different matter. He had treated me like a son and often told Mom of his hope that I would some day come to my senses and marry one of his two daughters.

I left it to the last possible moment, using the occasion of the weekend schnapps he liked to share with me in his living room to drop the bomb. "Fritz, I have a serious confession to make, and I don't know how to tell you, but it can't wait any longer." His response was immediate: "You knocked her up, didn't you?"

"No, Fritz—it's much more serious than that. I am leaving you. I am leaving the country."

Until that moment I never realized how much he had taken it for granted that I would become a permanent feature of his business. When he realized that I was serious, he sat in stunned silence, making little effort to hide his emotions. To his credit, he never tried to persuade me to reconsider, perhaps knowing it would be pointless. I felt sorry for Fritz, my good friend and benefactor, who was certainly not among those who made leaving my homeland less painful. My passport was issued on July 6, 1951. The Canadian office arranged the appointment for my medical, and on September 18 I was issued the visa.

But there was one last hurdle.

I had been assured by Rolf that all was in order on his side, and I asked the immigration officer if the two of us could travel together. To my dismay I was told that Rolf had never completed and filed his application.

"There must be a mistake," Rolf said when I confronted him, but by that time I knew him well enough to sense trouble.

It was his mother who visited me the following day, offering some feeble excuse why her son had had to reconsider. Even now I remember the shock I felt. What a cowardly thing to do. Knowing full well that I was dismantling my bridges to the past, he had offered not the slightest word of caution.

I never spoke to him again, but told his mother that what we had planned together for so long would require a certain amount of courage, something he was obviously lacking. Looking back, perhaps it was best that I learned beforehand what a coward my so-called friend was.

Actually, in retrospect, I did speak to Rolf Beller once more. Almost 50 years later, two years before he died, he joined 28 of our former classmates to pay Joan and me a visit in Canada. Enough time had passed and neither of us felt inclined to spoil the occasion by reminding one another of the unfulfilled pledge. He was accompanied by his daughter, a fine-looking, intelligent young woman, who told me something of her father's life. Through her story of her father's lifelong regrets and dreams of what could have been, she made the success of my own life and career appear that much sweeter and made it easier for me to forgive and forget.

For myself, I had passed the point of no return. My pride would never have allowed me to consider retreat. I would seek my fortune in the New World alone or perish trying. On October 2, 1951, I boarded the Italian liner *Vulcania* in Genoa for a voyage through the Mediterranean and across the Atlantic to Halifax.

CANADA

1951-1962

CHAPTER 12

The New World

America's greatest strength, and its greatest weakness, is our belief in second chances, our belief that we can always start over, that things can be made better.

—Anthony Walton, American historian

There were some conditions attached to Dad's letter of consent for me to emigrate. First, I had to promise that if I met up with hard times, I would find the courage to write and ask for help. Second, I was to make certain that I left on good terms with all our relatives, both in Forchheim and in Mörsch.

There were some, Emil no doubt among them, who greeted the news of my departure with relief. He was still secretly hoping that his daughter would find a more suitable companion, one more respectful and obedient to the order of the church. Grandfather Leibold, had he still been alive, would not have been surprised by my decision. It would have only confirmed what he thought of me all along: a gypsy and a vagabond who couldn't make an honest living at home. But he had passed away two years earlier.

I remember the discord over his death during Sunday lunch. Mom stormed away from the table in tears when Erich expressed his doubts that either he or I would be able to attend the funeral, while Dad delivered a stern lecture, insisting that even if we couldn't bring ourselves to honour the dead, we owed some respect to the living mourning his loss.

As was customary, my grandfather's coffin had been propped up in his living room, where for several nights it was attended by neighbours and friends, mostly women, whose special prayers and laments would light the way for his poor soul to the other world. On the day of the funeral, Father Dorer, with his entourage of altar boys in full regalia, had already arrived to lead the throng of mourners. They had gathered in the yard for the short ceremony and the procession through town to Grandfather's final resting place.

Everything was ready, except for two minor details: Erich was nowhere to be seen, and the pallbearers, even with the help of some of the bereaved, were unable to manoeuvre the coffin out of the front door and down the steep steps in a horizontal position. Just as it had been decided that a hay wagon would have to be positioned in front of the stairs as a scaffold, allowing the coffin to be lifted over the railing, everybody's head turned to look up the road. There Erich, sporting his long, black-market leather coat and his newly acquired NSU motorcycle, made his entrance.

"I'll wring his neck," Dad muttered under his breath, just as Erich gave the noisy beast one last boost, sending a cloud of exhaust smoke in Father Dorer's direction.

Quickly assessing the situation, Erich dismounted his bike and strode up to the scene, where he proved himself just enough taller than everyone else to be able to reach the coffin, precariously perched on top of the railing, and help guide it to the appointed place on top of a couple of sawhorses draped in bedsheets in the middle of the yard. The remainder of the funeral proceeded without further incident.

Aunt Johanna's reaction to my leaving was equally predictable. In her own mind, she never felt that she had done anything other than her Christian duty in looking after her sister's children in time of need. Had she not washed the sheets I had soiled in Grandfather's bed and shared what little she had to feed her own family? She and Uncle Otto wished me well.

"Don't forget where we are if you should happen to strike it rich!" Johanna shouted after me as I rode off on my bike.

Aunt Gretel, on the other hand, took me into the new store—which together with the print shop had been rebuilt and expanded since she and Uncle Otto had watched it burn—and asked me to pick out a farewell gift to remember them by. She was always very kind to us and very sincere in offering her advice. I chose a sizable book showing the maps of the world, which in the end turned out to be too bulky to fit into the cardboard suitcase that carried the rest of my worldly possessions. Despite that, Aunt Gretel does occupy a special happy place in my heart and memories.

Uncle Wilhelm, who was the proprietor of Forchheim's major painting and decorating business, was my next stop. Wilhelm had a very serious illness, in his wife's view, job-related. Apparently, after being exposed to a diet of harmful fumes escaping the paint containers, which needed constant stirring, he had developed a serious addiction to alcohol. On the day of my goodbye visit, the demon had struck a particularly serious blow, confining him to bed. He was the kind of drunk who turned mean and liked to shower his belligerence on anyone within earshot.

"Keep that gypsy vagabond out of my sight!" he shouted in response to his wife, who had timidly opened the door to his bedroom announcing my visit.

"*Bleib im Land und nähre dich redlich*" ["Remain in your country and feed yourself honestly"] was the last thing I heard, apart from a stream of obscenities that added to the polluted surroundings. Uncle Wilhelm, rest his soul, was the first of Grandfather Leibold's sons to join his father in the afterlife; he fell victim to his affliction not long after my departure.

Quite an assembly had gathered at the bus across the street from the new Leibold store to bid a final farewell. It was a tearful affair with everyone groping for words that would offer courage, something profound enough to keep the moment alive to be recalled at times of need.

Mother just kept repeating her wish that I would not have to embark on such an adventure alone. Hanna and I stood silently, holding hands, offering each other comfort. But for her the moment had a very special significance. She knew that my courage, for which everyone was giving me praise, would pale in comparison to the courage she would need before we met again.

Hanna accompanied me to the railway station in Karlsruhe, where Ludwig and Hilde, my new sister-in-law, met us to say

Hanna and Frank near Forchheim in 1951, just before Frank left for Canada.

173

their goodbyes. When the train finally pulled into the station, I could feel her whole body shaking, perhaps suppressing the urge to confess something she had been holding back from me, something that could have influenced my decision. But she remained resolute and strong then, just as she would throughout our lives. She would never have deprived me of any opportunity to chase my dreams or reproached me if things turned out wrong.

"Please take me with you," she whispered through her tears as we embraced for the last time. Oh, how I wished that it were possible.

It was a night train through Switzerland en route to Genoa on the Mediterranean, but my mixed emotions were competing for space in my mind, driving off any urge to sleep. A bright moon highlighted the peaks in the Swiss Alps, which had already adorned themselves with the season's first snow, and the train rattled and clanked its way through the unfamiliar terrain. Slowly the reality of the situation began to sink in. I had left behind people for whom I had learned to care deeply: Hanna, my parents, my siblings, and Erich in particular, because he was so close to me at such a critical time of my life. Berta, too, was among them, and Kneisel, the four Albecker girls—Christa, Veronika, Hilde, and Lore—all my classmates, and some other very good friends as well. Would I ever see any of them again?

People often think that immigrants have left nothing of value, fleeing from poverty and repression to find prosperity and freedom elsewhere. No doubt that's true in many cases. But for me and many others, leaving Germany meant leaving home. It meant leaving behind a network of friends and relatives, the universal social care offered by the state and the community, and a career as a baker—all for a very uncertain and risky future. The stories are legion of immigrants who died poor, desperately homesick for the rest of their lives. On the other hand, why would I ever wish to return to a place that had spawned such bitter memories? In the end, I resolved to clear my cluttered mind of any bitterness and to concentrate on the future unencumbered by the past in which I or any of my family needed to share any guilt. I was heading for a new life in a different part of the world, where a man would be judged not by the class, station, or reputation he had inherited, but by that which he had earned for himself.

I was young and full of hope and determination on that October day in 1951. Ahead was a long rocky road of loneliness, hardship, disillusionment, and at times despair that I couldn't have imagined in my wildest dreams. But for now, everything was new and exciting.

In no time at all I found myself in the midst of the hustle and bustle of the railway station in Genoa, which was crowded with people from all over Europe who, like myself, had booked passage to a new life.

"*Vulcania! Vulcania!*" shouted someone tending a large baggage cart. He collected our bags, giving us an introduction to the pitfalls awaiting the unwary traveller. Instead of delivering our luggage to the ship, which would have been available to us for boarding later in the day, our baggage handler made us unwilling guests in a rundown hotel instead. This was a serious problem because Germany, which had very tight currency controls in place at that time, limited the amount of money one could take out of the country to 40 marks. To assure themselves of payment that would have eaten up most people's available cash, including ours, the hotel management insisted on taking everyone's passports for safekeeping. They would only be returned at checkout.

It was a chaotic scene in the lobby the following morning as some of the people discovered that they would have to leave behind their luggage to settle their bill. Fortunately, I had befriended a young German couple who had travelled in Italy previously and were somewhat familiar with this particular ploy. Positioned just outside the place, we found a policeman who was undoubtedly well aware of the goings-on inside. Speculating that his business overhead would be much less than that of the hotel itself, we offered him payment for our room in return for our passports and luggage. This turned out to be a good bet. He only wanted five marks, which he tucked into his tunic as he elbowed his way to the front of the line of agitated patrons to demand our passports for inspection. He then explained to the clerk that he required our luggage as well, since he was placing us under arrest. Much to my relief, I was in the custody of the Italian police for less time than I was in Ernst Meier's. Just outside the door, the officer saluted us politely, gave us our passports, and wished us a pleasant journey.

Older and wiser, I was free to board the *Vulcania*. Our voyage would take us to Naples, then up to Cannes on the French coast, and from there to Palermo in Italy and Lisbon in Portugal, before crossing the Atlantic en route to Halifax.

It was nothing less than awe-inspiring to observe for the first time the ocean and the big ships that bridge the world. By today's standards the *Vulcania*, at 24,000 tonnes, was not very large, but for me there was no end to the things that aroused my curiosity. The cabin to which I was assigned was small and had to be shared with three other passengers. The two bunk beds occupied most of the space, and there was no porthole to the outside. But there was lots of space on deck and in the dining halls for entertainment and to get some exercise.

The Italians, I learned, had other ways that seemed peculiar to me. Compared to my own experience, their ways of saying goodbye were much more elaborate and emotional.

As the *Vulcania* made ready to depart late in the afternoon, a brass band on shore set the tone for a scene more dramatic than any Shakespearean play or Wagnerian opera. The dress code, it appeared, was black for both men and women—perhaps because most families, in Italy as well as in other European countries, were still mourning their war heroes, but it added to the ambience of the moment. As soon as their loved ones appeared on deck to wave their last goodbyes, the people left behind on shore shed every last vestige of composure. Their arms extended, they strained and stretched to bridge the void between ship and shore, which now, ever so slowly, began widening. They tore at their clothes, throwing themselves upon the dusty ground in convulsive heaps of unbearable agony, all the while giving expression to their grief with primal screams and floods of tears that threatened to raise the level of the sea which now, perhaps forever, separated them from the objects of their affection.

Even the most casual observer couldn't help but sympathize with the sorrow of our fellow passengers. Some of the women were undoubtedly en route to meet husbands or sweethearts who, like me, had preceded them to the Promised Land. Suffocating from grief, they were throwing themselves into the arms of total strangers, seeking comfort. Heroically, there were men who, throwing all caution to the wind, rushed to the rescue. Even before the mournful tunes from the brass band on shore were swallowed by the sea, such gestures of selflessness cemented new intimate relationships by which the participants would remember the voyage. Perhaps they were all direct descendants of Michelangelo who, to me at least, always seemed best able to depict a culture in which human agony and ecstasy draw life from the same breath.

It was my good fortune that among those heroes were two of my roommates, and since their shipboard romances were booked in second class, this freed up some space in my own cabin. I was to appreciate it when we hit the Atlantic.

Shore visits to Naples, Palermo, and Lisbon were an option, but my limited financial resources did not allow any extravagant exploration of the many wonders that were arousing my curiosity. I did see a little of Naples, the city in the shadow of Mount Vesuvius with its famous royal palace, opera house, and Castle Nuovo; Palermo, the capital city of Sicily, which was founded before Christ's birth in the eighth century BC; and Lisbon, capital of Portugal, with its graveyards in which the structures housing ancestral remains rival the homes of the living in size. There was not nearly enough time to satisfy my inquisitive mind, but I vowed to return someday to pay homage to the historic treasures of that region of the world.

However, it was now time to leave behind the Old World and focus on the future. Most of my fellow passengers could be found in groups discussing and sharing whatever information had been imparted to them by contacts in Canada or other reliable sources. Unlike any of the people I met, I did not have a fixed destination, so I was hungry for every morsel of information that might help in selecting a final goal. Most of the Italian passengers appeared to be on their way to Toronto, whereas the group of Germans I had attached myself to had booked themselves on the train from Halifax to Kitchener, a predominantly German community in Ontario that had once been named Berlin.

One young couple, who were en route to Vancouver on the continent's west coast, had been told that the eastern part of Canada offered nothing more than a poor copy of Europe. The real opportunities and excitement, their sources said, could only be found in the prairie provinces or the western wilderness on the Pacific. However, the West Coast would be as far away again as we had already come and quite out of my reach. I would have to be content to make my way in Halifax for whatever time it took to gather the means to support future plans.

The *Vulcania* pointed her bow toward the Atlantic late in the afternoon as she made her way out of Lisbon harbour. The reality of the situation caught up with me the following morning when I found myself, after falling off the top bunk, on top of my remaining roommate. He had wisely chosen a lower berth. As we discovered, the month of October was definitely not the best time to be crossing the Atlantic. I, most of the passengers, and even some members of the crew were deathly ill with seasickness for the remainder of the trip.

Nothing helped. Some people even risked being washed overboard by sleeping on deck rather than suffering the violence of the ship's motion from below. My stomach resisted any attempt to take on food in the dining hall and must have turned itself inside out so as to divest itself of even the most minute particle of foreign matter. Here was another occasion when God let me down, failing to answer my desperate appeals for Him to tame the waters, as He had done on at least one previous occasion.

Of course, you could say that it was His way of punishing the *Vulcania's* passengers for defying, in such blatant fashion, God's rules against adultery or the unsanctified sexual promiscuity that was in evidence throughout the vessel. Toward the end, some even prayed for death in preference to the relentless torture of seasickness. As I had done so often during my war years, I saw myself once again in the wrong place at the wrong time, in the company of people deserving God's wrath.

"You owe me one," I reminded Him in my prayers, hoping that if I survived the ordeal, I would be compensated for the torment to which I was subjected.

Finally, on the night of October 19, 1951, the *Vulcania* dropped anchor in Halifax harbour. To the anxious eyes of the passengers, the city presented itself as a desolate place, shrouded in a fog that only the lighthouse beacon was powerful enough to penetrate. An occasional foghorn broke the eerie silence lying over the place. I spent most of the following day on deck, leaning over the railing and trying to capture a glimpse of the place that would be my new home for the foreseeable future. When occasionally the fog lifted to reveal some of the harbour installations, with the city in the background, it did not inspire any hospitable feelings.

Since the weekend intervened, it was not until October 22 that we were allowed to disembark. We were docked on Pier 21, which today, thanks to a group of Nova Scotia historians, stands as a monument to the 1.5 million people who arrived in Canada through the port of Halifax in the years from 1927 to 1971.

Among them were refugees; soldiers returning from the war, whose lives had changed forever; and their brides and children. Over a million of them were immigrants, some escaping the horrors of war and famine in their respective homelands; others merely seeking to improve their social and economic situations; and some recruited or invited by the Canadian government, mostly for strategic reasons, to contribute their skills, energy, and resources to the building of our nation. Among them were some of today's leading citizens—industrial leaders, scientists and engineers, professionals of every discipline, and prominent artists and cultural icons—all of whom helped shape Canada's economic, cultural, and social landscape and the image by which we are recognized throughout the world.

Pier 21 in Halifax has been called the "Front Door to Canada," but at the time of my arrival it looked like a rickety wooden shed or an old warehouse with no redeeming architectural features. The reception we received on the inside was no more hospitable than the outside. Like cattle we were herded into pens, from which we were selected one by one to be interrogated by an official who offered little in terms of a welcome or helpful information. Among the last to be processed, I stood for several hours, waiting to learn my fate. The uniformed personnel conducting the interviews appeared rude, doing little or nothing to bridge the language barrier separating them from their clients.

It became increasingly difficult to crowd out the feelings of disappointment and even fear. The few words of English I had mastered failed me when it finally became my turn to be humiliated by the official representatives of the country in which I had invested so many of my hopes and dreams. Unlike all the other new arrivals, I had no forwarding address nor any sponsor responsible for looking after my travel or living arrangements. My entire fortune consisted of the princely sum of five Canadian dollars, which somehow Erich had earned for me on the black market back in Karlsruhe, the few marks I had left from the trip, and the contents of my suitcase—which included a dark blue pinstriped suit my mother had expropriated from Erich's wardrobe.

In Canada, the agent decided, my name would not be Franz, but Frank, and the stamp he pressed on page 14 of my German passport listed my status as that of "landed immigrant." Obviously I was wrong in assuming that a job or any living accommodation had been prearranged. Instead I was escorted to a secure holding area above the Halifax railway station that had been fitted to accommodate arrivals whose papers were incomplete or who claimed contacts in Canada that could not be verified. There, in the company of about a dozen shady-looking characters, I spent the first night in my new homeland, anxiously contemplating what the future might hold in store for me.

The following day, after a hearty breakfast, things looked better. The people in charge were friendly, at least toward me, offering helpful advice and information regarding my prospects for getting a job. I was allowed to come and go as I pleased, and until I was placed in a job and found some living accommodation on my own, I was welcome to room and board courtesy of the government. Reassured, I set out to explore the city.

It would be an understatement to say that the Halifax of 1951 was something much less than the cosmopolitan city it is today. I walked for hours through rain and fog, just happy to have my feet back on solid ground and to get a feel of the place. People seemed friendly and well-dressed. They drove large "American" automobiles, leaving me to speculate that, given the flimsy wooden houses in front of which they were parked, Canadians had different values and priorities than the ones to which I was accustomed. The railway station, the Chateau Halifax Hotel, and a number of magnificent churches were notable exceptions to the generally uninspired architectural landscape of the city.

The city had been founded in 1749 by British settlers, relatively recently from an Old Country perspective, and it was hard to understand how it could have become so rundown in such a short period of time. But perhaps the great explosion had something to do with it. On December 6, 1917, a Belgian ship collided with a French munitions carrier in the harbour. The munitions ship caught fire and exploded. It turned out to be the biggest human-made explosion before Hiroshima, flattening an area of more than two square kilometres. Almost 2,000 people were killed and thousands of others were maimed and injured.

The telling of the story is part of the city's culture even today. To aid the victims of the disaster, the government of Canada set up a relief fund administered by an agency that was still functioning 70 years later. As time went on, nobody in Ottawa had the heart to phase it out—until 1985, when a new government ordered a review of all federal departments and agencies for the purpose of giving a decent burial to those programs whose initial purpose could no longer be remembered.

Canada in 1951 had a population of just over 14 million. Louis St. Laurent was the prime minister. The Korean War had started a year earlier, after a United Nations police action turned into a full-scale conflict, and Canada, to my horror, was starting to play an increasingly important role in it. From what I could decipher in the newspapers, the U.S.-led UN forces were fighting for much the same things as the Allied forces were in the Second World War: democracy and freedom. The fact that my new homeland would likely never become a battleground for such conflicts was of little comfort to me at the time.

Day two in the "New World" started out even brighter. The sun was peeking through the clouds, casting a different light on the place and giving a much-needed lift to my spirits. And I had my first chance at a job in my adoptive country.

In the morning I was assigned to some housekeeping duties to earn my keep, but in the early afternoon I was sent for a job interview at the Green Lantern Restaurant on Barrington Street. As far as job interviews go, this one was notable in that it was mainly a mimed affair. Fortunately, the manager of the place was familiar with enough of the rudimentary skills I demonstrated with my hands to know that I had worked in a bakery before. In 10 minutes I had the job, and, as he pointed out via the clock on the wall, it would start the following morning at 7 a.m.—three hours later than I was accustomed to start work in any of my previous jobs.

There might have been some discussion about wages, but the outcome had not registered with me. I was just ecstatic to have a job that would sustain me until I became more familiar with the language and the customs of the place. I did not have to worry about rent yet. The boys at the lockup who had given me my new name hadn't indicated an end date to my tenure, and I felt no great urge to press the issue. So for the moment I was on easy street. The restaurant served us a meal at lunchtime and the government of Canada looked after me for supper. At this rate, I thought, I would be rich in no time.

Speaking of customs, I found some strange ones. Since I was the only one, apart from staff, allowed to leave the secure area above the railway station, I was regularly commissioned by the inmates to shop for essentials that were not supplied by our hosts. Aside from some drugstore items, beer was usually on top of the shopping list.

I must have explored every store in the city without finding any trace of beer being sold. I knew Canadians liked their beer. The army contingent of the Canadian military in Karlsruhe had certainly left no doubt about that. Finally, in desperation, my fellow inmates suggested trying a restaurant where they would surely serve, and perhaps sell, the precious brew. There was no evidence of any alcoholic beverage for sale at the Green Lantern, but eventually I did discover the source: a "beer parlour," where it became obvious why there was such a drought everywhere else.

The air in my new discovery, thick with smoke and blue in colour, obscured much of the scene that I came upon. There was an array of small tables stacked with glasses, some empty, some full, being attacked by the patrons, who appeared to be part of a contest to determine which among them could guzzle the most beer in the shortest period of time. The air prevented me from discerning the source of the liquid, which seemed to be the sole commodity giving the place its purpose. My eyes became fixed on a burly character close to me. He swallowed a glass of beer in one gulp without any discernible movement of his Adam's apple, indicating perhaps a genetic trait peculiar to Canadians.

Before I could tear myself away from this scene and consider what to do next, I was confronted by one of the bartenders who—so his gestures indicated—required some identification or credentials before I was allowed to participate in the contest. Unfortunately, with my language skills still minimal, I was unable to convince him that I was not there to challenge the record, or even to participate in the proceedings, but simply to buy some of the brew so as to practise at home.

I did show him my passport, which sealed my fate. He pointed to my birthdate and managed to explain that since I was 19—he worked this out on a piece of paper—I would have to wait for two more years before I could even enter the premises, never mind partake in the festivities. For the time being I had to be satisfied with my discovery that even though the consumption of it was practised in the most peculiar way, I would not be totally deprived of beer as an essential to sustain life in my new homeland.

The bartender's friendly demeanour did give me the courage to make another attempt. At the compound we spent the evening consulting the dictionary for the words to explain our desperate situation. The following night I returned to try to dislodge a few bottles of the precious liquid from the place to quench the thirst of my unfortunate compatriots. With great timidity I made my way through an open door, trying to be inconspicuous, forcing my eyes to penetrate the smoke, and hoping to identify and draw the attention of my friend of the previous night. As it turned out, he spotted me before my eyes could adjust to the din and the glare in the place, and this time he appeared to have no difficulty understanding the seriousness of my situation. Being the professional that he obviously was, he felt duty-bound to ignore his own safety to rescue a fellow human being from a fate worse than death.

With his eyes scanning the room, he took me by the shoulders and escorted me outside, where he pointed to another door at the end of the building, from which, he made me understand, he would discharge his duty. Sure enough, in very short order, paper bag in hand, he appeared on the scene, his eyes once again surveying the surrounding area, much like a bank robber fleeing the scene of his crime. The bag contained six bottles from which the tops had been removed. The contents smelled of beer.

Sensing that I was taking part in a conspiracy that, if discovered, might earn me a return trip to Forchheim, I paid the agreed price for the transaction and fled the scene. Back at the compound I was greeted like a conquering hero, but the euphoria was short-lived. After discovering the empty bottles the following morning, one of the guards delivered a stern lecture, leaving no one in doubt about the consequences of a repeat performance. Nevertheless, there were future attempts, but they were meticulously timed to coincide with schedules the guards kept, both in the evening, when the booty was smuggled in, and in the early morning, when the empty bottles—well concealed under one of the inmates' coats that was ideally tailored for just such a purpose—were removed and discarded.

It was only much later that I learned the reason for removing the caps from the illicit brew. Proprietors were required by law to account for the caps in an effort to discourage bootlegging. Obviously bureaucrats in Canada were no more burdened with common sense than their counterparts in the Old Country.

There was another occasion when I found myself walking a thin line and ended up in hot water with my hosts above the railway station. Returning home early one afternoon on an unseasonably bright day, I came upon a throng of people, thousands of them, behind a police barricade in front of the station. Flags were flying everywhere and the shiny boots of army and navy cadets were pounding the pavement. The bright red police uniforms added to the colour and the excitement of whatever warranted this occasion.

In order to get to my quarters I had to pass through a very tight police cordon. Boldly I elbowed my way to the front of the crowd, presenting the pass I had been issued to the first officer blocking my way. He and one of his colleagues gave it only a cursory glance before they ordered me to proceed.

High-ranking police and military personnel and what appeared to be all of the city's dignitaries, none of whom paid the slightest attention to me, were crowding the inside of the place. Caught up by all the excitement, I decided to hang around to discover the cause of the commotion. I didn't have to wait long before everyone's attention focused on the arrival of a train, and the crowd began positioning itself in order of rank and importance on the station platform. I discreetly snuck behind the most important-looking personages. Since I was the only one among the thousands there who didn't know what the fuss was all about, I considered it only fair that I should have the best vantage point from which to observe the proceedings.

A military band began to play as the train slowly made its way into the station. Coming to a stop, it disgorged more personnel in parade uniforms, preparing the scene for the arrival of Her Royal Highness Princess Elizabeth and her husband, the Duke of Edinburgh. Standing no more than 20 feet away from our future Queen, I could hardly breathe, but I didn't worry. There were only two eyes that were fixed on me rather than on Her Royal Highness. One of the guards of the compound had spotted me, but too late to interrupt the spirit of the moment. However, as the procession began to make its way to greet the cheering masses outside, he snatched me by the scruff of my neck to escort me back to the compound, where he withdrew my pass and the freedom to leave the premises.

How would I get to work? I raised the question with a night-shift guard who had taken a liking to me and was giving me English lessons to fight the boredom of his job. He found the whole situation funny and promised to clear the matter up in the morning. He even offered me a ride to work. The matter was not mentioned again until much later, when I found an occasion to share the story with Prince Philip during one of Her Majesty's official visits to Ottawa. It got a good laugh.

My job at the Green Lantern posed no challenge to the skills that I had acquired in the bakery and pastry trade. Obsessed with overcoming my shortcomings in language skills, I spent all of my spare time studying English. The most valuable textbook I discovered was an old Eaton's Catalogue, which I had found at the compound. My friend the guard exercised limitless patience in satisfying my curiosity, insisting on just the right pronunciation of every word. I set a target of at least 20 words a day, which I would repeat even in my sleep. No formal language training could possibly match the pace and the scope of the approach I had chosen. In no time at all I was familiar with the entire range of sports equipment Eaton's was offering, as well as tools and hardware items, furniture and household fixtures, and even the most delicate and discreet items from their line of ladies' lingerie.

My friend manned one of the reception desks every time a ship docked carrying new arrivals from Germany. So rapid was my progress that toward the end of my stay at the compound, he engaged my services as an interpreter to assist those making connections to trains and buses or retrieving luggage and personal effects that needed to be transhipped once they had been cleared. Arrangements were made with my employers for time off on such occasions.

Eventually, however, I was encouraged to find my own lodging, which revealed the inadequacy of the remuneration I was earning at the Green Lantern. My wages roughly equalled what I would have to pay Mrs. MacIsaac, who ran a rooming house at 66 Hollis Street down near the water, for my lodging and some groceries to supplement the meals I was getting at work. I was left with little to spare for other necessities, let alone enough for savings. My situation was once again desperate.

From what I learned during interviews at the Pier, I began to realize that I had settled in the wrong place. Most of the newcomers were on their way to the "Golden Triangle" near Toronto. Some who had contacts in the west talked of the kind of life and opportunities to which I had attached my dreams. But with the prospects for other employment in Halifax almost non-existent, how would I get there? I tried to console myself with the fact that my Halifax stay was giving me time to learn the language and the leisure to look out for other opportunities. I had been in much worse situations. But then I received some news from Germany that would deprive me of even that small comfort. It was my first letter from home bearing my new address.

Mrs. MacIsaac greeted me with it as I came back from work one late afternoon. It was not written in Hanna's familiar script, but in her sister Cilli's. Sensing the news would not be good, I sat on my bed, too afraid to open it, trying to speculate what could have motivated Cilli to write to me directly.

There could only be one explanation. Emil, with me out of the way, had decided that he would not allow his daughter to attach herself to a man who had chosen a gypsy's existence, a life of adventure, instead of pursuing the opportunities that had offered themselves at home. I felt my anger boiling inside me. I knew my love for Hanna was the only thing stronger than my pride, and she would be the only reason I would ever abandon my dream and return home. The news Cilli conveyed instead must have been infinitely more devastating to Emil and Berta than it was to me. It could not have come at a worse time. Their daughter was five months' pregnant.

At that time in Forchheim it would have been inconceivable for parents to commit their lives to guiding a son into the priesthood while being burdened with the shame of a daughter carrying an illegitimate child. Cilli offered to manage the situation as much as possible by herself, but she counselled that I should attempt to make my way back to accept my part of the responsibility.

I was devastated. Why would Hanna have kept from me something she must have known about, or at least suspected, long before my departure? Why had she not written herself? Contemplating her situation, I felt utterly helpless. Once her secret was revealed, she would undoubtedly be rejected by her family and closest relatives. She would have to cope with the most unimaginable shame, pain, and suffering. For a whole day I walked around in a daze. Even if I took Dad up on the promise he had extracted from me and asked my parents for help, I knew how difficult it would be for them to mobilize what it would take to book a return passage for me. I seriously contemplated stowing away on one of the regular passenger or freight ships departing Halifax for Europe.

Finally I composed some letters, first of all to my parents. I informed them of the situation, pleading with them to act on my behalf in offering Hanna whatever possible comfort and support they could. I even told my dad that if he should fail and abandon me again, it would be the last they would hear from me. Then, in that little room on 66 Hollis Street in Halifax, I sat down to compose perhaps the most difficult letter I would ever have to write—the one to Hanna. First, I wanted her to know that my love for her was strengthened by the news and that I would dedicate the rest of my life to making up for what she would have to endure during the next few months. But I also had to confess to her that for the foreseeable future it would be difficult for me to concentrate on anything but my own tenuous situation. With our dream so far resembling more of a nightmare, I said that I would leave it up to her to decide whether we should abandon it or whether, despite our new responsibilities, I should continue to follow the rainbow and try to find us a place suited to our ambitions and dreams.

I couldn't know, of course, that she had made that decision before I left. She knew that revealing her condition to me would trap us into a life we were both desperate to escape. If it now meant that only one of us would have that opportunity, she was prepared to make the sacrifice for me. Reading her response, I felt more frustrated, more lonely and helpless than I had in all my life. I pounded my fists against the walls of my room, tears streaming down my face. Once again I would have to depend on others to help me out of a desperate situation. I chose to wait for Dad's response and perhaps fatherly advice before deciding on what to do.

It wasn't long in coming. Were it not for what I had left behind, he wrote, he would have told me to never set foot in his house again. How could I possibly doubt that he and Mom would even for a moment hesitate to accept their responsibility in this matter? How cruel of me to make the connection to our separation in the war years, which had burdened their lives forever with guilt and remorse. Given what I had written, and after meeting Hanna to invite her into our family, he now had doubts that I could ever be worthy of her love and her total commitment to me. He also reminded me of the shame I had brought on my own family as well. Already some people, including some of our relatives, were offering the opinion around town that another Oberle was following in the footsteps of his father, escaping his responsibilities and leaving others to clean up after him.

Yet, despite all of that, he tended to agree with Hanna. Coming back, even if it could be arranged, was no solution. If I kept alive the dream we had hatched for a new life together, it would give her added strength to cope with her situation. I was left with no other option but to accept that the love Hanna and I felt for one another would be put to its most difficult test under conditions where both of us would have to face the ordeal alone. It would test our commitment to one another to the extreme, but it would also help prepare us for a life that would take us from the depths of despair to the dizziest heights of success, accomplishment, and exhilaration.

Neither of the letters did much to improve my spirits. I had to find a way to save enough money to extricate myself from the trap I was in. I managed to add another four hours to my workday and began helping out on weekends, washing dishes and doing odd chores in the kitchen of the Green Lantern. Since I was now practically living at the restaurant, I managed to scrounge enough food to satisfy my enormous appetite. By Christmas I was able to begin making plans for my next adventure.

Halifax in 1951 might have had a lot of shortcomings, but the people more than made up for it. Everyone at work was involved in my language training. Not once, as I remember, did anyone laugh at my pronunciation of some of the more difficult words. Everyone took pride in my progress. I had several invitations for Christmas dinner but turned them all down, choosing instead to work the extra hours I could get from people who preferred to spend them with their families. Despite such kindness, that Christmas season was the loneliest time I ever spent.

The route back to my dingy room at Mrs. MacIsaac's took me past the beautiful old church on Barrington Street, not too far from the restaurant. The city was blanketed with a thick layer of fresh snow that added to the lights and the sounds coming from the church and gave the scene a surreal, mystical ambience. As if someone were taking me by the hand, I felt drawn toward the familiar sounds of the timeless Christmas carols coming from within the church.

The mass itself was in Latin, just as it would have been at St. Martin's Church in Forchheim. Someone politely invited me into one of the pews to share in the prayer, but my emotions were too powerful to concentrate on the familiar phrases. My mind was elsewhere, trapped by the memories and traditions of past Christmasses at home with the family. It made me recall a particular night some years back when, just as on this night, I was dead tired and, after leaving work late, was going home to spend Christmas Eve with the family.

I made my way through the forest on a stormy night with rain and sleet whipping at my face. The darkness was so complete that I actually became disoriented, stumbling over roots and debris. After some time, when I had I managed to find the railway tracks running parallel to the path, I was too confused to know the direction from which I had come. Dad, worried as the evening wore on, set out to look for me. I had never much been afraid of the dark, but I must confess I was greatly relieved to hear his voice penetrating the darkness.

All was ready when we got home. Dad had spent the day in his annual ritual of competing with God in the creation of the perfect tree. God always ended up losing, since His tree was never quite perfect until Dad had added a branch here and there and done some trimming in just the right places. Decorating the tree was part of the ritual, which could begin only after everyone was home and in the mood to be embraced by the spirit of the occasion. All of us were blessed with good voices that could be heard all over the neighbourhood, and while the gifts were modest, they came from the heart. In any case, we were all grown-up by then and the value of the gift was no longer a measure of the joy and contentment that filled our hearts. These were rare and precious occasions when we managed to come together to celebrate the good fortune of being alive and spared from the hunger and the despair we had all suffered during those terrible years of the war.

Humble and modest as these moments were at the time, they now occupied my consciousness in that Halifax church as something I overwhelmingly desired to re-create once Hanna and I were established in a home of our own with our own children. On this, my first Christmas in Canada, I found my voice failing me. The mass was nearing the end, the organ leading the congregation in "Silent Night." My eyes released a flood of tears as I stumbled out of the church onto the snow-covered street. It must have been close to midnight before I got back to my room, where my kindly landlady had deposited some pine branches decorated with tinsel and a small gift as a gesture of her friendship. Thank you, Mrs. MacIsaac. You will never know how much that small gesture meant to me that night.

Early in January I was introduced to Bill De Louhy who, like me, had arrived in Halifax without a job or sufficient means to travel to another destination. He was given a job in the Green Lantern's kitchen and a room at my boarding house. Right from the start we hit it off well enough to plot our future plans together. He, too, had heard glowing reports about the opportunities that awaited eager, hard-working, and ambitious people in the western part of Canada.

Mrs. MacIsaac, who was a widow, offered Bill a free room in exchange for doing some much-needed repairs to her place. This gave us the flexibility to plan the next phase of our adventure, on which we would be ready to embark by about the end of March 1952. Unfortunately, as much as I liked the people at work who had all been so kind to me, I ended up having to leave earlier than anticipated and not on very good terms.

It started innocently enough. The staff at the bakery had decided to make a fancy cake to help celebrate the manager's birthday. I volunteered to contribute my considerable artistic talents to decorating it. Well, Pope

Paul III could not have been more pleased with Michelangelo's work on the Sistine Chapel's ceiling than the management of the Green Lantern was with my masterpiece. When I arrived at work the following morning I was called to the office and informed that my talents had obviously been wasted. They were hardly telling me anything new, but their offer to reassign me to the pastry store to deal with special-order cakes, with a substantial increase in wages, came as a surprise.

My first instinct was to reject the offer and tell them of my plans to make a career change. However, the extra money and the chance to unleash my artistic talents were too enticing. It was my first introduction to Canada's peculiar and archaic labour-relations practices and, needless to say, it did not have a happy outcome.

The person who was to familiarize me with the intricacies of the new job, when told that I would be her replacement, quit without notice. It was hardly surprising since she had held the job for as long as anyone could remember. Overnight, no one in the place would talk to me. Gone were the friendly greetings that had brightened my mornings, and the instructions that came with the special orders were passed on only reluctantly and were deliberately distorted. In one case I produced a "Hapy Birdsday" cake, resulting in a very unhappy customer.

To make matters worse, no one offered to explain the sudden change in attitude toward me. Finally Bill, engaging the bakery foreman in an exercise of great linguistic acrobatics, managed to piece together the story. Apparently the woman I had replaced was a single mother with two teenaged children and a baby, whom she sometimes had brought to work. She would have the greatest difficulty feeding them without the income from the job I had stolen from her.

I was devastated. Bill even thought that his conversation might have contained a subtle hint for me to watch my back. Clearly my days at the Lantern were numbered.

A consolidated statement of the combined fortune Bill and I had accumulated by that time revealed enough cash to cover the rail fare to Vancouver, but very little to spare to cover any living expenses after we got there. In the interests of caution, we decided to venture only as far as Winnipeg. There we would examine any prospects for jobs before embarking on the final leg of our journey to the Pacific.

The following Friday I gained some satisfaction from telling George, the foreman, when he delivered the week's pay packet, that I had no intention of working for an employer who treated his people as shabbily as my predecessor had been treated and that I was giving the same notice she had been given. There was no one else trained in the art of decorating cakes, and Saturday was usually the busiest day of the week, so the Green Lantern was left with little choice but to reinstate the poor woman I had replaced. Thus I quit my first job in Canada. A warm and friendly handshake and George's best wish for good luck and good fortune indicated my redemption with him and the rest of the crew.

Mrs. MacIsaac was disappointed to see us leave. People in the west, she lamented, were totally unsympathetic and boorish in their demeanour. She was certain two such nice and refined young gentlemen as we were would find it difficult to establish ourselves among them. Having added the words "unsympathetic," "boorish," and "demeanour" to my expanding English vocabulary, we boarded the train for Winnipeg the following Monday morning.

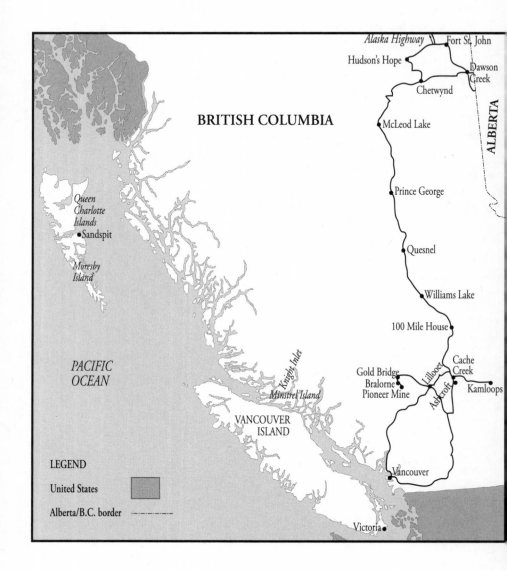

CHAPTER 13

Go West, Young Man

It's choice—not chance—that determines your destiny.
—Jean Nidetch, founder of Weight Watchers International

As a rite of citizenship in our great country of Canada, it should be obligatory to travel the entire length and breadth of it at least once. For me, coming from a region of the world where a trip of 300 kilometres might take in several countries, it was hard to imagine how one could spend six days and five nights on a train travelling in one direction without crossing an international border. It was an even greater challenge to imagine the kind of raw courage and commitment that must have driven those people who travelled this vast expanse of territory in very recent history—from a European perspective at least—by canoe, on foot, or on horseback, and who surveyed and mapped the land and engineered and built the railways and roads.

Even more, what kind of courage and commitment would it take to settle the land that had thus become accessible, but had yet to be tamed or cultivated to yield even the basics needed to sustain life? I could only speculate on what might have motivated the early settlers to subject themselves to the hardships and deprivation that would overwhelm their lives. Perhaps their past experiences were no less extreme than my own, making it easy for them to exchange the cultural or social bonds they had in their country of origin for the loneliness, isolation, and hardship of the New World.

What would the life I was heading toward be like? Aiming for a job on a new frontier would likely be just as difficult and perhaps even dangerous. There were long hours of sleepless nights with time to reflect on the past and to consider what might lie ahead. Would I, in pursuit of my dreams, have to face challenges similar to those of the early pioneers who shaped this land? At the end of this journey there were now well-established, even modern, cities. But if the Halifax experience was any indication, these were nothing more than bad attempts to copy the great cities I had seen and visited in Europe. In any case, it was not in the comfort of well-established cities that fortunes were made. Would I have the courage for the kind of adventure I would have to face, reaching beyond the ordinary to break out from under the limited horizons of the station in life into which I had been born?

I was confident I would not lack the courage. Given the opportunity, I would dispel the demons that kept reminding me of my past. I would not shy away from making tough decisions. To do otherwise would betray the trust Hanna had invested in our dream. In the end, Hanna was my touchstone. If I felt self-doubt or moments of loneliness, they were insignificant compared to the sacrifice Hanna was making by herself, depending in part, at least, on strangers to help her through the worst of her situation. Her courage would be the measure against which I would gauge my own. I would do whatever it took to raise the money for her to join me and chase our dreams.

It was February 1952, just three months since I'd arrived in Halifax, and the landscape of Canada's middle provinces was bleak. Of course I had brought with me my trusted Eaton's Catalogue to pass the time, and having a friend to share one's thoughts and impressions with made the journey easier. Bill, who was two years my senior, had spent the last few days of the war in Berlin. Trained in the hospitality industry, he was more inclined to get established in a city than I was. He also spoke some French and was further advanced in English than I, something that, together with his good looks and pleasant personality, would be an advantage to him in finding work in his chosen field.

The towns along the way, at which the Canadian Pacific train made its brief stops to take on fuel and water, appeared desolate, blanketed in snow. The engine spewed out angry puffs of white steam, as if to answer the barks and yelps of the dog population aroused by the intrusion. Only the larger cities, few and far between, featured small kiosks in the station where we could buy an apple or some cheese to supplement the diet of *gummibrot* [rubber bread] sandwiches available on the train. Then, for hours on end, there would be nothing but a barren landscape covered in its winter coat. Sometime during the night there might be a single light in the far distance, leaving one to wonder who the inhabitants were and what was sustaining them in such a desolate place.

Finally we arrived in Winnipeg, Manitoba, but it was a disappointing and, as it turned out, brief rendezvous.

Bill and I left the station full of anticipation and relieved to be free of the rhythmic clatter of the train. I remember the shock of the first gulp of frigid air that gripped the city with a temperature of -30°F. We were ill-prepared. I was wearing a rather light windbreaker, which I pulled up over my ears to keep them from falling off, leaving my bare hands to alternate between my pants' pockets and the handle of the suitcase. Neither of us had any headgear, and by the time we had covered the short distance from the station to the stately old Fort Garry Hotel, I had frozen the tips of my earlobes. Shock turned to terror.

To make matters worse, we immediately encountered the first of the people Mrs. MacIsaac had warned us about. The staff at the hotel, once it was established that we were not paying guests, showed little sympathy for us and rudely discouraged us from becoming too comfortable in their lobby. Braving the elements once more, we were forced to trot back to the railway station, fighting the bitter cold. It's a miracle we survived the ordeal without more serious harm to our tender parts.

We hurriedly re-evaluated our situation. Fortunately Winnipeg qualified for a longer-than-usual stopover, giving us ample time to conduct another detailed audit of our finances and to purchase tickets for Vancouver. By being careful about what money we would invest in meals for the rest of the trip, we would arrive in British Columbia with about $25 or $30 between us. As the train pulled out of the station, puffing and snorting to regain speed and momentum for its journey to the Pacific, I became deeply conscious of the additional distance I was putting between myself and the responsibilities I had left behind.

I was playing my last card. I would have to find the end of the rainbow or else join the ranks of the thousands of people whose sad stories are told in German folklore and song. The monotony of the desolate prairie winter landscape through which the train was now making its way did little to improve our spirits. Not knowing what to expect, but realizing that at this journey's end there would be no place further to go, added to the anxiety.

Later in life I would make the trip innumerable times, by much faster means of transportation, but never without thinking back to the first time.

The most exhilarating part remains the trip through the Rockies, half in Alberta and half in B.C., and I still remember the stunning impact it had on me then. Our eyes were riveted to the spectacularly rugged terrain and breathtaking beauty of the mountainous landscape through which the train now laboured toward the country's western extremity at the Pacific. In no time at all we were winding our way through the Fraser Canyon, following the path the great river had carved for itself to find an outlet to the ocean. In places, the mountain peaks conspired to block out any view of the sky.

This at last felt like being part of a great adventure. No time here for any negative thought: It made no sense to let the fear of failure block my view of the stars or sap me of the energy and courage to chase whatever opportunity presented itself at the end of this journey.

Then, on the final stretch, the sky opened up and the mountains receded to expose a lush green valley into which the river, in its timeless journey from the glaciers high in the Rockies, had deposited its cargo of silt and fertile soil. It was a typical Vancouver winter day. I didn't know what to expect, but I was utterly amazed not to be greeted by another winter storm and, what's more, not to find any snow at all. Still, as the train pulled into the Main Street railway station, I couldn't help but be reminded of an earlier disembarkation. It was now February 15, 1952, almost seven years to the day since I'd got off that train in Dresden.

We arrived at the station late in the afternoon, 38 days before my 20th birthday. The fresh air spiced by the ocean, the lush greenery that adorned the perimeter of the station, and the friendly demeanour of the first people we met, belying Mrs. MacIsaac's opinion of them, made our spirits soar. Even in 1952 the hotels along Main Street were no longer the ritziest in the world; the architecture and the state of cleanliness and repair of the buildings hardly matched the image of the "New" World I had in mind. But the price for our first night's stay in one of them was all right, and the flaws could not dampen the almost festive mood by which we felt embraced.

If our intended use for our room was to sleep, we wasted our money. Our minds were too busy recording the images taken in that first night and full of anticipation of what the next day might bring. We didn't even bother to unpack our suitcases before we set out to get acquainted with the place. First we had to assure ourselves that we had actually arrived at the Pacific Ocean. Somewhere near where today's luxury cruise ships have their berth, we dipped our toes into the water just to make sure. Then for many hours, and long into the night, we followed the bright lights leading us up Granville Street to the centre of the city. At one point we could see the brightly illuminated letters YMCA mounted high on the side of a building on Burrard Street, and following some suggestions we decided on it for our first contact the following day.

The next morning turned out to be relatively warm and sunny as we made our way downtown. With the help and advice of the good people at the YMCA, we were checked in before noon at a nicely furnished housekeeping room in a cozy old three-storey wooden house on Nelson Street.

To our pleasant surprise, having paid a week's rent in advance, and after a thorough raid of the Chinese grocery store nearby, we gave ourselves 10 days to two weeks before our finances ran out. That was plenty of time to get acquainted and impress people with our looks and talents.

By European standards the city of Vancouver was in its embryonic stage. Forchheim, just prior to my departure, had celebrated its thousand-year history. On my arrival in 1952, Vancouver was just 66 years old. The arrival of the first transcontinental train in 1887 followed the incorporation of the town by one year. Between 1885, when the Canadian Pacific Railway announced that Vancouver would be its western terminus, and 1891, the town had grown from just 400 to 13,000 people. With the docking of the first ocean-going ship from China, also in 1887, Vancouver's destiny as the gateway to the Pacific began to manifest itself.

We had arrived in Vancouver at a time when the pace of post-war reconstruction and development of some of the Pacific Rim countries was, in part at least, determined by the volume of raw material harvested from forests and mines in the north and up the B.C. coast that could be channelled through the port of Vancouver. Price was no object, as buyers from all over the world were breaking down suppliers' doors to increase their shipments. The population of Vancouver had grown to over half a million people.

From what we'd been told, the prospects for jobs in the city were not that bright, but Vancouver was also the staging ground for major projects on the frontier catering to the world's demand for access to Canada's rich storehouse of natural resources. Companies were offering wages many times what one could expect in the city. Clearly we had come to the right place. Even Bill became interested as we set out to look for hiring offices without being selective about the kind of work they might have to offer.

It was again at the YMCA, on the third or fourth day after our arrival, that we found the pot of gold I knew was waiting for our discovery. We would hang out there in the evenings, using the swimming pool and gathering information from other patrons in similar situations to ours. The pot of gold came in the person of Bill Lekei, who was a logger with his own falling crew, putting in time until the camp to which he was attached in the Queen Charlotte Islands opened up after an extended holiday shutdown.

Bill was of German-Ukrainian descent and was intrigued by the familiar German dialect I spoke, which was similar to the one he had learned from his parents. Like so many of the people who settled our prairie provinces, Bill's ancestors were among the thousands of Germans who answered the call of Catherine the Great of Russia in the 19th century and settled in the Ukraine with the promise of land and an exemption from military service. His parents escaped the revolution in Russia in the early 1920s and moved to North America, enticed by Canadian-government promises of land and other forms of assistance tied to the settlement of the prairies. The family suffered with everyone else through the 1930s, but managed to survive and prosper, finally exchanging the substantial farm enterprise they had built for a sizable fruit orchard in B.C.'s Okanagan valley.

Neither Bill nor his parents had ever set foot on German soil, but they still spoke the language flawlessly and could not have been more patriotic and in love with their ancestral homeland. Bill had an insatiable appetite for stories and information about Germany to add to and compare with what he had learned from his parents. He was particularly interested, of course, in the war years. Like his mother and father and so many others of his ethnic group, Bill was hoping that the truth had fallen victim to the propaganda of the war or that one could rationalize what had taken place, find some justification to wipe away the stain that had sullied their romantic image of the land and the people to which they still felt so strong an emotional attachment.

Bill spent hours with us, walking the streets or sitting in restaurants, stubbornly clinging to his favourite topic of conversation. As long as he offered to pick up the tab, we were more than willing to satisfy his curiosity.

Bill was an unlikely specimen for a faller in one of the coastal logging camps. His physique matched the image all right, but his dress and demeanour were those of a gentleman who was not at all out of place in some of the city's finer restaurants. After a few encounters with him, he suggested that, should we be interested, he would talk with his partner, Chic, to get his okay to offer one of us a job with his falling crew. He would leave it up to us to decide who it would be, but he wanted us to know that while the pay was lucrative, it was commensurate with the hardship and danger that came with the job.

Even though I had no idea what an incredible opportunity it would be for a greenhorn such as me to land one of the most prestigious and lucrative jobs in the bush at that time, I knew instantly that this was the chance I was looking for. I was ready to sell my soul to the devil in pursuing it. Bill De Louhy and I avoided the subject for several days, each hoping the other would make the first offer to stand aside. Perhaps motivated less by altruism toward my more pressing situation than by a tinge of fear at the danger and challenge the job presented, Bill finally suggested that I should go. In turn, I promised to support him for whatever time it would take to find his own job.

While he spent his days pounding the streets looking for work, I used the remainder of the time before my departure to immerse myself completely in my English studies. Bill Lekei preferred to speak German with us, by way of practice, so I enlisted the second-best friend we had made in Vancouver by that time: Mr. Chou. The grocer at the convenience store down the street from our lodging, he spent hours teaching me, often at the expense of neglecting his regular customers.

His method was to insist that I know every single item of his entire inventory in the store. Since he was from China, he had the usual trouble with unfamiliar English consonants and vowels.

"Today we wolk in the ploduce section," he would declare as I entered the store in the morning. By the time I left in the afternoon, I would know all about peas, "callots," lettuce, and the rich "valiety" of "fluits" and vegetables he was carrying. My brain must have worked like a sponge, eager to absorb and stubbornly refusing to release anything it had taken in. At the end I emerged from the experience with a very strong Chinese accent that took me a whole year to shed.

In return for his kindness, I helped with stacking the shelves, sweeping the floor, or making myself useful in other ways. It was a most amicable arrangement that earned me an introduction to everyone who came in the store—not an unsympathetic person among them—as "my fliend Flank." And to top it all off, at the end of every day Mr. Chou would press a bag full of groceries into my hand, enough even to replenish the landlady's stores at the rooming house.

My first step toward fulfilling my pledge to Hanna began near the end of February, when we finally left for the logging camp in the Queen Charlotte Islands. Bill Lekei had made a great effort to tutor me on what to expect, but nothing could have prepared me for the great adventure that started with my first airplane ride up the west coast of the province. I was about to meet B.C.'s real pioneers and pioneer culture, armed with nothing but Karl May's notions and Bill's promises.

There must have been about 20 passengers sharing the crowded space with Bill, Chic, and me on the old DC-3 that was to take us to Sandspit, the only major town on the islands. I assumed that the two pilots were sober, which, together with Bill and me, made four of us. The rest of our fellow passengers, including Chic, had to be assisted on board by a specially trained ground crew. Chic's excuses were his claustrophobia and his fear of flying, which he managed to temporarily suspend with a 48-ounce bottle of whisky hidden in the "barf bag." Much of its contents, after Chic tried to open the closed end of the bag and failed, ended up on my lap a short distance into the flight, still sufficiently potent to provide me with several happy hours of spiritual intake.

Without exception, everyone else on board was a chronic alcoholic. They were strapped to their seats with what must have been lockable seat belts, and after having relieved themselves of every conceivable profanity, they fell asleep, a comatose mass of human cadavers emitting offensive burps, rivalling the thunder of the engines, and foul air from every orifice of their bodies. Even though to me, with my limited English, the profanity sounded like another strange language, I was taken aback. If these were the people with whom I would have to share my life for the foreseeable future, I was not looking forward to it.

Bill could sense my anxiety and kept reassuring me that once I got to know them in a sober state, I would learn to like them. I wished I could believe him, but instead I began to doubt his stories about the legendary skills and prowess loggers on the B.C. coast brought to the job. According to those stories, a logger, if attacked by a grizzly bear, could wrestle it to the ground with one arm and keep operating the power saw with the other. But at this point, the only thing that made me think of a grizzly bear was the smell of my fellow passengers.

To some extent the scenery outside the windows of the plane ameliorated the discomfort inside. It was love at first sight. Not having seen much of the world by that time in my life, I found it hard to imagine that any place on earth could rival this coast for its natural beauty and splendour. Our final destination was the south end of Moresby Island, the area that in 1988 was designated a national park, aptly named Gwaii Haanas [island of beauty and wonder], and is listed as a United Nations World Heritage Site. The remoteness of the place, 130 kilometres west of the mainland and 640 kilometres north of Vancouver, guarantees that, given the curtailment of all commercial exploitation, only those willing to risk their spirits being captured by the magic would now venture to visit the place. I will always feel a tinge of guilt for having been part of the army of 20th-century intruders that sought to subdue and conquer the resident spirits and interrupt their timeless rituals, but I also feel privileged to be among the few who, like the world-renowned artists Emily Carr and Bill Reid, experienced the mystique of this natural treasure.

Throughout the trip, which in Europe would have taken us from Barcelona in Spain to Frankfurt in Germany, there was hardly a sign of human life or activity. One could get lost here without ever again having to look in the eyes of any monster in human disguise. I briefly recalled the terror from my childhood, when my mind had blocked out any considerations other than the search for food, a safe place to hide, escape from death, and the need to cling to my miserable life. I felt anxious and perhaps even fearful about my new companions, realizing that this wilderness, inhabited as it must be by creatures hostile to human intruders, would pose its own challenges. Yet I also knew that people native to the area since time immemorial had managed to live in harmony with their natural world without ever having to go hungry or be without shelter. I regarded what my eyes were taking in with a feeling that this might be the end of the rainbow, the part of the world where Hanna and I would find our pot of gold and carve out the place shaped by our dreams, a place our children could call home.

The stopover in Sandspit was brief. Company officials, obviously experienced in the task, were on hand to transfer the human cargo to a boat ramp for transhipment to camp. Bill, Chic, and I, thanks to our elite status, boarded a small seaplane to take us to our destination. Low clouds forced the pilots to keep the craft low to the water and along the shoreline, giving us an introduction to the rugged, spectacularly beautiful scenery that was to become our home for the next five months.

The camp, ideally situated near the shore of a deep, sheltered bay, consisted of about a dozen primitive wooden one-room shacks housing from 8 to 10 men each. There was a large cookhouse, a central facility for toilets and showers, a store or commissary, a service and repair garage for machinery and equipment, and an assortment of other nondescript structures.

There were no roads. Logs were transported to the site by a narrow-gauge rail system and dumped into the ocean to be bundled into huge rafts, which were then towed to mills on the mainland. Being among the first to arrive, we settled in the bunkhouse closest to shore, choosing whatever beds offered the most privacy or space.

The first two days were taken up with getting outfitted in the required footwear and clothes. There was no exchange of cash, since most of us were in the same dire financial situation. The bill, which to my horror I found to be astronomic, would simply be deducted from the first month's pay. I remember asking Bill if he thought one month's pay would cover the cost. He assured me that the investment was worth it. As well, Bill and Chic gave me a crash course in servicing the very latest models of motorized saws Bill had acquired for the job. Chic and some of the other "buckers" still preferred to use six- and eight-foot crosscut saws.

On the third day the rickety little train carrying the gear and supplies we would need for the task at hand puffed its way along the coast and some way into the rugged interior. Just as morning was breaking, we found ourselves gazing up the mountain we would have to scale to get access to the cutblock that had been assigned to our crew. Part of the route would take us over mountains of the previous season's fallen timber and other debris that required the skill and dexterity of a squirrel to navigate. There was a light drizzle, which made the ascent, with over 300 pounds of equipment—power saws, axes, wedges, gasoline containers, not to mention our provisions for lunch and coffee breaks—even more treacherous than usual.

My two companions shouldered a power saw each. The main one, a seven-horsepower McCulloch, weighed 80 pounds alone, without the blade. I was given a bundle of wedges in a canvas bag and told to take my time until I became accustomed to the terrain. By the time Bill and Chic got back for the second load, I had progressed no more than a hundred yards and was looking up about 15 feet from under a pile of timber. Both my partners had made three trips and were enjoying a leisurely coffee break by the time I arrived on the scene. I was close to tears, certain that I would never be able to pull my weight and that Bill's charity would have its limits.

I was sure that my career as a logger would end as quickly as it began. The now heavy rain, which was being absorbed by my heavy woollen clothes, must have doubled my weight, and I doubted I could make my way back without breaking my neck in the process. But Bill, the good friend that he turned out to be, proved himself as sensitive and compassionate as he was tough. As he set out with the scaler, who had arrived shortly after me to instruct us on the limits of our cutblock, Bill suggested to Chic that he give me some basic lessons in the art of tightrope walking.

My thoughts took me back to my first lesson in swimming. I was faced with another "swim or sink" situation. If I wanted to get back to camp that night—indeed, if I wanted to continue on this career path—I had to overcome my fear of heights and learn to trust my brand-new $25 spiked boots to give me the footing I needed to balance my way from one fallen log to another via a small limb or a two-metre jump.

Well, I did make it back that night, albeit with numerous cuts and bruises. It's amazing how one's mind can focus when the alternative is sleeping with monstrous black bears who, upon waking from their winter sleep, hungry and mean, discover their home has been invaded by noisy, smelly, ravenous intruders intent on wrecking everything in sight. Moreover, I now knew that going uphill was only half as difficult as down. I was almost looking forward to the following morning.

But first we had to contend with the new arrivals who had moved into our humble abode in our absence. They were among those who had been on the plane from Vancouver with us, and there was little discernible improvement in their condition or demeanour. From Bill, I had learned that they would spend the first week to 10 days as guests of the company, undergoing a crash rehabilitation program. The treatment was basic: No booze of any kind, no place to escape to, and no mercy. For the rest of us, sharing the living quarters, it was sheer torture. It came as a relief every morning to hear Bill turn on his radio, signalling the time to escape camp for another day on the trapeze.

The camp was headed up by "Panicky Bell," among the last of a breed of "bulls of the woods." Panicky Bell, it was said, would grind a bulldozer over his own grandmother were she to stand in its way. Fortunately the falling crews, hired on a contract basis, were in the main spared his temper tantrums, which always resulted in someone being fired or demoted.

Some said he also had a peculiar sense of humour. I saw a demonstration of it on one occasion when he, tickled by his funny bone, in the company of a group of men having lunch, shouted to one of the chokermen sitting on a stump some distance up the hill, "Hey you, can you see Vancouver from there?"

Looking around in all directions to make absolutely certain, the innocent fellow, sensing what might be coming, answered in the negative.

"That's too bad," Bell replied, "but never mind. You'll be on the plane out tomorrow for a better view." And, true to his word, the next day the choker was fired. To add to the poor fellow's problems, the company, in the case of dismissal, always deducted the airfare from the final cheque.

Bell refused to be tamed or intimidated by the new breed of militant union bosses who were beginning to assert power and influence gained through the open-ended agreements they had won in the post-war period. The Marshall Plan in Europe and the cost-plus-delivery contracts tailored to the ravenous appetite of the Japanese construction industry had enticed the forest industry to cater to even the most ridiculous demands the newly organized unions were making. As long as the profits were measured by the amount spent in the production, all other rules or business disciplines remained suspended.

No one, certainly not the provincial government, showed the slightest concern for the future of the resource, let alone the environmental or ecological consequences that had to result from the rape to which the forests everywhere up and down the coast were subjected.

My six-day-a-week routine started with a quick trip to the common washroom. I soon discovered it was worth the loss of half an hour's sleep to get there early. Breakfast at 6:30 a.m. was followed by a shopping trip through the lunch boutique, an antechamber to the cook shack. Here we were treated to an endless variety of sandwiches and all sorts of fruit. Most men carried two thermos bottles: one for coffee, another for either milk or juice.

"Just follow me and do what I do," Bill advised me. Despite the fact that only the fallers were at work on this first day and a more leisurely inspection of the merchandise was possible, there was only one line, and the pressure from behind was intense. Following Bill's advice, I ended up with enough sandwiches and cookies to completely stuff my regular tin lunch box.

The two thermos bottles were carried in a special pouch built into the back of the heavy woollen coat, which appeared to be standard equipment. Two apples and two oranges found room in the side pockets. The abundance led me to think initially that I had misunderstood the routine. Were we to stay at the work site for a week's duration? During our 1945 trek, Joachim and I could have survived on these rations for at least a month and a half. But no, it was intended to be just a regular day's supply of food and drink.

Everything was a new and awe-inspiring experience for me, but perhaps the menu and the lunch room most of all. The eating habits of my fellow travellers, and the culinary delights that were offered, defy any description. The menus anticipated and satisfied the crew's every possible wish and demand. We could never possibly have devoured the entire contents of our lunch boxes, but it was nevertheless necessary to fill them in order to multiply the double layers of meat or whatever spread was chosen by simply discarding one layer of bread and putting the meaty parts together for a more nutritious helping.

At 7:30 a.m. it was off for the 10-kilometre trip to meet the day. Once at the site, we took time to have another cup of coffee and to catch our breath before starting the power saws, the monsters that shattered the serenity of the cathedral-like natural architecture. The smoke from the exhaust blended with the fog that usually shrouded the surrounding hills before either rain or sun dispelled it for the day.

The ravens on south Moresby were the size of small turkeys. They were the only ones among God's creatures that were unafraid of our presence and also naturally curious. Much to our delight, they kept us entertained during lunch breaks, earning their rewards of the surplus bread by performing all kinds of acrobatic stunts to keep our attention. They also raided any unguarded lunch box of its contents, including rings, wristwatches, or any other shiny objects with which they adorned their nests.

At mid-morning there was a short break, and another at mid-afternoon, with an hour for lunch in-between. Then, at the end of our workday, the whistle of the steam locomotive as it made its way out along the shore served as a reminder to be beside the track at about 5 p.m. for the trip back to camp. Missing the train meant spending the night under the stars.

The dining hall opened for business at six o'clock sharp, astonishing

Bill Lekei, right, and Frank tackle a forest giant in the Queen Charlottes.

me all over again. Like a bunch of hungry wolves circling prey, the crowd would start to assemble about 20 minutes ahead of that time, jostling for position close to the door. Each table would accommodate 12 of us. They were stocked with at least three kinds of meat, chicken, and fish. There were mashed potatoes, gravy, a variety of vegetables, and salads. For dessert we were treated to coffee or tea, several kinds of cake, pies, or cookies, and of course ice cream. Finally, it would seem, that huge appetite of mine, which had so annoyed Tante Johanna, was satisfied.

The customary table manners required some getting used to. Salt, pepper, ketchup, and meat sauces were all within easy reach, but any attempt at reaching for anything else that was not directly in front of you was punished by having one's hand scorched with a cup of boiling hot coffee or whacked with a spoon. Apparently the reason loggers—and as I discovered later, Canadians generally—don't eat with knife and fork is to keep one hand free at all times to prevent their table partner from grabbing for anything out of his reach. All this happened without anyone looking up or losing concentration on getting as much food into his mouth as possible in the shortest period of time. If a salt shaker proved constipated, it was tossed over a shoulder to land in the middle of the floor, and someone would quickly scramble to find a replacement.

The only words that were exchanged related to the replenishment of one's plate. Pass the meat, fish, chicken, and so on. Each of the tables was assigned a "flunky," who in concert with his colleagues and the kitchen crew operated with military precision to assure the uninterrupted supply of the various items on the menu. None of the serving dishes or platters was ever allowed to be empty. In fact, I remember that on one occasion I caused a near riot just by uttering the words "Pass the ice cream."

Ice cream was served in a big two-gallon stainless steel bowl and was eaten with tablespoons. Instead of the bowl making its way in my direction from the head of the table, I noticed the person closest to it picking up his spoon and pounding it on the table in the manner of the chairman of an unruly parliamentary committee using his gavel, and with the same authority. The bowl was empty. There was a mad rush and some urgent dialogue among the flunkies, leading to speculation that no new supply was to be expected from the kitchen. The drumbeat was now joined by the rest of the crew on my table. In desperation, one of the senior members of the kitchen staff reached for the nearly full ice-cream bowl at an adjoining table. He was rewarded with a hammerlock applied to him by the first of the combatants on the bench.

Everyone in the hall was now pounding the tables except for some men who were so annoyed by the commotion that they started pitching some of the used dishes and implements against the wall. Only the arrival of Panicky Bell himself and some of the camp supervisors restored a measure of order. Having chased the kitchen staff from the room, he made a short speech promising to personally attend to any "loose ends" in the food supply area. Everyone knew that meant firing half the kitchen staff.

Indeed, there was never again any shortage of supply of either ice cream or any other menu items. To my absolute disgust, I discovered later that all leftover food, at least as much as was actually consumed, ended up in the garbage dump, which perhaps explains why, even today, black bears on the Queen Charlotte Islands are almost twice the size of their compatriots on the mainland.

It was during those early days at camp that I was first introduced to the strange language I had heard on the plane and the concept behind it. According to Bill, it was a form of bilingualism. Bill explained that, unlike the German experience, where different regions of the country spoke different versions of the same language, the version of English spoken at the camp was gender based. Not yet totally familiar with his peculiar sense of humour, I might have failed to register some of the nuances in his explanation. In Canada, he said, men—gifted with greater intellectual assets—tended to speak a somewhat enriched version of the same language as women, but only in the company of other men. This was why, he explained, beer parlours in the cities were separated into sections set aside for "Men Only" and others for "Ladies and Escorts." The men were perfectly free to attend in the company of ladies, but ladies, unable to speak this enriched language, were naturally forbidden by law to enter the men's section. It was not absolutely necessary to learn this new language to live life in Canada, Bill said, but if I wanted to get along with my new companions, it was essential that I do.

I scarcely had the opportunity during my working day to add to my language skills. There was precious little time to think of anything much besides staying alive. In the evenings, particularly during the initial period, I was so totally drained of any energy that it became a struggle to take off my clothes before climbing into bed. However, since there were no ladies to be found anywhere within a 100-kilometre radius, it appeared that I had to start learning my English all over again.

To my great relief, what at first sounded extremely difficult turned out not to be very complicated at all. There were only about half a dozen new words to be learned. What required skill and gave flavour to the new language was the innovative ways these words were woven together with the conventional version.

Bill wasn't much help. He had been brought up in a strict, traditional, God-fearing environment that not only made it hard for him to advance his own linguistic skills, but also made it impossible for him to explain the new words' meanings. Chic tried his best but didn't have the necessary aptitude in mime. Still, once my mind had absorbed the mostly simple four-letter words—without worrying about their actual meaning—I found myself conversing with much greater ease. Sure, the ordinary sentence appeared to have become twice as long, but with every second word chosen from the new category, look at the gain in variety.

Meanwhile, my plans for Hanna and a home were always in the back of my mind. As the first week ended, I was anxious to find out what my pay would be. Bill had already explained that since we were working on contract with the company, we would only get an advance at the end of every week, with a more detailed accounting to follow at the end of the month. When I got my cheque, it was for $72. I quickly multiplied this number by four to convert the amount to Deutschmarks, which at the time were trading at 25 cents to the dollar, and was euphoric to discover that in the first week as a logger I had earned at least four times the amount I had earned as a baker after three hard years of training. The real shock came when Bill pointed out that the $72 was the net amount of the advance, after my room and board and the purchases I had made at the commissary had been deducted. The gross amount of the cheque was close to $250, which, Bill explained, I could expect to be the amount of the following week's advance.

My initial enthusiasm was dimmed by the fact I was deeply conscious that I hadn't earned a nickel of it. I offered Bill and Chic my portion of the earnings after deductions for at least the first two weeks, but neither of them would even consider it. I kept my cheque, and for the first month of the job each of us made just under $1,200. I couldn't believe my luck. Not even my wildest dreams could have led me to expect such good fortune, and what's more, I could actually sense that I was beginning to pull my weight at the job.

Even Bill's promise that I would get to like some of the dire alcoholics I'd met on the Vancouver flight was turning out to be true. Once they were fit enough to start working, their demeanour changed. I had never before seen men who performed as they did under the conditions that prevailed in the industry at that time. They emerged as tough, hard-working, highly skilled, and conscientious individuals who earned every penny of what they were paid. Among them were some who, like Bill and me, were there for the money to pursue other dreams, but even the ones who spent their spare time playing poker or listening to the scratchy sounds of a radio turned out to be fair and even kind to me. Not once did I sense any hostility toward me on account of my background. On the contrary, several of the fellows I met at the camp had served overseas during the war and were curious about my experiences. They were well aware what we had to endure and showed sympathy and some remorse.

That first paycheque was as if someone had turned on the light. Overnight my outlook on life came into much sharper focus. Sure, I would not be able to bring Hanna and our child to live with me at camp, but so what? I could set them up and support them in the city for the time it would take to save enough money to get myself into a less demanding job or perhaps even start our own business. It was time to start dreaming again.

Bill and I were walking along the track by the office one rare bright sunny afternoon when someone shouted, "Hey, Bill, tell your Kraut friend there's a telegram here for him. Can't read what it says." I could feel the blood draining from my face, and my legs barely carried me up the wooden steps to the office. My hands were shaking as I unfolded the little scrap of paper:

Forchheim bei Karlsruhe 15 März 1952. Heute um 18:30 wurde Deine Tochter geboren. Beide—Hanna und Kind haben die Geburt gut überstanden. Herzlichster Glückwunsch von uns allen, Erich Oberle.

[Forchheim near Karlsruhe March 15, 1952. Today at 18:30 hours your daughter was born. Hanna and the child are both well. Heartiest congratulations from us all, Erich Oberle.]

Feeling the loss of my composure, I let my shaky knees carry me to the door. Bill, fearing the worst, tried to console me, but I managed to tell him that the news wasn't bad but very good. Nevertheless, I walked away. I needed to be alone to deal with the emotions that at that moment deprived me of my senses.

There was a trail I favoured that led from camp to an isolated sheltered bay that would give me the solace to collect my thoughts. Everything seemed to converge. Happiness, of course, but also shame and anger, loneliness and despair. I never knew I had so many tears, but I let them flow freely and I prayed: "O God, whoever and wherever you are, if you never grant me another favour, please take my place to comfort her and help her manage until we can be reunited as surely you must have intended us to be. Make her feel my love and give her the strength she will need to cope with the shame we have brought on her family."

I felt utterly helpless. The fact that the telegram, because of the time difference, reached me four hours before my daughter was officially born made me realize how far I was removed from the scene and how enormous the distances were that separated us.

Bill and Chic came looking for me just as the sun was vacating its place in the sky for a dip in the ocean far off on the horizon. They had begun to worry when I failed to show up for the evening meal. They brought some sandwiches and coffee, pointing out how selfish it was of me not to include them in celebrating the birth of my daughter. How good it felt, despite my obsession to not ever become dependent on anyone again, to be among true friends. The list of people to whom I am indebted and whose friendship I have enjoyed throughout my life is very long. Bill Lekei is the first on the list of Canadians to whom I shall be eternally grateful.

Hanna and I had exchanged ideas about the name we might give our son or daughter, and I know she would have liked to make me happy by accepting Isabella as my preference, but she felt obliged to please my mother. Thankfully, Mom had showered Hanna with love and affection and had given her all the comfort and support she so sorely needed during the last months of her pregnancy. Mom had earned herself the privilege. Who was I to argue with her choice? It was "Ursula."

CHAPTER 14

Welcome to Vancouver

Only the curious will learn and only the resolute overcome the obstacles to learning. The quest quotient has always excited me more than the intelligence quotient.

—Eugene S. Wilson, American author, critic, and educator

I began to work out my frustrations on the job, as if Ursula's birth had given me some new energy, new enthusiasm. Often it was I who was first back on my feet after a lunch break or who suggested that there was enough time to attack another few trees at the end of the shift. Back in camp I volunteered to take responsibility to chop the firewood to feed the pot-belly stove and helped Bill until late into the night, sharpening the tools and servicing the machines. In fact, I traded my frustrations for the courage to try new things to the point where Bill had to caution me for being too reckless.

But all too soon time was running out on my first high-paying job in the New World. We were due to return to Vancouver in August. The camp was built to last no longer than the time it took to cut and slash and scorch every stick of timber within an area that could reasonably be serviced by the rail system. In no more than three or four seasons, all of the useful fibre would be gone, at which time nature would be allowed to reclaim the site.

Living quarters and personal habits were equally casual. The bunkhouses were equipped only with the basic necessities. A converted oil drum served as the central heating system, providing comfort on the principle that if one's feet rested on a block of ice and one's head on hot coals, a person should on average be okay. The beds were positioned parallel against the walls, which were neither insulated nor double-sheeted. It was a constant battle to stay relatively comfortable, rolling one's body every few minutes to expose it to the side that was either too hot or too cold. The only furnishings were a rough table and a couple of benches. Our personal belongings were stored under the bed, except for our work clothes. We hung these from the rafters around

Bill Lekei (right), a co-worker, and the author (left) at the Queen Charlottes logging camp.

the stove, which thus also served as a humidifier, vaporizing the mixture of sweat and rain and giving the place its special aroma. During the night, when the stove's red glow cast shadows of the woollen long johns, their flaps dancing around the room in ghostly choreography, it was reminiscent of a scene in a Wagnerian opera.

As far as I know, Bill and I were the only ones who periodically bothered to wash at least our underwear. The rest simply wore them until one morning they became too stubborn to put on, at which time they were deposited in the garbage dump, the theory being that the smell would discourage the bears from venturing too close to camp. I remember at first worrying about exposing myself in front of other men, perhaps when standing in line in the shower room, which had no partition, or while waiting to use one of four or five shower heads that served the entire population. I needn't have worried. Only on very rare occasions did I observe anyone making use of these facilities.

Once the camp routine had developed, it was interrupted and enriched only by the monthly visit of a supply ship or the periodic landing of an airplane to evacuate accident victims or, in at least one case, the remains of someone who had not survived the injury he suffered when crushed by a tree. There were several occasions when my guiding angel had to work far beyond the call of duty to spare me from serious injuries save some rather nasty cuts and bruises.

Not all the injuries at the camp were job-related. There was the occasional visit, usually around the time of a payday, of certain professionals who dedicated their lives to teaching the finer art of playing poker to anyone with enough money, curiosity, and courage to learn. Invariably these sessions ended with the hasty departure of the visitors, who left behind broken bones, shattered dentures, and rearranged facial features, making it easy the following day to recognize the participants in the lectures.

The last few days at camp were hectic and came earlier than expected. The provincial forest service had announced a shutdown of all commercial forest activity because of an exceptionally hot summer and the heightened danger of fires. No one, including me, was too disappointed. After five months of camp life everyone was ready for a visit to the outside world. For people like Bill and me and Chic, who had a wife and five children waiting for him in Vancouver, a visit to the bright lights would be a welcome respite. For most of the others it would mean renewed acquaintance with their demons. They would spend the entire time away from camp in some flophouse, totally oblivious to the affairs of the world around them.

Our last mission was to fell one of the remaining great Sitka spruces that had been designated as spar trees. It had been intended to facilitate the removal of the mountains of fallen timber surrounding it, but was now considered surplus. The day started with an exceptionally difficult ascent to the top of a steep mountain with all the gear we would need to tackle this seven-foot-diameter specimen. By the time we reached the site, the wind, which had caused some concern in the morning, had subsided, allowing us to choose the optimum position to land the tree—which stood 75 metres tall—to limit the danger of it breaking up. We decided to fortify ourselves with an early lunch and then work out the strategy for attacking the monster. The fact that the ravens, which normally would have given us their attention, were nowhere to be seen should have been an omen. They had vacated the area, just as we were about to do, perhaps never to return to this desolate landscape, at least in their lifetime.

Just as we finished the undercut, we noticed a slight breeze from the direction least expected. It was pushing against the now totally exposed tree. The prudent course would have been to abandon the project for the day to await more favourable wind conditions. But as it was, we only had until about five-thirty, when the whistle of the last train back to camp for the season would summon us to the valley below. We decided to pick up the pace.

First we drove the seven-foot blade into the backside of the monster. As soon as it had gouged its way deep enough, Chic went to work filling in the space behind with all the wedges we had brought, trying to nudge the beast forward. For a time it looked as if we might win, but once we got deep enough to expect the tree to yield, the wind picked up even more, frustrating any efforts to fight it. Finally the mighty trunk yielded to the wind and settled back to jam the chain of the power saw, its seven-horsepower motor pitifully inadequate to resist the force. We were left with no other option but to abandon the project and the site, knowing that the tree could come crashing down at any time and in any direction.

We did risk the time to salvage the motor by detaching it from the blade before we made our escape. Unfortunately, the least likely path for the tree to fall, offering the best chance for us to get out of harm's way, led us even farther uphill, away from the rendezvous with the little steam engine, whose whistle had already summoned us from below. We put a respectable distance between ourselves and the potential danger and, carefully staying upwind of the tree, began making our way down the slope. About halfway to the tracks, disaster struck. The giant chose to ignore both the direction we had chosen for it to fall and the direction the wind was pushing it. As if it were driven by revenge or guided by a mystical force, it chose to come after us, straight down the mountain.

On its first impact the whole mountain, littered with fallen trees and debris, began to move. The three of us were on top of a fair-sized log about 10 feet off the ground when it began to shift, taking our feet out from under us. My hard hat flew off in one direction, the lunch bucket in another, as I scrambled to reach for some loose limbs in an effort to break the fall into the abyss. Landing with my back against a stump below, I was left with the presence of mind to scramble for shelter behind the trunk of a giant cedar that, after being blown over by a windstorm, had died of natural causes some time ago. Struggling to regain the breath knocked out of me by the impact of the fall, with the avalanche of debris still passing overhead and the prospect for survival in grave doubt, it was time to pull the ripcord on Father Dorer's emergency chute to assure my salvation in heaven.

"God, honestly, I believe in you, and if in the past I had some doubt as to my guilt over some of the awful things Hanna and I did and, of course, all that other stuff that may have offended you, I am deeply sorry." Crouched in a fetal position, my hands covering my head as a substitute for the hard hat, I was still mumbling the lines of the Lord's Prayer when Bill grabbed me from behind to inquire about the state of my health. Chic was already making his way up the pile of logs to survey the situation. Miraculously, aside from a few bruises, none of us suffered any ill-effects.

My prayers may have spared our lives, but we still weren't out of trouble. The monster we had unleashed carried on down the mountain, gaining speed as it went. At the bottom, its pointed top found the rail tracks at just the right angle and with enough force to carry them another 200 feet to the edge of the water, where they ended up grotesquely suspended in mid-air. We arrived on the scene, having salvaged nothing more than our own skins, the motor of our seven-horse McCulloch, and a double-bladed axe. In the distance we could hear the whistle of the steam engine, which had picked up several other crews, with similar missions to our own, further up the coast. Needless to say, we were not greeted as conquering heroes as the engine came to a screeching halt behind the wreckage.

What made the situation even worse was a strong if unconfirmed rumour that someone had witnessed the unloading of a case of whiskey and several cases of beer from a floatplane the previous day. They were intended to liven up the farewell party scheduled that evening after dinner, a rare event indeed since it was a misdemeanour to be in possession of any form of alcohol, including shaving lotion and other such products, anywhere on company property except during special occasions. It did not help the mood that most in our company could taste a bottle of whiskey 10 miles away, roughly the distance that separated us from camp, while their chances of getting close to one would likely have to be postponed by as much time as it would take for us to make our way to camp on foot. With the train trapped on the wrong side of the wreckage, our fellow travellers could expect to miss both the dinner and the party, and the longer they missed them, the meaner they got.

Meanwhile, back at camp the missing train was the last thing on anyone's mind. It was very late in the evening, with the festivities in full swing, before our absence was discovered and a rescue mission dispatched. Fortunately, someone had the foresight to equip the mission with a case of beer and a bottle of whiskey, which for the second time that day might have saved us from an untimely and premature meeting with our maker.

The next day we waved our goodbyes to the rest of the crew from the pontoons of the seaplane that took us back to Sandspit, after promising to see each other again in the fall. Privately Bill had some doubt about that. He was of the opinion, later confirmed, that the company had inflicted enough damage in this particular part of the island and would be required to relocate.

The landscape we left behind had undergone a change from its surreal, supernatural splendour to a chaotic scene of utter destruction. As far as the eye could see, it resembled the scenes of devastated cities I remembered from back home after the Allied bombing raids. Only the odd giant Sitka spruce, the spar trees, remained standing as monuments to lost glories.

Even at the time I questioned the morality of this kind of careless and brutal assault on the natural system. I began to wonder what Grandfather would have had to say about such indiscriminate forestry practices. Not that it would have made much sense to make a comparison to the meticulously cultured forest along the Rhine valley under his care. For thousands of years it had provided shelter and sustenance to countless generations of people, whereas we were the first European intruders into this ancient rain forest, some of which had been spared by the ice age, the glacier sheet that covered most of the coastal areas of British Columbia as recently as 10,000 years ago. Grandfather would have looked silly with his little hammer coaxing one of the giants, boasting a three-metre diameter, to reveal much about the state of health at its core. Perhaps it's naive to think that any other type of logging practice could make sense at a location so remote from human settlement or the market for which the fibre was destined.

Still, for many years I wondered whether, and to what extent, nature had managed to heal the scars we had inflicted. In the early 1980s, 30 years later, I had the opportunity to visit Moresby Island and fly over the area in a small private aircraft. To my absolute astonishment I could not even identify the precise location of the camp. From the air there was not the slightest sign of the traumatic events that had been visited upon the area during my short stay there. On the ground, only the giant stumps, adorned with ferns and moss, remained as stark reminders of the splendour of a past era. But the ancient giants had left behind their splendid genetic lineage, and the area had not suffered any lasting climatic change that would have deprived it of its reputation as perhaps one of the most prolific and productive forestry sites anywhere in the world.

Mother Nature had re-established her domain, and it gives me great satisfaction to know the place that spawned my lifelong love affair with the west coast of British Columbia, and to which I will always be drawn, is now protected for all time from any commercial exploitation, except perhaps for the limited use the Aboriginal population might make of the trees for cultural and ceremonial purposes.

Bill was right about more than the relocation. Even as we said our fond farewells, he strongly suggested we avoid contact with any of our new friends after they became reacquainted with the darker side of the lives that awaited them in Vancouver. The seriousness of this advice was reflected in his panic-stricken eyes just two days later, when the two of us, out for an innocent stroll on Granville Street, were forced into an unscheduled reunion with a couple of them. A taxi had come to a screeching stop in the middle of the street. In the back seat a passenger had one of his arms around the driver's neck and the other pushing on the horn. His friend, half his body leaning out the back window, was using all his vocal capacity to get our attention.

"Hey, Kraut! Hey, Bill! Get your sorry asses in here—we're having a party," he yelled. It was a couple of our crewmates, Al and Bert.

"Don't look around, just keep on walking," Bill urged me under his breath, but it was no use. The traffic had come to a complete halt, and everyone's attention was focussed on us. The taxi driver's face was developing a purplish tint, his eyes pleading with us to save his life. We had no choice.

Our first stop was the old Belmont Hotel on Granville Street. The driver was instructed to wait with his meter running since the various planned stops might be brief, as indeed the first one turned out to be.

Apart from my brief introduction to the beer parlour in Halifax, it was my first real experience with the finer points of this particular cultural pursuit in my new homeland. The place was packed, the air thick, the noise deafening. We managed to secure a table close to the bar. Almost immediately a waiter was on hand to clear the table and to wipe the Arborite top with one expert motion, using a rag the size of a bath towel.

There appeared to be no need to debate the menu since its variety was limited to just two items: beer (whatever kind happened to be on tap) and tomato juice. There was no evidence of food on any of the tables. Let the fun begin.

In bare seconds the waiter was back with a tray full of brew. With swift, expert motions he plunked not one but two glasses in front of everyone but me before he moved on to the next table. Al, who had resided in the cabin next to ours in camp, reached over to grab the waiter's arm, drawing his attention to the fact that he had missed me.

"He is too young," the waiter explained. "Get him out of here."

Al reached for the tray with one hand and the waiter's throat with the other. With his free hand the waiter threw a full glass of beer into Al's face. The fight was on. At first it looked as if this time I would end up on the winning side of a war. Several patrons got up from neighbouring tables to deflect the intervention of a couple of big, mean-looking specimens who, I was later told, were the bar's bouncers and main entertainment, while the rest of the clientele seemed content to cheer for our side. However, a booming voice from behind the bar, enhanced by a loudspeaker, announced the suspension of service until the hostilities had ceased, and the momentum quickly shifted away from us. It was time to move on. Bert had the presence of mind to drain one of the glasses left on the table before joining the melee, but the only taste of the brew Al got was from licking his face once we were back in the taxi nursing our bruises.

If I'd thought my age would provide me with the excuse to leave the party early, my hopes were soon dashed. Al simply plunked his new cowboy hat, which he had acquired in the same pawnshop where he'd hocked his boots, on my head. "To make you look like a man," he said. To my surprise, it worked. The rest of the night unfolded without further incident, except for the final chapter.

We didn't manage to patronize every beer parlour in town, but we must have come close to it. At the end, around one in the morning, the taxi driver calculated the bill to be about $20, which would include depositing Bill and me at our destination. Al kept peeling off the twenties until he had a bundle big enough to amount to perhaps $200. The driver was obviously embarrassed by such a generous gratuity on top of a bill already well-padded. Bill and I, only slightly less inebriated, offered to help him out of his predicament, suggesting that he reduce the tip to double the amount of the bill and let us take custody of the rest. We promised to return it to the donor the following day.

Unfortunately, Al misunderstood and let loose with a barrage of verbiage that, once stripped of most of the "masculine" four-letter words, amounted to calling us a couple of cheap bastards who were trying to steal his money. He was coming for us both—arms flailing, but thankfully much less coordinated than he would have been at an earlier stage of the festivities—when Bert, with the suggestion of another drink, finally helped us make our escape.

I came away from the camp with more than enough money to pay for what it would cost to bring Hanna and Ursula to join me, and the more I learned about the city, the more I felt at home. Vancouver had everything. The ocean, the mountains, the pace and excitement of a large metropolis, and yet, in 1952, it still had enough of a small-town atmosphere to nourish my rural roots. However, both Hanna and I thought it prudent for me to get established in a more permanent job before making a move in that direction.

Meanwhile, it was great just to bum around for the first few days, exploring the city and feasting on the sights. There was some anxiety about how long the interruption of the job might last, but for the moment that was overshadowed by all the new experiences I was taking in. My language training progressed to a more advanced stage by adding the movie theatres as a source of learning. For the princely sum of 25 cents, I could immerse myself all day in this form of schooling, and there were several venues from which to choose. I watched at least two movies every day, often more than once if I found some sequence or scene particularly interesting. *The African Queen* with Humphrey Bogart and Katharine Hepburn and Marlon Brando's *A Streetcar Named Desire* were among the ones I watched several times over.

Bill De Louhy still had the apartment on Nelson Street and offered to share it with me again. He was happy and content with his job at the Devonshire Hotel next to the Georgia. He had a steady girlfriend and was making plans to set up house with her. My friend Mr. Chou, the grocer, greeted me like a lost son and was very impressed with the progress I was making with my English, although he had to remind me on a couple of occasions to be more careful in the use of my newly acquired enriched version of the language.

Bill Lekei then invited me to visit with his parents and family in West Summerland until we were recalled to camp. Bill's mother greeted me as one of her own, making up for all the deprivation she imagined we had suffered during our time away from home. In my case, she was determined to fatten me up and restore my body with all that it might have lacked during the war. Like Bill, she was nostalgic about her ancestral home and eager to have news of Germany. I was surprised to find that though the family had lived in Canada for over 30 years, she could not speak a word of English. Even Bill's dad had trouble carrying on an intelligent conversation in anything but German.

As time wore on, we became anxious to get back to work. A neighbouring farmer had a contract cutting railway ties for the CNR and invited Bill and me to help out until we could get back to the coast. It would have been a fun job had it not been for the same heat wave that had forced the closure of our camp at the coast. It was even worse in the Okanagan. During the day it was next to impossible to work. Even the horses we were using to skid logs to the mill flatly refused to move from the shade. We tried to get a few hours of work by starting at four in the morning, but by about seven, the mosquitoes, big enough to heft the power saw, stopped us from carrying on. We spent much of the day submerged in Okanagan Lake before making another effort late in the evening. The experience cured me for all time of the urge most northerners acquire during the long winter months to relocate or perhaps some day retire in the Okanagan Valley.

Finally, in early August, we got word that we were to present ourselves at the company's offices to be reassigned to a new camp. The fire season was over. To my disappointment, Bill decided to make a career change, staying closer to home so he could help his aging father with the operation of the orchard and take up an offer to go into partnership in his neighbour's tie-milling operation. The family and the neighbour offered to let me stay on, but the lure of the green gold and the tall trees, together with the fear of developing webbed feet from lying in the lake all day, was too strong.

Bill assured me that I would have little difficulty hiring out with one of the companies, given my credentials as a faller, even though I would likely have to settle for a lesser position. Fortified by Mrs. Lekei's farewell banquet in my honour and a bear hug to her ample bosom, I returned to Vancouver where I struck it lucky with my first contact. The Powell River Logging Corporation offered me a job as a chokerman at its Minstrel Island camp, starting the very next day. The pay would not be anywhere near what I had earned as a faller, but still many times more than I could expect to earn in the city.

Minstrel Island was another remote location, this time 280 kilometres up the coast from Vancouver in Knight Inlet. The rules were much the same and the work just as hard and hazardous. However, there was one peculiar factor that affected the turnover rate at camp significantly.

Across the bay from camp was a small settlement boasting a hotel with a beer parlour (the masculine type only) and a marina. The company boat made regular trips to the supply depot at the marina, and while none of us were allowed on it, there was never any shortage of enterprising locals who could be persuaded, for a handsome fee, to provide a ferry service and to supplement their income with a bit of bootlegging. However, anyone caught at camp with booze or in the slightest state of inebriation was fired on the spot and given a free ride across the bay, returning him to the comfort of the beer parlour. As a result, the company maintained a three-crew rotating employment strategy. One crew, recently fired, would be leaving as another was coming and a third was actually at work.

I was assigned to a crew working on a high-line operation. A long cable, perhaps two- to three-hundred yards in length, was stretched across the valley, the dead end anchored to a number of large trees and the live end to a "steam donkey." With the help of pulleys on both ends, this dredged logs, some of them weighing several tonnes, to a central site. From there they were loaded on trucks for shipment to tidewater.

It was extremely dangerous. We were working in the midst of an area of perhaps two square kilometres that had been clear-cut the previous season. Again the devastation was complete. I was part of a crew of four chokermen and a foreman, who also controlled the movement of the cable, communicating with the operator of the steam engine by means of a loud horn. There were four choker cables, each the thickness of my forearm, attached to the main line. It was no less than an acrobatic feat to first catch the wildly swinging cable with its attached bell and then to fasten it to a log, all the while dancing precariously from log to log and limb to limb. Often, once the chokers were set and the machine began its pull, the whole hillside started to move, making it almost impossible to maintain one's footing. I consider myself extremely lucky to have survived the experience with all my limbs and other faculties intact.

Our foreman, on the other hand, who must have received his training under Panicky Bell and who had earned his own nickname, "Bullmoose," was not so lucky. He was as skilled and innovative in the use of profanity as he was obnoxious. For eight hours every day he would exercise his vocal cords, relieving himself of torrents of profanity for even the slightest delay in wrestling the stubborn steel snake around the butt-end of a log. Unfortunately, it had to be me who triggered the accident he had long been inviting with his belligerence.

I was struggling beneath a huge pile of debris to attach a choker to a monstrous cedar log that had been on the ground for some time and was overgrown with mosses and ferns. Because of its size it was to be a single pull. Two of us were struggling to dig a hole below the log for the cable to pass through. Bullmoose was perched high above, accusing us of being the offspring of female dogs and of sexually violating our own mothers.

His fatal mistake was to intervene personally, insisting on showing us the easy way. Down he came, pushing aside my partner, who was digging on the opposite side of the log, to apply himself to the task. Finally he managed to feed the knobbed end of the cable underneath, where I could get my hands on it to pull and pass it back over the top to complete the loop. It took every ounce of my strength and both of my hands to tame the stubborn beast. When I had it in a position where he could grab it from the other side, he told me to let go.

That was the last thing any of us ever heard him say. The cable, intent on going in a direction other than where I was pointing it, snapped sideways, missing Bullmoose's meaty fist, but not its real target. As if it too had had enough of all the noise, filth, and obscenity coming from his mouth in a steady stream, it smashed him right smack in the middle of his face. He was out like a light, his face a grotesque mess of blood and tissue, and his nose pushed back to keep his palate company. For the first time the place shrouded itself in an eerie silence.

It took us the longest time to break the spell. Horror-stricken, someone managed to find the signal horn to alert the rest of the crew, but it must have taken more than an hour to move the lifeless body to the road, where an ambulance was standing by to rush him to camp. By the time we got there ourselves, he had been evacuated to a Vancouver hospital by air ambulance.

Afterward to my surprise and absolute dismay, I was treated like a conquering hero by the rest of the camp's population. The rumour had spread quickly. "Hear about Bullmoose? The Kraut shut him up for good. He coaxed him under a pile of logs and punched his ticket." So universal was the hatred our tormentor had earned for himself that there was no doubt in anyone's mind that the act had been intentional. The respect it earned me I would gladly have done without, especially since it triggered an RCMP investigation into the incident that cast serious doubt about our friend's chance for survival. Thankfully, in the minds of the police at least, I was exonerated.

Bullmoose did survive, but I never met anyone who had either seen him or recognized him after his release from hospital.

My career as a chokerman was all too short—just long enough, in fact, for me to make my first acquaintance with one of our more notorious labour unions. A month into my new job, we were ordered out on strike.

I could see no justification at all for calling it. Sure, the conditions in the camps left much to be desired, and so did the treatment the men were given by the industry's bosses. But in most instances the men got what they deserved and were compensated generously for the hardship they had to endure. Perhaps the union felt it was a patriotic duty to help correct the sluggish economy by recirculating—via the urinals of Vancouver's beer parlours—the money its members had just earned. If so, there was certainly no call for a long strike. In most cases it took less than a few days to spill what had been earned during our short work time since the end of the fire season. Some of my compatriots never even made it to the bright lights of the city. Thanks to our final party, they barely made it as far as the hotel and beer parlour at Minstrel Island Hotel.

Friday was the last day of work and so, strike or no strike, the boys wanted to celebrate. They advanced the reasonable request that the company dispatch the boat on Thursday night to get some supplies for a farewell party. Everyone chipped in a few dollars to bankroll the mission, which was to be carried out by four of our colleagues considered best suited for such a delicate task. It was late in the evening before they made it back, given that the wares had to be sampled before procurement.

How they made it across the bay is still a puzzle to me. The sea was less than calm, and the heavy load on board had elevated the waterline to within four inches of spilling into the boat. Fortunately, two of our friends didn't show up for the return trip, having fallen victim to unforeseen circumstances that kept them shackled to the bar at Minstrel. The heroes who did return never even attempted to tie up at the dock. They simply rammed the boat into the rocks, where 50 sets of outstretched arms and eager hands assisted in rescuing the precious cargo.

Needless to say, the party did not wait until the Friday night. I had acquired a bit of a thirst myself during the long wait, and feeling somewhat compelled to consume at least the worth of what I contributed to the enterprise, I was feeling no pain at all when I retired to bed around midnight. It was not to be a restful sleep. At about two in the morning the celebrants decided to teach the company a lesson to remember us by. Mobilizing a couple of the heavy-duty vehicles on site, they began dismantling the camp. I awoke as the cabin in which I had blissfully fallen asleep began making its way toward the water, minus the log foundation on which it had been constructed. It ended up perilously teetering on a rock, with the doorway over the edge and requiring a three-metre jump to reach solid ground.

It was not a pretty sight and neither was the rest of the camp. Even the cookhouse had been modified to stand at a 45-degree angle, rendering it useless as the venue for breakfast next morning, thus forcing its cancellation. This missed meal, ironically, became part of the grievances the union listed against the company as the rationale for calling the strike in the first place. No work was possible, and the operation was shut down a day earlier than planned. The farewell party continued, on the other hand. It merely shifted to the Minstrel Island Hotel, to which we were evacuated by private water taxi. The company, perhaps because of the extensive damage suffered by the boat during its last trip, no longer felt obliged as part of the contract to provide transportation back to Vancouver.

Always on the lookout for more work, I had one last experience as a west-coast logger. During our short stay at camp I had befriended a millwright whom I considered to be among the more stable of the crew. Ernie was about twice my age and always ready with some fatherly advice. He claimed to be acquainted with a private, non-union contractor in the area who might offer us work during the strike, and he offered to pursue the prospect. It looked like the strike might have a silver lining, but as it turned out, tying myself to my friend's proposition very nearly cost me my life.

The episode started innocently enough. We arrived at the Minstrel Island Motel late in the afternoon and were assigned a room with two single beds. The bathroom, equipped with only a toilet and a sink, was down the hall and had to be shared with the other 8 to 10 rooms on the floor. Once settled, Ernie offered to buy me a beer before supper, but recalling Bill Lekei's advice after the Queen Charlotte Islands adventure and still suffering from the hangover of the previous night, I declined. In any case, I was still six months short of the legal drinking age. Instead, I asked the proprietors of the place about the possibility of a hot bath. Since it was the first occasion in all the time they'd owned the place that anyone had made such a request, they generously offered to let me use their own private facility.

After supper I went for a stroll on the wooden walks along the shore, which were populated by dozens of private yachts and boats of all descriptions. The sunset over the water and the scenery were nothing less than spectacular. I doubted if I could ever find a place more beautiful and more serene on God's earth than this idyllic spot. My curiosity was rewarded with an invitation to board one of the larger vessels sporting an American flag, where I spent the rest of the evening in the most pleasant company of an elderly couple on their way to Alaska. I began feeling like a human being again.

It was late when I got back to the hotel, where I was confronted with an urgent message from Ernie. He needed to see me right away. We retired to the room, where he confessed to a slight problem with alcoholism. He had to get back to the bar to meet with a foreman who had promised to help us secure the job with the private contractor, but he would need me to keep him out of trouble. Sounding most reasonable and still quite coherent, he requested that I look after his money for the rest of the night to save him from his usual temptation of challenging the patrons of the bar to help drink the place dry at his expense. Under no circumstance, he stressed, was I to relent to any request he might make later in the night to retrieve some of the not-inconsiderable wad of cash he pressed into my hand for safekeeping.

I should have known better. It wasn't more than an hour before he was back for a draw, which he now needed to cinch his deal with our future boss. True to my word, I declined and even managed to persuade him to call it a night. He staggered out of the room to use the facilities, but must have become distracted on the way. By the time he returned, I was sound asleep. To my good fortune he had trouble finding the handle of the door and started to kick at it with his foot before he gained entry, trailing a steady stream of obscenities, accusing me of stealing his money and threatening to fix the cheap "DP"—displaced person, a common slur—son of a bitch for good. Even so, I never even had time to get out of bed.

The room's small window had not been washed since its installation about 20 years earlier, but the full moon still managed to penetrate the dirt enough to reflect on the blade of the mean-looking hunting knife Ernie was brandishing as he came for me. Still somewhat dopey, I summoned enough presence of mind to meet his advance. Too late to set my feet on the floor, I planted them with all the force I could muster in just the right place in his fat gut. He landed against the wall gasping for breath, giving me enough time to make my escape down the stairs to summon help.

To my relief the proprietor, himself aroused by the commotion, met me at the bottom of the stairs. He went back to his quarters for a shotgun, which fortunately was not needed. We found Ernie still on the floor where he had hit the wall, either asleep or unconscious. I never bothered to find out. The owner, obviously not a novice in dealing with situations like this, simply grabbed my friend by one arm, pulled him to the top of the stairs, and, with a swift kick, sent his limp body tumbling to the bottom. It took both of us to install him in a secure area that also served as the laundry in the basement.

The image of him I took away with me was of a not very healthy specimen. I spent the rest of the night terrified that this time I might have succeeded in killing a man. I could only hope that his involuntary descent of the stairs would prove to be the cause for his demise. However, Ernie did survive the ordeal to drink another day, but I'd had enough. I didn't even bother to stay for breakfast. I deposited Ernie's money with the hotel and headed for the dock to catch the first seaplane back to civilization.

So here it was September, just a little over a month since I'd left Bill Lekei, and I was back on the streets of Vancouver, trying to make sense of it all. It was lucky Hanna and I had decided not to do anything rash and arrange for her and Ursula to travel over before I had a more permanent job. My first priority now was to wait out the strike and find some kind of menial work that would sustain me without my having to draw on the money I had managed to save.

I had no luck marketing the bakery skills I had so painfully acquired, so I was forced to branch out into yet another career. In the Clancy Skye

Diner on Granville Street, just down from the Birks store, I spotted a sign: "Help wanted. Part time Short-Order Cook." I had no idea what a short-order cook was, nor was I any keener then than I am now to spend a lot of time in the kitchen. But, necessity being the mother of invention, I applied for the position. Unable to offer any credentials or point to any experience in the field but declaring myself eager to learn, I was offered a dishwashing job instead, running from eight in the evening until midnight, four days a week including weekends. The pay, which included one meal per day, was enough of an inducement for me to sign on.

Franz Farber, an Austrian immigrant, also worked there. He had graduated to a full-time position that included other duties such as clearing tables in the dining area, allowing him not only to pick up the odd piece of change the waitress might have overlooked, but also to pick up some gossip from the patrons munching their meals. Through him I learned of Joe Banana, who was in town for treatment of an injury to his eyes resulting from an accident at a gold mine where he was earning big money. The last bit was the key part.

Joe Banana—no one ever knew his real name—was Prussian by extraction and therefore, as far as an Austrian like Franz was concerned, had to be regarded with a high degree of skepticism. Nevertheless, my sensory faculties immediately shifted into the highest state of alert. Being entitled to a break around this time, I was sitting across the table from Joe faster than he could crumble crackers into his soup. Now, anyone who met Joe could expect to hear his life story, with particular emphasis on his war experiences, apparently so legendary that you wondered why Germany had come out on the losing end. As a result, it took me some time to get Joe to focus on the subject in which I was interested—the address of the hiring office.

Armed with this and Joe's assurance that the mere mention of his name would guarantee us a job, Franz and I were positioned in front of the office an hour before it opened the following morning. Neither of us was surprised to learn that no one there had ever heard of Joe Banana. The reception was nevertheless friendly and encouraging. We were invited to come back after the month-end, which was a week away, to file an application, and our next visit promptly resulted in the repositioning of the "Help Wanted" sign at the Clancy Skye Diner. Without the foggiest idea of what it entailed, we had a job with Pioneer Gold Mines as hardrock miners—as soon as we could get there.

Reaching Pioneer, high above the Bridge River valley in the interior of the province, turned out to be almost as big an adventure as the new job. Franz, who became a great friend, had vastly different priorities than I. He saw the mining job as a chance to realize his dream of owning his own car. He bought one, a grey, pre-war model Studebaker that had seen better days, paying less than $200 for it at a used car lot on Broadway. This was to be our transport to Pioneer. Franz hadn't bothered to worry about a driver's licence, so the deal we struck committed him to supplying the car and me to teaching him how to drive and get acquainted with the subject of his dreams. We were on our way.

We started out on a beautiful Indian summer day, perhaps the best time of the year to travel through the Fraser Valley, with the last crop of hay drying in the fields, the hillsides draped with all the colours of the rainbow—all in all, a feast for the senses. As we got closer to the mountains, the radio in the Studebaker began to fade, so we gave expression to our soaring spirits by exercising our vocal cords with all the folk songs we could remember glorifying God's wondrous world and the blessings He had bestowed upon His creation. Beside us ran the Fraser River, which had carved its way to the Pacific, giving shape to the land, sustenance to the Native people, whose recorded history in the area dates back 6,000 years, and access to the early fur traders and settlers. It was to be the first of many trips I would make through this area, every one of them an awe-inspiring experience, every one of them a new adventure.

In Lytton the highway shifted to track the Thompson River, but we kept following the Fraser to Lillooet along an unimproved, treacherous road carved into the side of the mountains. Franz was at the wheel while I, aided by the hot afternoon sun and the effects of a bottle of beer, was resting my eyes for a spell. Suddenly Franz alerted me to the fact that the car seemed to be losing power and was not responding to his efforts to keep it to the centre of the road. I suggested he stop to explore the cause of the problem. By the time Franz's blood began circulating again through the knuckles of his hands, we were parked perilously close to the edge of a 300-foot cliff with little in the way to impede a crash into the Fraser below. Moreover, we had a serious problem. The right front wheel pointed straight toward the cliff, whereas the opposite one indicated a more sensible direction toward the ditch on the other side. The left end of the tie-rod, designed to keep the two wheels working in harmony, had come apart. We were in the middle of nowhere without any tools or even the most basic understanding of the anatomy of an automobile.

It was at times like these that the ingenuity and self-reliance I had acquired during the war years came in handy. Franz, a year or so my senior, had his own experiences that allowed him to remain unfazed as well. Much to our credit, we managed, with the help of a piece of wire we dismantled from a nearby cattle fence, to bind the two ends of the tie-rod back together to resume the journey. Franz stayed behind the wheel with instructions to keep the monster in first gear. I chose to lie flat on the running board outside to keep an eye on the repair, with perhaps a bit of a selfish motive to be in better position to abandon ship in case of any other emergencies. In this fashion we manoeuvred the last 15 miles to Lillooet, arriving as the mountains began to cast their long shadows to signal the end of another eventful day.

That night we slept in the car, parked on a service station lot. The proprietor was a very resourceful person, which, as I was to find out some years later, one has to be to survive in Canada's outback. He had us back on the road with a used part salvaged from some wreck in his yard before noon the next day.

In 1952 there was no road into the Bridge River valley, so the car had to be loaded on the railway and carried along Seton Lake to Shalath, where another primitive road would take us along Carpenter Lake to Gold Bridge. From there it was a few more kilometres straight up the mountain to our final destination. There would be a three-hour wait for the train, ample time to explore the town, meet some of the locals, and, for me, make an important contact.

Father Schweitzer was an Oblate priest, no relation to the African missionary but equally as dedicated. No doubt inspired, as I was, by the literary genius of Karl May, he had left his native Germany convinced that he would spend his life among the most perfect of the human species, noble primitives whose sole desire was to be baptized in the Catholic faith as the only way to convert their earthly paradise to salvation in heaven. Apart from the quaint little church, there was little indication that the message was taking root.

This was my first encounter with Native people, and I gained the impression that Karl May might have lied to me as well. He described the North American Native as a proud, superior race of people, endowed with the finest of human traits, dignified, self-assured, and yet respectful of the natural world in which they had been placed by the creator. This certainly seemed to be at odds with my first impression of Father Schweitzer's parishioners milling around the entrance of the Lillooet beer parlour. At least May could be forgiven in that he had never set foot on the North American continent and had never actually met an Aboriginal person. In fact, most of his books were written in jail, where his contemporaries kept him to protect their society from being carried away by his lively imagination. But this is something I learned later. For the moment, despite the gap between my expectations and reality, I kept an open mind on the subject, not letting this first encounter dampen my keen interest in getting to know the original inhabitants of my new country.

There was a much more immediate subject I wanted to discuss with the Father, who had introduced himself as the church's only representative in the entire region. Once again all my thoughts were consumed with the prospect of meeting my daughter and being reunited with Hanna. I didn't expect Pioneer and my job at the gold mine to fit the bill for what we had envisaged our home to be, but it could be the start we would need to earn enough money and become better acquainted with the customs and the people in our new homeland. Her image was in my mind's eye, and the memory of her sweet embrace shut out most other considerations. Father Schweitzer would obviously be playing a major part in bringing us together.

As part of Hanna's application to emigrate, she needed a sponsor and a commitment from me to marry her within 30 days of her arrival. Father Schweitzer was delighted by the prospect and promised to visit me during his occasional trips to Pioneer and the nearby town of Bralorne, where he had established a little house for God to reside and to meet his faithful.

After a short trip by rail, Franz and I drove the final stretch of what was identified on the map as a road, but would better have been described as a primitive trail. With a cloud of dust trailing behind us for miles, we pulled into Pioneer late in the evening. For the Studebaker, the town would be its final destination. Franz still drove it for some time and spent much of his hard-earned money on it, but in the end he had to leave it behind in some Pioneer backyard to be reclaimed by nature.

CHAPTER 15

Digging for Gold

Courage is doing what you're afraid to do. There can be no courage unless you're scared.

—Eddie Rickenbacker, American First World War flying ace

Pioneer is nestled in a small valley surrounded by towering mountains of the Chilcotin range. I assumed that since Pioneer had its own post office, it was qualified to be called a town. But in 1952, counting men, women, children, and dogs, the population might have reached 400. The "downtown" consisted of the company store, the administration and survey office, and a cookhouse, complete with a dining area for the occupants of the single-quarters bunkhouses.

Five kilometres to the south was Bralorne, the larger of the two mining towns, which boasted two beer parlours catering to the thirsty: the Legion and the Stope. This constituted the sum total of the amenities dedicated to culture and recreation. As for medical services, there was a hospital operated by Bralorne Mines with a single doctor, Dr. Lippset, who was the only physician within 320 kilometres.

The valley's inhabitants broke down into mine employees, their families, the beer parlour staff, and two non-mine officials: an RCMP constable and the legendary Charlie Cunningham, who served as magistrate, justice of the peace, insurance broker, government agent, and legal counsellor. Immigrants made up a large part of the workforce. The company seemed to be partial to hiring mostly German and Austrian immigrants, with some Greeks and Italians thrown in, right off the boat. Most showed up at the mine with only the most rudimentary language skills.

In my five years at the mine I was to make a lot of good friends among my compatriots, including the Hintereggers, who came from Austria, and

The Pioneer mine in 1952. Now the site is a ghost town.

later Fred and Christel Sachs, and the Winterfeld and Seebacher families. I also owe a good deal to kindly co-workers like Nick Labuschka, who first trained me, and Pat Miller and Sid Simonds, two of my bosses. But on my arrival that October day it was all strange to me, and my initiation to the world of hardrock mining was no less traumatic, no less terrifying, than my first days in the woods.

Franz and I were put up in the single men's bunkhouses, which were well appointed relative to my previous camp experience. There was a room attached to the cookhouse that was equipped with pool tables, dart boards, and a single movie projector used once a week to show the latest five-year-old Hollywood creation. Franz's first assignment was a supply job on the surface. Mine was to assist the pipefitter, whose responsibility it was to keep the underground supplied with the water and air needed to sustain life—at 800 metres straight down toward the centre of the earth.

My new partner was Nick Labuschka. He was a kindly old gentleman who had spent all his working life in the mines and had been on his present job as long as anyone could remember. He tried his best to help me become acclimatized to the conditions in which I would spend a good part of my life over the next few years, but my first descent, down a vertical shaft in a 2- by 2-metre steel cage hanging from a single cable, was a frightening experience. Most of the stations, at 30 metres apart, were illuminated by only a single light bulb. Anything beyond the station was draped in absolute darkness. It took me days to learn to trust the beam of the lamp fastened to my hard hat as the only means of orientation.

The drift, or tunnel, leading hundreds of metres to the vein was perhaps no more than 2.5 metres wide and about the same height. The vein, a body of white quartz-like rock from which the gold was extracted, ran diagonally, following the contour of the mountain to the bottom of the shaft. It ranged in thickness from not much more than a metre to, in some cases, 2.5 and 3 metres.

Once down at the lower levels, my system immediately rebelled against the sudden change in altitude. Right from the first day on the job, I acquired an excruciatingly painful headache that would be my constant companion while at work underground—and sometimes after work. Having contributed little if anything to Nick's work, I emerged from that first shift in a state of deep depression, doubting I could bring myself to repeat the ordeal the following day.

Franz tried to console me with the prospect of joining him, but his pay was much less than mine and I was here to get rich. Not even the friendly atmosphere at the cookhouse and the well-presented meals helped raise my spirits. I was angry with myself and totally dejected, too sick and tired to eat. Nick, no doubt sensitive to how I felt, came to visit me after supper with a case of beer under his arm. He assured me that what I felt was normal and that most people at first suffer from claustrophobia, something they get over in just a few days.

"Why, in no time," he said, "you'll ask to be assigned to a drilling crew, where the big money is."

That would be the fabulous paycheque Joe Banana had told us about. Most of the underground jobs were based on a daily rate plus generous production bonuses. The base rate was $8.35 per day, just over a dollar per hour. On some jobs the bonuses amounted to several times that amount.

Good old Nick is one of my heroes. Had it not been for him and the prospect of having to write Hanna that our reunion had to be postponed even longer, I might not have found the courage to show up for work the following day.

Another legend was Pat Miller. He was the man in charge of traffic up and down the two shafts. He was also the chief steward for the Mine,

Mill, and Smelter Workers Union. If he wasn't seen, he was heard, his deep, gravelly, booming voice echoing through the tunnels promoting "solidarity forever" and singing the praises of Joe Hill, the legendary martyr who fell victim to the greed of the capitalists in the mining business. I can still hear him:

> I dreamed I saw Joe Hill last night,
> Alive as you and me.
> Says I, "But Joe, you're 10 years dead."
> "I never died," said he,
> "I never died," said he.

> "The Copper Bosses killed you, Joe,
> They shot you Joe," says I.
> "Takes more than guns to kill a man,"
> Says Joe, "I didn't die"
> Says Joe, "I didn't die"

> From San Diego up to Maine,
> In every mine and mill,
> Where working-men defend their rights,
> It's there you find Joe Hill,
> It's there you find Joe Hill!

> I dreamed I saw Joe Hill last night,
> Alive as you and me.
> Says I, "But Joe, you're 10 years dead."
> "I never died," said he,
> "I never died," said he.

It was Pat Miller who inherited me as a helper after graduation from Nick's orientation school. I became one of his cage tenders. Pat was a nice enough guy to work with, even though he found it hard to disguise his dislike of the flood of "DPs" crowding out, as he put it, honest, hard-working Canadians and assigning them to the soup kitchens in the city.

"Not only did we have to fight and die to rid the world of these mother-fucking Huns," he would say, "but we are now expected to starve to make room for the cocksuckers in our own country."

Frank in full mining gear at Pioneer.

For some reason, maybe because by now I could speak some passable English, I never felt that Pat resented me personally. He did insist, of course, that I attend all the union meetings and participate in all their activities. He even had me appointed to a bargaining committee to make it appear that the "Krauts"—whom, when challenged, he would admit he hated less than the capitalists in management— were in support of the union and its demands.

There was also the mine superintendent, Jack Genest. I suppose in every situation where men are challenged and pressed to the limits of their endurance there has to be someone like him. A man who, like Panicky Bell in the logging camp or some commander in the life-and-death situations of war, must be cruel and obnoxious enough to keep the crew in line. At Pioneer it was Jack Genest or, as he was known, "Rough on Rats Jack."

It was said of him that he would choose in favour of getting an extra tonne of muck to the surface over wasting time rescuing his own grandmother from a cave-in. I witnessed one occasion when he took a telephone call informing him that a man had fried himself by touching the exposed high-tension line powering the trains at the 2,500-foot level with a scaling bar. After eliciting only a cursory explanation about the mishap, he instructed the person on the other end of the line to make sure to bring up his lamp.

In his defence, it can be said that the batteries powering the lamps were a critical part of a miner's equipment and very expensive to supply and maintain.

Fatal accidents were not at all uncommon in the conditions to which we were exposed for eight hours a day. It was stifling hot and damp. The foul-smelling air was supplied by compressor and pumped to the dead ends of the various workings, where it absorbed the smoke and residue from the previous shift's rock blasting before drifting toward the only escape up the shafts. It wasn't until several years after my arrival that government standards required the management at Pioneer to install a ventilation shaft that supplied fresh air to the main drifts. In 1952, even the rights Joe Hill might have been fighting for were as basic as the right to breathe.

There were some brief moments, I must admit, when even I managed to find some enthusiasm for keeping an eye out for Joe Hill and Pat Miller's union interests. Almost every other month there was some accident, more often than not fatal, resulting from cave-ins or mishaps involving a piece of machinery. Mind you, the men themselves were not blameless. Motivated by the promise of rich rewards and production bonuses, they threw all caution to the wind to capture another foot of space at the end of the drift or add another tonne of quartz to the bins.

In the end, Nick was proved right. Gradually I managed to shed my phobia, fear, and anxiety and learn to live with the conditions, and within months I was invited to take on a new challenge as the operator of a train that supplied the crews with equipment and transported the harvest to the mill. The work was rewarded with a share of production bonuses, and there was ample opportunity to work extra hours at 1.5 times the regular pay. With my bank account showing some modest but steady gains, things were looking up.

I also became a key part of the town's unusual social scene. Cage tenders in mines are like taxi drivers in the city. They are privy to all the gossip imparted by everyone entering and leaving the mine, from the lowliest mucker to the superintendent. Of course, information comes in very small bits and has to be properly massaged, summarized, cross-checked, and compiled into stories to be planted with "reliable sources," who then share them with a wider audience. Pat Miller was the resident expert in that field.

The town was equipped with three separate telephone services. The first covered the mine itself, linking the underground to the administration offices through the hoist room. Another was a party line linking residences to the store and the company offices. This network could be connected to the provincial telephone network through an operator at the office. The mine network could also be connected to the party line, but only at the discretion of the hoist man, who had to assess the urgency of the message. Only the underground network was set up to accommodate the specially enhanced version of the English language.

People who like to gossip often make strange bedfellows. One of the shift bosses maintained a regular network of contributors in strategic positions, such as the hoist room and the administration office, that provided full-time monitoring of the various telephone systems. Between Pat, the cage tender, and Bud Drury, one of the shift bosses, not even the tiniest morsel of juicy information was lost.

Since the women had their own ways of working the party line, the town's network was restricted to feminine versions of English only. Here the immigrant newcomers had an advantage in that, by conversing in their own language, they could be assured at least some privacy. To overcome this impediment to the proper dissemination of useful town gossip, it was decreed that all underground communication had to be conducted in English, as did all conversations that were channelled from underground to the party line. Since many women had not yet acquired the necessary language skills, urgent messages had to be conveyed through reliable third parties. I frequently found myself pressed into service.

The company store was another important source of vital information. Bud's wife was a clerk there and was just as keen as her husband to volunteer her time and talents to keeping a steady flow of reliable information in the pipeline. For instance, any woman neglecting to buy her regular monthly supply of sanitary napkins was immediately identified as being pregnant. It was not unusual for the happy father to learn of his good fortune from Pat Miller while descending the mine shaft at 10 metres a second—and long before the expectant mother found the right occasion to share the good news with him herself.

Besides gossip, the town's other main occupation was drinking. Unlike logging camps, where it was easy to enforce total prohibition, the mine had only one rule that was rigorously enforced: drinking on the job was forbidden and anyone detected going to work with alcohol on his breath was sent back to the bunkhouse. This did not mean that minors were less demonized by alcohol than loggers were; it just meant that they had learned to manage their addiction differently.

The conditions of employment, for example, allowed for periodic "binge holidays" for those men who found the three days' time off at shift changes was not sufficient to quench all their thirst and cleanse their bodies of all the dust that had accumulated during working hours. For most of the single men in town, a normal day consisted of eight hours at work, eight hours in the beer parlour, and eight hours of sleep, in that order. Any hours spared by those requiring less sleep were added to the drinking time.

Nick Labuschka was among those who regularly deposited all their paycheques not in the local bank, but in one of Bralorne's beer parlours. The proprietor was Tony Branca, a brother of Angelo Branca, at the time B.C.'s most prominent criminal lawyer. Tony was Nick's banker. Whenever Nick needed a few dollars to buy tobacco and other incidentals, Tony would advance him a modest amount.

Then one day Nick failed to show up for work. A search of his room provided few clues to his whereabouts. He had simply gathered whatever few belongings he had acquired over the years—Bud Drury figured there would have been about 53 items: a deck of playing cards and a grip-board—and faded into thin air. At the time, his account at Branca's was overdrawn by about $200. Tony was philosophical. After cashing every one of Nick's paycheques for at least the last 15 years, he was not about to lose a lot of sleep over the loss. I never found out what happened to my friend. Nick was gone for good. I would like to believe that he had the good sense to opt for a new start somewhere in a different environment, but it is doubtful that he could ever have made the transition to a normal life.

Booze accounted for the only things the area had in common with the big city: a "rush hour" and a high number of accidents. The most critical times were just before 10 a.m., when the beer parlours opened, and at 5 p.m., shortly after the day shift got off work. Most of the accidents, however, happened after closing time, as the patrons attempted to negotiate the hazardous curves and avoid the huge boulders on the road between the two towns.

Surprisingly, few accidents ever caused serious injury. The reason was that car passengers were usually packed in like sardines on their way to and from the watering holes.

I recall one occasion in the middle of winter when I was crowded into a car with seven others on our way to one of the Bralorne drinking establishments. On this particular day the boys had decided to patronize the Legion instead of the Stope, on account of the former being closest. The building, rather like a primitive Quonset hut, was situated just above the main road, with a driveway parallel to it. As it happened, the operator of the snowplough had misjudged the width of the driveway, extending it out over the abyss. Taking a run at the hill leading up to the driveway, we ended up with too much momentum, infringing on the vacant space the snowplough had left. Just as the car came to a halt, both left wheels disappeared over the edge. Gently we rolled sideways down the embankment, but miraculously, after three or four revolutions—who keeps count of such trivia?—the car came to rest back on its wheels, right in the middle of the main road.

"Ah, fuck it," the driver said once everyone's legs, arms, and bodies were sorted out and back in an upright position. "We should have gone down to the Stope in the first place." Frankly, I was relieved because it seldom failed that someone in the Legion's establishment, knowing my background, insisted on refighting the Second World War, and if there's one thing I hate, it's a sore winner.

It didn't take me any time at all to be accepted into the social life of my compatriots from different parts of Germany and Austria. Most of them had either immigrated with their families or were well enough established to have their wives join them. Like me, none had been trained in mining, nor were any of us accustomed to the harsh life of a remote mining camp, isolated from family and from cultural and social amenities. But we were all young and willing to make whatever sacrifices were necessary in the short term to be accepted eventually and to share in the benefits and the promises of the land we had chosen as our new home.

To cope with the ever-present dangers at the workplace, amplified by our inexperience and lack of language skills, the men developed a dependency on one another that shaped strong bonds of friendship. The women, too, turned to each other for help with children, setting up their homes and making the best of things with the limited resources available to them. Members of our close-knit group enjoyed a level of comfort and security that at least in part replaced universal health care and those other social benefits to which Europeans had become accustomed over half a century before the Great War. The Canada Pension Plan and the Health Act were still years away from being enshrined as features of our own social benefits structure. Life would certainly have been much less bearable without our circle of friends like Lotte and Frank Hinteregger, Rudi and

Poldi Reibenschuh, Trudel and Willie Winterfeld, with whom we shared a lifelong friendship.

In fact, after only a short time of bunkhouse living and camp food, I was invited to live with Frank and Lotte until I could establish a home for my own family. Frank was trained in optical engineering, and both of them were ardent students of history, knowledgeable in many diverse areas of interest. They no doubt inspired some of my own curiosity. Their two children, Peter and Margaret, were a delight to be with. It actually felt good to be part of a family again, part of a regular routine. I will be eternally grateful to them for their unreserved friendship, kindness, and support at this critical juncture of my life.

Frank was not one of those Austrians who profess to be among the first oppressed by Hitler's regime. He was old enough at the time to understand people's early enthusiasm for Hitler's politics. His parents were among those who found hope and inspiration in the promises the Nazis were making. Germans speak of Austrians as being among the best diplomats in the world if for no other reason than their success in convincing the world that Beethoven was Austrian and Hitler German. Frank helped everyone who wanted to be educated on this subject to dispel this myth. He spoke fondly of his experiences as a Hitler Youth, where he developed the love for flying that he shared with me on many occasions.

Naturally, his world collapsed together with the Nazi regime when the truth of its atrocities was revealed. Perhaps, like me, he found it too difficult to reinvest his loyalty and trust in the country that had so deceived him in his youth. He even rejected the church, declaring himself an atheist and choosing to find other moorings to rebuild his life in another part of the world. Tragically, it took the accidental death of their grandson, many years later, to help Lotte and Frank restore their faith.

In spite of the warmth and generosity of such people, Pioneer was not the home of my dreams. The miners themselves appeared to show no interest in anything but getting to their assigned work site and concentrating on staying alive while there. They were a miserable lot as they congregated at the station platforms at shift's end to be lifted to the surface, anxious for a breath of fresh air. Their bodies were caked in mud and dirt, their eyes without expression. Like a herd of cattle they crowded into the cage to claim a space to safety and freedom for another 16 hours. The sight of them often reminded me of the scene that had made such a lasting impression on me back home: the moment when I tried to pick out my father from the multitudes of dull, expressionless faces pushing through the factory gate in Karlsruhe.

I had vowed then never to get caught in such a hopeless situation, but as time went on I realized that the Pioneer mine was as good a place as any in my new homeland to get established and be reunited with my family. That thought, coupled with its sweet memories, became an obsession, and it often helped me find the extra strength and courage to soldier on, to reach beyond the limits of my endurance. I yearned for the sweetness of the love Hanna and I had experienced together, for her companionship to share my pain, my experiences. With her by my side, no obstacle would be great enough to keep us from realizing our dreams, and everything would turn out all right.

The next step toward our dream was a final piece of documentation in support of her application to immigrate. I needed a notarized affidavit committing myself to getting married within 30 days of her arrival. I visited the lone RCMP constable, who directed me to Charlie Cunningham.

Charlie acted as judge, jury, and executioner in Pioneer and Bralorne. For example, since he was the only agent in the valley selling automobile insurance, Charlie was the man to see. In the case of accidents, he instructed his clients not to report to the constable until he had made the initial assessment and until all traces of the most probable cause, alcohol, had been expunged by a good night's sleep.

Despite the weighty responsibilities Charlie carried on his shoulders, he did not have an office. That is to say, he did not have a conventional office. His office was his car, a big Ford Town and Country station wagon that had once had decorative wooden mouldings adorning its sides. If you needed Charlie, you would flag down his car, or you could approach him in the coffee shop that was part of the Bralorne mine cookhouse. It was from here, when stationary, that he administered his domain.

It was no light matter to call on the great Charlie Cunningham. Anxious to get Hanna's application dealt with, I stayed awake after a graveyard shift to get an early start. Dressed up in my dark blue pinstriped suit and polished shoes, I found the car in front of the coffee shop and went in. I asked for Charlie at the counter, but he was busy with another client at a table in the corner, so I decided to stay at a discreet distance until I could get his attention.

The cafe was crowded, and when I said Charlie's name, the whole place went into a mode of suspended animation. All 40 sets of eyes were riveted on me. One of the waitresses, her hair wound up in dozens of curlers, leaned on the counter, a piece of toast hanging from the side of her mouth, which she seemed unable to close. As I realized much later, it was doubtful that anyone in the room had ever met a person done up in a suit, white shirt, tie, and polished shoes, certainly not in the Bralorne coffee shop. Not even my maiden speech in Parliament caused me more stage fright. I suppose I could have simply ordered a cup of coffee, but I had just finished my breakfast and wasn't inclined to such frivolous wasting of a dime. So I leaned against a wall near the window, trying to look nonchalant, as if unaware of the snickering in the room.

I was greatly relieved when Charlie approached me to inquire about my needs. He was a large, imposing man dressed in blue jeans and a jacket that at one time might have been red. His speech was impaired by a cleft palate. Not being able to understand a word he was saying to me, I simply pulled the required form from my inner pocket and showed it to him.

"No problem, just step into my office," he said, making his way toward the car parked outside. The actual transaction, simple as it was, was conducted on the hood because, despite the humongous size of the contraption, there was not enough room inside to accommodate both of us. Charlie extracted his official seal from a filing cabinet on the front passenger seat. With his sleeve he wiped a quarter inch of dust from the hood, converting it to his office desk. He then asked me to raise my right hand and repeat the text prescribed in the document.

"I swear that I…" I dutifully repeated what I thought he said, all the while keeping half an eye focussed on the windows of the coffee shop, every inch of which was covered with the faces of curious onlookers.

The price of the transaction was one dollar, which included his signature and, above it, his imposing-looking seal.

I learned later that I was not the only one confounded by Charlie's manner of speaking. His business required the frequent use of the coin phone at the coffee shop, which was connected to the province-wide network. The quality of service left much to be desired at the best of times. On one occasion Charlie was having a particularly hard time making the operator understand the number to which he wished to be connected. The fact that he felt the need to raise the level of his voice to match the distance he was attempting to bridge did not help the situation. The operator at the switchboard kept asking him to repeat the numbers. Finally she must have suggested he try to "round out" the numbers for her, to which Charlie, to the delight of all the patrons of the Bralorne coffee shop, replied in a booming voice: "Assholes, assholes! Is that round enough for you?!"

The hard-won affidavit did the trick. Early in 1953 Hanna reported that her application to emigrate had been approved, and with the baby almost a year old, she was ready to make travel plans. While she did that, I looked around for a home for us.

For reasons of stability, the mining company naturally preferred to employ married people. There was an ample inventory of modest but comfortable homes from which to choose. I selected a three-room apartment in a converted bunkhouse. It was perhaps a kilometre up the valley at an idyllic location, adjacent to a creek that was fed by the Coast Mountain glaciers. Every one of my new friends chipped in with the painting and decorating and with selecting some furniture from the town's lively second-hand market. I began counting down the days and hours.

Finally Hanna and I managed to book a berth for her from Bremerhaven to Halifax for early March. She would then take the cross-Canada train and I would be waiting for her in Lytton. Bob Coleman, an English friend working in the survey office, was the only one of my close friends with a car at the time. He generously offered to take the day off work to make the trip to Lytton with me.

Rösel, my mother, was kind enough to accompany Hanna and the baby on the first part of the journey by train from Karlsruhe to Bremerhaven, Germany's second-biggest seaport next to Hamburg. Hanna's spring voyage across the Atlantic was no less eventful than my own, except that in addition to fighting seasickness herself, she had the extra burden of caring for the baby. I know just how relieved she must have been to set foot in the New World through Pier 21 in Halifax, but for her the ordeal was far from over. It is never easy for a European to comprehend the vast distances that separate the various parts of our great country. The conductor on her train indicated Saturday as the day she would arrive in Lytton. Since the train left Halifax on a Saturday—by coincidence on Ursula's birthday, March 15— she had a whole week to become acquainted with the geographic reality of her new homeland.

My knees were literally shaking as the train pulled into the station. I still could not believe that it was actually happening. Only a few people got off, and none of them looked like Hanna. She had warned me that she had changed, so I gave everyone a good second look, but there was no sign of her.

Finally, after most people had already left the station platform, I saw the porter trying to extricate someone with a baby clinging to her from one of the cars. She just stood there, her eyes surveying the surroundings, anxiously looking for a familiar face. For days I had practised some thoughtful phrases befitting the occasion: something to say to make her feel welcome, something by which the moment could be recalled. In the end, the flood of emotions we both felt rendered words meaningless, even if we had been able to utter them.

As it turned out, it was Ursula who dominated the scene. Throughout the journey she had reacted with a blood-curdling scream every time a stranger—sometimes trying to afford her mother a moment of respite— came close to her. Hanna was worried how I might react to being rejected by her as well. But Ursula saved the moment with her wide open black eyes that seemed to recognize me as someone familiar, someone to whom she could tentatively submit for a gentle touch and embrace.

No matter how majestic the church, how solemn the ceremony, or how many people in attendance to sanction the union, nothing could ever come close to that simple moment when our tormented souls finally met, where without words we pledged to one another never to be separated again.

The return trip was uneventful except that Bob, worried perhaps about how this refined young lady would take to the rather primitive home I had selected for her, pointed at all the most dilapidated shacks we passed as being similar to what she should expect when she arrived at the end of the world. I am sure that, at the time, Hanna could not have cared less. As primitive as our place was, it was equipped with a central heating system, hot and cold running water, and indoor plumbing, things the average house in Forchheim could not yet boast of.

The reception at Pioneer was overwhelming. Everyone in the building was excited by the prospect of having a child to spoil. Christel Sachs had prepared a pot of my favourite pea soup, which had to be washed down with several welcome drinks. None of us was sensitive enough to understand that while everyone was perfectly acquainted with Hanna—after all, they had heard me talking about nothing else for months—she felt most intimidated being among all these strangers with whom she would have to compete for my affection. It was hours before we finally closed the apartment door behind us to begin the process of getting to know each other again. We needed to adjust to the maturity we both had gained from our experiences since we parted at the train station in Karlsruhe just 18 month earlier, but now a lifetime away in the past.

The harrowing events both of us had lived through during that time had spawned in us an instinct for caution, a change of character that would not easily yield to any shared relationship. Both of us had just turned 21, and while still attached to our dreams, we were much more mature now and acutely conscious of the reality of our situation. It took us several days to bridge whatever it was that had come between us and to overcome any caution not to offend as we sought intimacy. Both of us realized that Pioneer was not the end of the road, and our little abode was cozy and comfortable. But Hanna, finding me now almost a stranger, no doubt felt trapped in a situation from which there could be no escape. Mercifully, with some special care and consideration, the help of my friends, and Ursula's unwitting reminders of our parental duties, we soon managed to span the rift our separation had caused. We rediscovered our love for each other, and it was strong enough to sustain a partnership to which we could surrender our personal independence.

We still had our marriage ceremony to go through. Conscious of the 30-day time limit, I wasted no time sending word to Father Schweitzer in Lillooet of our intention to get married at the earliest possible moment. Dutifully, the good Father came to visit us a week or so later to discuss the arrangements. However, upon learning that we already had a daughter without claiming the benefit of Immaculate Conception, he became suspicious that Hanna might have had a previous nuptial arrangement. Nothing could persuade him to grace us with the Holy Sacrament without a letter from the priest in Forchheim testifying to the purity of our status. Furthermore, understanding though he was of the necessity of us living together in our apartment, he needed to be assured that the arrangement was on a brother-and-sister basis. In fact, during several subsequent visits he raised the issue, sympathetically inquiring whether we still had the strength to fight temptation.

A letter to Germany at that time took up to two weeks to be delivered, and even if Father Danner, who had succeeded Father Dorer in Forchheim by that time, replied immediately, the one-month deadline would be breached. In desperation, we decided to visit the local police constable to confess the dilemma and perhaps seek an extension.

The office of the RCMP was a one-room shack leased from the Bralorne mine. The constable's desk was behind a single-pane window that had a view of the main street and was obscured with a heavy layer of the same kind of dust that covered Charlie Cunningham's car. Hanna, using the excuse that she would not understand what was said anyway, chose to wait for me outside. The real reason was the paranoia she had acquired during the war of any authority in uniform; it was a fear she would be unable to shed for the rest of her life. However, it was just as well. There was barely enough room to accommodate even a single visitor in the humble office.

The constable could think of no way to facilitate a legal extension of the contract, but offered a much simpler solution to the problem: a civil ceremony that he himself, given the nature of his posting, could conduct. When I inquired about a suitable date he said that, if we were willing, now would be as good a time as any. Knowing it would save us the inconvenience of another trip to Bralorne, I decided to seize the opportunity. I pounded on the window to disturb enough of the dust to get the lucky bride's attention and waved to her to come in. Sure enough, as the constable had said, it was really quite a simple procedure. To ease matters along, the constable, noting that Hanna was identified as Johanna in her passport, helpfully suggested that Joan, rather than Hanna, would be a more customary Canadian abbreviation of the name. She being willing, he could think of no reason why the marriage certificate couldn't serve the dual purpose of effecting the change. Hanna, possibly because she'd never been that fond of her name, and even more because of her reluctance to question the constable's wisdom, readily agreed.

In just a few minutes the necessary forms were ready.

We signed, and our signatures were followed by a handshake and the constable's wishes for a happy life. Hanna, now Joan, had not the slightest idea of what had transpired during the brief encounter. I am certain that I never saw anyone more surprised than when, holding both her hands and looking into her eyes right there in the middle of the dusty street in downtown Bralorne, I said to her, "Let me be the second to congratulate you, Frau Oberle. We are now married, and you now have both a new first and second name."

Later, of course, there was a church wedding to make things right in the eyes of God, but it was a rather primitive affair. Father Schweitzer did eventually satisfy himself that the rules of the church were broad enough to sanction our union. So on May 31, 1953, on a beautiful sunny Sunday morning, we made our way to the little church in Bralorne, early enough to allow the Father to hear our confession before the mass.

As would have been the custom back home, we expected to have to testify to the number of occasions—with perhaps some details—on which we had committed our sexual misdeeds. We agreed on a plausible story to satisfy the priest's curiosity. Mercifully, much unlike Father Dorer, we found Father Schweitzer to be perfectly satisfied with a statement of generalities without description of any specifics. What a relief! For us, it was one thing for a practising Catholic to ask forgiveness for sins for which he does not feel remorse, but quite another to bend the truth in the confessional. (Without doubt, either in Father Dorer's book would have warranted a sentence in purgatory of several millennia.)

Another problem was that all the friends we had made in Pioneer by that time were Protestant and therefore not eligible to enter a Catholic church, much less qualify as witnesses to the signing ceremony. But Father Schweitzer assured us that he would find someone among the 20 or so faithful attending the service that morning to fill the void. True to his word, he simply asked the congregation if anyone in attendance would be willing to help out. Two hands belonging to a Martha and Frank Bruekel shot up as if they had waited for just such an occasion to perform their good deed for the day. Another reason might have been that they had heard about us on the party line and were looking for a chance to introduce themselves as fellow Brigandines—the nickname for the good burghers of Karlsruhe. What a small world! And what a pleasant surprise.

The local bishop's annual visit to Schweitzer's far-flung parish coincided with our wedding. How nice it would have been to report to Berta back home that our bond was sealed under the watchful eye of a bishop. But that was not to be. Instead, we took our satisfaction after the ceremony from observing the holy man sitting in his automobile, near total exhaustion, the sweltering heat draining his body of whatever liquid it had stored through pores in his skin that looked like the ends of sewer pipes.

The good Father invited the rest of his congregation to stay for the wedding if they wished, but warned them that, in courtesy to the bride, who could not speak English, he would conduct the ceremony in German. Unfortunately, Father Schweitzer, after a 50-year absence from Germany, during which he would have had only a few occasions to practise his mother tongue, found his skills wanting. His failing eyesight and the dilapidated state of the little book he had dug up specially for the occasion added to his problem. Several times he leaned over to ask for help with the pronunciation of a certain word or phrase, and finally, out of sheer frustration, he simply handed the booklet to me to read. The other novelty was that the bottle from which he dispensed the holy water, which we Catholics use to seal our contracts and fend off evil spirits, still carried its original label: "Eau de Cologne."

If God was watching, he must have been amused. I am sure Joan, who had attended many weddings at St. Martin's Church in Forchheim with never a flaw in the prescribed ritual, harboured some doubt as to the legitimacy of what we were doing. But given Father Dorer's interpretation of God's law, both of us were already burdened with several of the deadly sins of the flesh and were destined to spend eternity in a very hot place anyway. At the moment we just wanted to be left alone to get on with our lives here on earth.

CHAPTER 16

Old Customs, New Roots

A pessimist sees the difficulty in every opportunity; an optimist sees the opportunity in every difficulty.

—Sir Winston Churchill, British prime minister

As it turned out, Father Schweitzer's holy water must have been of a very special blend indeed to keep the two of us, who would tempt fate at every juncture of our lives, united by the bond we sealed that day. Once we had bridged the gap of our separation, we quickly settled into the kind of home life we had longed for. Joan set to work redecorating our humble abode with some of the linens and tableware she had acquired before she left home. Greenery from the forest and, later on, wildflowers, tastefully arranged, adorned the table and shelves we had fastened to the walls. There were two little bedrooms and a combination living room and kitchen. It is said that the way to a man's heart leads through his stomach, and Joan spared no effort to satisfy my hunger for the delights of her culinary artistry.

Life in Pioneer settled into a comfortable routine. Apart from the ever-present danger at the workplace and my constant headaches, it was a happy, carefree existence with ample time to cultivate friendships, explore and enjoy the natural surroundings, and read and further our education. Why not enjoy the time spent in accumulating the savings we would need?

Our plan was to become independent by starting a little business of our own, something that was always part of our dreams. My experience working in the mine helped strengthen our resolve toward that end. Joan and I disciplined ourselves to live within a strict budget of $100 a month. In exchange for looking after the central heating system in the building and changing the odd light bulb, we enjoyed free rent. Whatever other necessities we needed were supplied by the company store, at generously subsidized prices.

However, there were some gaps in the culinary offerings the store could supply that had to be filled. As much as possible, the women managed to improvise. None of us, for example, ever acquired a taste for *gummibrot*, the standard white bread that was the only fare available at the store, so the women baked their own. And any of us travelling to Vancouver would fill the trunks of our cars with better-quality wine, for which the local liquor store had no demand before our arrival. Still, our diets lacked one group of vital ingredients. We were totally deprived of sausage, smoked ham, and all the other delights produced by the German butcher. We were desperate.

For a time I contemplated persuading my old friend Kneisel back in Forchheim to embark on a mission of mercy by emigrating to Canada, where undoubtedly his art would make him a fortune in no time at all. Later I discovered that some of my compatriots were thinking along the same lines and were praying for a similar deliverance from the drought. God's answer was the butcher David Seebacher. Together with his industrious wife, he answered the call and left the comfort of Vienna to fill the void in Pioneer.

The expectations were high. A couple of his fellow Austrians, Rudi and Poldi Reibenschuh, had briefed him well on the situation. He arrived, equipped with all the tools, spices, and other ingredients required for a *Schlachtfest*, to a reception befitting a conquering hero. With my own considerable experience on the subject, the stage was set.

First, we had to recruit the principal actor, who would have to be in the 200- to 250-pound weight range, no more then two years old, and either a spayed female or a gelded male. Four of us volunteered to embark on a mission to Lillooet, where some farming enterprises involving livestock had been observed. Willie Winterfeld, the most senior among us, was chosen as the intellectual leader of the mission. His lack of comprehension of English was balanced against his extensive business experience. After the war he had developed an innovative way to use the German post office to market a birth-control calendar based on the rhythm method. The idea, even though sanctioned by the church, was against all the rules of the postal authorities and could have landed poor Willie in jail had he not chosen to emigrate to Canada instead.

Another of our compatriots, Barney Berger, supplied the transportation, a fair-sized station wagon modified and outfitted with a wooden cage we had nailed together to contain our passenger during the return trip. Rudi was the third volunteer and I was the fourth. Thus began the great pig adventure.

We left in time to catch the Friday evening train from Shalath to Lillooet, allowing ourselves the rest of the weekend to complete the mission without missing any work. The first night we somehow managed to sleep in the station wagon, no mean feat in itself. My trip to the local barber shop the following morning, where I treated myself to a haircut (Joan had not yet acquired the skill to perform that task herself), paid off in that another of the patrons was able to provide directions to a neighbour's farm where he was sure we would find just what we were looking for.

What a stroke of luck! The place, even though some distance from town, was not hard to find, and the farmer, obviously alerted by his neighbour over the phone, met us at the front gate to confirm that his inventory did indeed include a specimen of the type we had described. However, there was a problem: the beast had grunted itself into the hearts of the children, who were treating it as a member of the family. Some time would be required to evacuate them to another location before he could allow us onto the property for the next stage of our mission. He assured us that as far as the price went, we would find him easy to deal with.

The delay afforded us time to work out the strategy we would use to strike an acceptable bargain. Obviously I would have to do the talking, but Willie, dressed in a dark suit and hat, was to be introduced as the expert in the trade who would assess the animal for its suitability and fix the price we would be prepared to offer. Willie, who had grown up in Berlin and had spent his entire life in the city, assured us that the farmer would never know that he was barely able to distinguish a pig from the other species milling around in the barnyard.

It was love at first sight. It appeared to be the kind of pig of which even Kneisel back home would have been proud. It would yield enormous-sized hams and vast quantities of *Schmaltz* [lard]. The bargaining turned out to be anticlimactic. Hesitantly, the farmer mentioned a price that turned out to be way below our expectation. Willie nevertheless rolled his eyes and shook his head in reaction to my translation.

"Does Mr. Winterfeld have a price in mind?" the farmer wanted to know. This precipitated a discussion among the rest of the group, which was disinclined to miss out on a good deal. But Willie insisted on reducing the amount mentioned by half, which I was most embarrassed to relay to the farmer as a counteroffer. To my astonishment, it was accepted with startling and, at the time, inexplicable alacrity.

What followed, if captured on film, could have made for a great episode of the Keystone Cops. The beast seemed to sense our intentions and resisted every effort the farmer made to coax it into the back of the station wagon. To force the issue he grabbed it by the ear and told Willie, the "expert," to twist its tail while the rest of us pushed it toward the tailgate. It was to no avail. The beast was just too strong and, once free, would not allow any of us to come close again. The chase must have lasted over an hour and covered the entirety of the estate. At one point Willie lost his hat, and somebody stepped on it, pasting it with chicken manure. Several times we had the beast cornered in a shed, but in desperation it charged directly at us, sending everyone scrambling for cover.

At last the farmer lost his patience. Fearing perhaps the return of his wife and kids, who would undoubtedly complicate matters even further by joining the pig's side of the war, he managed to administer a sort of narcosis by hitting it over the head with what looked like a solid fence post. Barney backed up the car, and after much heaving and prying and grunting we managed to install our new passenger in his designated place before he regained consciousness.

We stopped on the way back to treat some of the injuries and dishevelment we had suffered during our version of the Boar War and arrived at Lillooet just in time to see the afternoon train pull out of the station on its scenic trip along Seton Lake. Not to worry, we thought. Had we not earned a night out on the town after making such a good bargain and risking life and limb to do it?

We weren't much inclined to spend another night in the car, particularly since the additional passenger hogged two of the places that had been available to us the night before, so we decided to procure a room in Lillooet's only hotel and to patronize the local beer parlour to quench our thirst. Willie even suggested that, at 10 cents a glass, we use some of the brew to spike the water the farmer had suggested we keep on hand to lubricate our passenger during the trip toward his destiny. Blissfully content with the day's accomplishments, with only the melodious sounds emanating from the various orifices of our beer-fed bodies piercing the quiet, we drifted off to sleep in our hotel room. But the adventure was not yet over. At about two in the morning we were subjected to a rather rude awakening.

In the hallway there were loud voices, and the banging on our door sounded more like someone attempting to break it down than merely trying to get our attention. The street in front of the hotel had come back to life, with people shouting and the sound of a car horn going at full blast. When I opened the door I was overrun by half a dozen people, led by the local police constable, spilling into the room and demanding to know who owned the fancy "pig-chauffeured" station wagon parked in front of the hotel.

Only half dressed and still half asleep, we went downstairs and encountered a totally chaotic scene, illuminated by the headlights of the police cruiser. It was a sight to behold. Our friend, not accustomed to sleeping in such tight quarters, had decided to modify his situation by breaking apart the cage and appropriating for himself the much more comfortable front seat to sleep on. Unfortunately, this meant that part of his ample posterior had come to rest on the horn.

Unlike ourselves, the locals were in a festive mood, offering comments and opinions. One smartass pointed out to the constable that just because pigs couldn't fly didn't necessarily mean they couldn't drive.

In fairness, they were quite helpful in bringing the situation back under control. Someone produced a sturdy rope, and with the help of much pushing and pulling, the beast was restored to his rightful place. The constable, telling us that we would only get in the way, ordered us to stand aside as skilful hands, aided by tools and materials appearing out of nowhere, reconstructed and reinforced the rickety cage around our passenger.

Unfortunately, by now the monster was wide awake and once again asserting himself with all kinds of menacing gestures. Someone offered the suggestion that having the car in motion would be a calming influence on the beast, and so it was that for the rest of the night, until it was time to load the car onto the train in the morning, we spelled each other off at hourly intervals to keep the mission in motion with only the occasional grunt of contentment coming from the rear.

The rest of the trip was uneventful except that the smell, which remained in the car for the rest of its natural life, became unbearable, requiring us to keep the windows down at all times despite the big clouds of dust that drifted through the car every time we met or passed another vehicle.

Back in Pioneer, people had not been idle. Under Seebacher's direction, the tub was disconnected from our bathroom and positioned in the yard behind the apartment building. Every stove in the vicinity had been appropriated to supply the boiling water needed for the first act following the slaughter. Everyone in the neighbourhood was on hand to celebrate our return and greet us with a rousing welcome. People crowded around the car to meet the newcomer who would spend the remainder of his short life with us.

Seebacher was anxious to hasten his departure. With a fair-sized hammer of the underground rock-breaking variety in hand, he ordered the tailgate lowered and the spectators to step aside. Much to our surprise, the beast now expended as much effort to resist his removal from his cage as he did being put there. A rope was fastened around the monster's neck to pull the head out far enough in the open for David to swing the hammer, but perhaps because of the concern that the beast could change tactics and leap forward for another attack, this technique had to be abandoned.

"Anyone have a gun?" David demanded. Someone produced a 22-calibre rifle, and David unceremoniously pressed the barrel against the pig's forehead and pulled the trigger. As if in one last act of defiance and revenge, the bullet glanced off the thick head and exited the scene through the roof of poor Barney's car. "Never mind," someone suggested later. "You are going to need some additional ventilation anyway."

Finally the desired effect had been achieved, if only long enough to allow the executioner to administer a more permanent *coup de grâce* by slitting the throat to provide an opening for the blood. An important ingredient in some of the sausage, it was allowed to escape into a large container, where it had to be stirred to keep it from gelling.

It was only after our prize pig had been eviscerated and placed into the bathtub to be scrubbed and scraped that David had time to conduct a closer inspection of the remains. Our farmer in Lillooet had definitely had the last laugh. No doubt he would gladly have let us take the beast for nothing, just to get rid of it. And the helpful patrons of the barber shop must still be laughing at the memories of our visit. The teeth, those that had not already fallen out, showed signs of a long life—in excess of 10 years, David figured. Even more disconcerting was the fact that, until recently, the specimen had carried his male appendages between his hind legs, something that should have made him ineligible to perform in the role in which he had been cast.

In summary, David told us bluntly: "I'll cut it up and make you whatever sausage you want, but don't expect me to eat any of it."

Frank, Joan, Ursula, and their friends pose proudly with the pig brought from Lillooet.

After this ill-fated adventure, we found another method of supplying our ham and sausage needs. Willie Winterfeld, ever the entrepreneur, returned from a Vancouver car-buying expedition as agent for the first German butcher to set up shop in the city. In fact the new car, a Nash Rambler with all kinds of cargo space, was loaded to the brim with samples of the culinary delights he would be distributing in Pioneer as a sideline to his mining career. For most of us it meant the restoration of our faith in God, but sadly it also taught us the lesson that business and friendship make poor companions.

Willie, you see, was not greedy, but it appeared to us that he was planning to pay for his fancy new car with the initial inventory of meat, sausages and other delicatessen items that he had crammed into it. Signing on as his customers for future delights would have meant a budgetary adjustment of at least $20 every month, something we could ill afford. Willie clearly had to be reined in, and soon, while he was still very much dependent on the help of his friends at work.

Willie had a terrible time understanding and conversing in English and needed a translator, so arrangements had been made for one of our band to stay close to him as we passed by the shift boss's wicket to receive our instructions for the day. Willie would then have to rely on that person to translate his orders.

At first we chose to give our sausage agent the silent treatment and refused to relay instructions. But, having made his down payment for a ticket to freedom, Willie was ingenious enough to muddle through for some time.

His next lesson helped him get the message we intended to convey, but it also nearly got him fired. Underground workers not directly involved in the mining and transportation of the ore were assigned to general maintenance or cleanup duties. The shift bosses would usually tell Willie to keep doing what he was doing the day before, or they would tell him, "Go and fuck around until I get there later on in the day." One particular day he was told to do some general cleanup along the tracks at the 25th level, but to make sure to stay away from the traffic. Fred Sachs, Christel's husband, overheard the instructions and gave Willie a somewhat modified translation on the way down the shaft. Instead of cleaning out from between the tracks any materials spilled from the fast-moving trains, Fred told him to scour the drift for loose material hanging from the ceiling or the walls.

At the time, the 25th level was the main working area of the entire operation, with trains running at a frantic pace to keep up with the accumulation of materials from the various sites. In no time at all, Willie had scaled enough loose rock onto the track to bring the entire operation to a grinding halt. One of the main trains operated by Hans Manthy, a neighbour in our apartment complex, had been derailed, spilling most of its cargo. The cleanup and repair would take the rest of the day.

No one was very amused, least of all the crews who would sacrifice their bonuses for the day. By the time Rough on Rats Jack appeared on the scene, the guys were making threatening motions to send Willie to the sump at the bottom of the shaft without an elevator. Jack went ballistic. He ordered Willie to report to the office and await his fate there. It might mean the end of his mining career, and even more serious for the rest of us, was the prospect of severing our pipeline to the sausage factory. Naturally, this was the very last thing we had intended. It was time to bring Pat Miller into the picture.

As it happened, just a few days earlier I had come as close to meeting my maker as I ever had. During a lunch break I felt the urge to pay a visit to one of the makeshift toilets (a used powder box filled with sawdust and placed under a crude one-hole arrangement) that was positioned just off the main drift. I have never been among those who could rush through this daily ritual, but this was not the most hospitable or comfortable place in which to linger any longer than absolutely necessary. I stayed only briefly, and I had no sooner covered the hundred or so feet back to where we had lunch than the quiet was shattered by what everybody instinctively knew to be a major cave-in.

In Pioneer this was not an infrequent event, but nevertheless, every time one occurred it struck panic into the heart of anyone close by. The thought of being trapped behind a major cave-in 800 metres below the surface was enough to send shivers down the spines of even the most seasoned of miners. This particular collapse was massive in scale, with tens of tonnes of rock exploding to cover the space surrounding it. Fortunately it did not affect the main drift, leaving open a route to escape. Instead, it happened precisely over the makeshift outhouse where just seconds before I had blissfully relaxed to relieve my bowels of the residue of my previous day's intake, which no doubt included some of Willie's sausage.

Needless to say, the incident gave rise to endless jokes at my expense. Bud Drury, the shift boss, told everyone that he was seeking my co-operation to examine the feasibility of harnessing whatever it was I deposited into the "honey box" to save the mine a lot of money spent on much less potent dynamite. Even Joan got into the act, lamenting the challenge she would have had for the rest her life, trying to explain the manner in which her husband met his demise.

But out of evil came good. The incident became a bargaining chip in the Winterfeld situation and strengthened the argument the union's safety committee had been making for some time that the area had become unstable and was long overdue for what should have been regular maintenance work. We succeeded in coaching Pat Miller to threaten management with serious action unless remedial work was ordered forthwith. He also made it clear that the severity of the union's response would depend on the degree of disciplinary action planned against Willie, who had only done what management was obliged to do anyway. Even Rough on Rats had to concede that we had a point. Willie was reassigned to work with a partner more adept at taking instructions, and things did get back to normal. On the meat delivery side, after a solid weekend of soul-searching, Willie negotiated significant price concessions for his closest friends and customers, and the whole thing, except for the valuable lesson, was forgotten.

The plans Joan and I had for our new life did include a large family, but the timing of our new arrivals was always inopportune. Isabell decided to make her grand entrance just about the time we and every one of our friends were starting to think seriously about a career change. The pattern by which she chose to live her life was shaped even before she was born. She was always in a hurry.

We had no sooner discovered that Joan was pregnant than things started to get complicated. About five months into the pregnancy she started hemorrhaging. Dr. Lippset, the Bralorne doctor, decided to terminate the pregnancy. Just a minor procedure, he promised, an overnight stay at the hospital. The operation was done, but when I went to visit her at the end of my shift, things had taken a turn for the worse. Joan was burning up with fever, something the nurses told me was highly unusual and dangerous after an operation. Worse, the doctor was away on another emergency, and when he did arrive, he told me not to worry. Everything was under control. The following afternoon, hoping that I could take her home with me after shift, I found Joan shaking so badly that her bed was literally moving about the room. Lippset, I was told, had consulted with some colleagues who suggested that, as a precautionary measure, she be evacuated to a Vancouver hospital. He told me to start making arrangements for an ambulance as soon as she was stable enough to be moved.

We were into our first major crisis. It was the middle of winter. The lakes that during the summer accommodated floatplanes equipped as air ambulances were frozen over. The only options were to summon a conventional ambulance all the way from the city, the cost of which would have eaten up most of our savings, or to take a chance and drive her there myself.

In the end it was Willie and Trudel Winterfeld who took charge, proving themselves the great friends they were. He insisted I take his car, which was equipped with Pullman seats that could serve as a bed. Trudel would look after Ursula during our absence. The whole town, of course, knew of the situation, and I was flooded with offers for help from every quarter. The biggest surprise I got was from, of all people, Rough on Rats Jack.

On the day before I was finally able to take Joan out of the hospital,

I had a visit from Jack, who normally had no reason to climb the 300 wooden steps to the hoist tower, where I was now working.

"I understand you have some trouble at home," he said. (The party line had been buzzing for days, fed undoubtedly by contributions from inside the hospital.) "Have you talked to the man above?" His eyes rolled toward the ceiling, indicating that he might mean someone in another realm because there simply was no other person living or working in the area at an altitude higher than the hoist room. Then he walked over to where I was sitting and put his hand on my shoulder.

"God," he said, "you know I would never question your wisdom, but I ask you in the name of your son Jesus Christ to protect these kids and help them over their crisis." Then he invited me to join him in saying the Lord's Prayer. "Just say it in German if you don't yet know the English version," he said.

Yes, Jack turned out to be a devout Catholic, and he had a human side very few people would have recognized him by. For some reason he had taken a liking to me, and he took an interest in my future career. Many years later he even visited me in Parliament, where I invited him for dinner in the parliamentary restaurant. To my great embarrassment, at the end of the meal I watched out of the corner of my eye as he picked up a ceramic ashtray adorned with a picture of the Parliament Buildings and let it slide into his pocket. Somehow I couldn't get mad at him, even though I was sure that it was much less stressful for him to confess the indiscretion to his God than it was for me to confess to the manager of the restaurant what kind of scoundrels I invited to the place.

The first leg of the trip in our makeshift ambulance turned into a nightmare. Willie's car was in great shape, but had just reached the point where the tires should have been replaced—something he hadn't got around to doing. We left very early on a bitterly cold winter morning to make absolutely certain that we wouldn't miss the train at Shalath. I made it to within about five kilometres before we had the first flat. Parked on a downslope, the car slid closer to the edge of the road, beyond which was a 150-metre cliff, every time I attempted to jack it off the ground to install the spare. My hands were frozen and my face was numb when, with only a few minutes to reach our destination, we were finally back on the road. How we made it without going over the cliff I will never know.

After two more flats, I could no longer avoid the expense of equipping

Willie's car with a new set of tires. It was late in the evening before the bright lights of Vancouver raised our spirits. It was Joan's first visit to the city about which I had spoken in such glowing terms. Surprisingly, she felt well enough to ask for the seat to be raised halfway so she could enjoy the view.

She would have to suffer one more traumatic experience before we arrived at the emergency entrance of the Vancouver General. One of Vancouver's finest took exception to the Rambler shooting through a red light and came after us, sirens blaring. My attempt to make light of it, by explaining to Joan that it had to be a welcoming committee, had little effect. Her innate fear triggered a response that made it easy to convince the cop there was a reason for my being in a hurry to get to the hospital. He was very polite and ushered us on with good wishes and a suggestion that perhaps I should park the car at the hotel until I was ready to leave again for the hinterland. If I had any doubt about his sincerity, it was dispelled two nights later when, as luck would have it, the same cop got in my way as I drove in the wrong direction on a one-way street. This time he was kind enough to inquire about Joan's condition and seemed genuinely pleased when I told him the good news.

In fact, the news was almost too good to be true. The doctor cheerfully told me that Joan was feeling just fine and so was the baby she would deliver in about two months' time.

"Any fool," he said, "could hear the child's heartbeat, and whatever they scraped out at the Bralorne hospital was not your wife's uterus." Since we were planning on going back there, he would conduct a series of additional tests to make sure of her condition, but he could see no reason at all why we couldn't be on our way in a couple of days.

Isabell must have overheard the doctor. After surviving Dr. Lippset's attempts to terminate her, she decided to get on with it and arrived on February 23, 1955, one month and one day ahead of schedule. She was tiny. Hospital staff called her and another baby, also born prematurely, Peanut One and Peanut Two. To his credit, Dr. Lippset spared none of his talents and contributed his very best efforts to help our new daughter into the world and to guide her through her first critical hours and days. Even then, we had a final hurdle.

When he released her to our care, it was with clear instructions to feed her every two hours around the clock. It took us an hour to coax the fragile little body to absorb even the tiniest fraction of her prescribed formula, and with me manning the night shift at the mine and trying to get some sleep during the day, it became a nightmare for both of us. Joan never got any sleep at all. After about two weeks I began acting like Jack Genest and Panicky Bell. We were at our wits' end.

Knowing what sleep deprivation felt like to us, we thought it was reasonable to assume that being torn from her sleep every two hours was absolute torture for the child. We decided to ignore the instructions and let Isabell choose her own mealtimes. When we took her for her first checkup at the hospital, she had gained considerable weight and had begun to show some interest in the world around her. This was in sharp contrast to the other premature child, whose parents were still feeding her on schedule. Needless to say, we passed on our experience. Following our own instincts may well have saved both children's lives.

Our traumatic experience with northern medical services was not unusual. Besides David Seebacher, the Hintereggers and Reibenschuhs had persuaded another close friend to leave Vienna and join them in Pioneer. Only a few weeks after his arrival with his family, he met a tragic end.

He was still assigned to light duties underground when one day, just barely into the day's shift, he was found unconscious in one of the drifts. Apart from a sizable bump on his head, there was no other visible sign of injury. He was rushed to the hospital, where the staff, with the sparse equipment at their disposal, could shed little light on the mystery of his condition. Jack Genest rendered the opinion that he must have suffered a stroke and bumped his head when he fell, but the Workers' Compensation Board insisted on a more expert opinion and an air ambulance to evacuate him to a Vancouver facility.

It was just a single-engine floatplane that touched down at Gun Lake for the mission. His wife and one of his friends who spoke English wanted to accompany him on the trip, but the pilot insisted on a nurse instead to fill the only other available space in the small craft. The plane, ill-equipped to cope with the typical treacherous conditions over the Coast Mountains, crashed into a peak, killing everyone aboard. It took the poor widow years to get any satisfaction for her claim for compensation from either the mine or the air-charter company.

Stories like this are legion. Canadians pay heavy penalties for choosing to live and work in the more isolated parts of the country. There were no incentives then for the professions to locate north of the 100-mile corridor along the American border, and even now, the premiums on wages in the north are quickly eaten up by the much higher cost of living. Consequently, most of the one-industry towns have ended up with only the basic health care, educational, and cultural amenities. For any nation so dependent on its resource industries, it is nothing less than scandalous to allow these conditions to exist. This was one of the factors that many years later motivated me to pursue a career in politics.

As my family grew, I became increasingly aware of sacrifices people were required to make, living and working in such isolated areas. Sure, our bank account was growing steadily, but what would happen to my family if I was hurt or killed?

By 1955 I had graduated to the position of hoist man and was assigned to operate the equipment at a newly installed but rather primitive hoist station servicing a new shaft that started at the 2,500-foot level and that, unlike the two main shafts, was built on an incline following the vein for another 300 feet. We were well into a graveyard shift, hoisting some of the higher-grade materials to a transfer station, when without any warning a wall of water came cascading into the hoist room, rushing past the operations platform and down the shaft.

My first concern was for the crew below who, judging by the volume of water gushing past me, would drown like rats in no time at all. Apart from my own crew tending the chute and lifts at the other end of the cable, there would have been two crews at the lower level, assigned to general maintenance duties, and a steel sharpener, Heinrich, making his rounds to the various head-stations. I managed to reach all but the latter by phone and ordered them to abandon their stations to be lifted to the top.

The call from the shift office on the surface added to the gravity of the situation. It was assumed that through some inexplicable phenomenon, the river above had found its way into the workings of the mine. I was told that a Code 1 emergency procedure had been implemented, and it wasn't long before the strong, nauseating smell of onions—fed into the air supply as a signal to evacuate the mine—became noticeable. Despite that, I was ordered to remain at my station until all the crew were accounted for. Once I had got them as far as my level, I was to direct everyone to make their way to the No. 3 hoist in the main shaft to be lifted to safety. A sharp click, resonating like a rifle shot from the direction of the electrical breaker switches, indicated the flooding of the pumping station at the bottom just as the cage, with four of my companions sitting in water up to their chests, their panic-stricken faces peeking over the top, entered the platform. They did not have to be ordered to get to the main shaft. They were on the run before I could ask them about the whereabouts of Heinrich, the steel sharpener.

Heinrich was a fellow countryman who had worked himself into this important but cushy job of sharpening or replacing worn-out drill bits. On a normal day it would take him no more than three or four hours to complete this task, after which he could be found slumbering in some obscure drift for the rest of the night. I knew he had gone down, but I could not recall him intercepting the lift to come back up. He was either sleeping somewhere below or had made his way up the array of ladders rather than interrupt the flow of material—something that always earned him a torrent of profanity from the crew trying to pad their bonus cheques.

It might not have been more than 10 minutes, but it seemed like eternity until I was joined by Sid Simonds, one of the shift bosses who came running from the direction of the No. 3 in water up over his ankles. I offered to wait as Sid ventured down the ladders to make a closer inspection of the situation and explore some of the places Heinrich would have attended during his rounds. He returned a few minutes later, having determined that the level of the water had risen to the second to last drift, but none the wiser as to the whereabouts of the missing Heinrich. Mysteriously, the torrent of water had slowed to a trickle, but we still decided that it was time to abandon the station and head for safety. On the surface, no one had left the site. We were greeted with thunderous applause as we stepped out of the cage, the last to leave the mine, with only one person unaccounted for.

Jack Genest, aided by a quickly assembled rescue team, had already determined the cause of the flood. Instead of the river, it was the new ventilation shaft, which had just been commissioned, that was the source of the problem. A number of high-volume fans had been pumping the valley's freezing winter air down the new installation, causing the entrances to the upper levels to slowly seal themselves behind a wall of solid ice and damming up water that normally seeped from the rocks. The warm spring air had now reversed the process, causing the ice to melt and the dams to disintegrate. The crisis was over, but it would take several days to pump out the lower parts of the mine and restore its production.

Heinrich's situation had a happy ending as well, even though the rescue team could not find hide nor hair of him anywhere. Early in the morning Jack appointed a delegation to visit Heinrich's wife and alert her to the fact that he might have been the victim of the night's disaster. No one was keen to go, but they needn't have worried. When they got there, they were met by Elsa's rosy-cheeked face peering out from behind the screen door.

"You vant Heinrich?" she inquired. "He schleep. I go wake." And sure enough, seconds later the elusive Heinrich presented himself, well rested indeed. Having completed his nightly chores halfway through his shift, he could think of no reason why he shouldn't spend the rest of the night in his own bed, cuddled up to Elsa's ample and warm body, instead of sleeping on his workbench in a cold, damp and miserable place in the mine.

One thing must be said in favour of the management of the mine: with only one exception that I can recall, no one ever got fired. Sure, Heinrich had to endure a half-hour of Jack's entire repertoire of enhanced English adjectives, listening as he was described as a person who would violate his own mother and would delight in sucking male genitals, but he was back on duty sharpening tools on the very same day that the mine reopened.

It was another of my countrymen, Fritz, who was the exception to the rule. It started innocently enough. He had settled for a lesser-paying position than the rest of us, in the mill where the ore was processed. We saw little of the actual gold, the fruits of all this labour, since it was barely visible in the mine, embedded as it was in the quartz-like rock. However, Fritz came in contact with much higher concentrations of the precious stuff.

No one, he reasoned, would mind if he skimmed off just a small amount for a souvenir. His hobby might also, he thought, net him enough extra income someday to make up the difference between his measly paycheque and that of his friends underground. The trouble was that he had no idea how much gold was contained in the black-looking froth he carried home every day in his thermos bottle or how he could convert it to cash.

At the time the price per ounce of gold was pegged at $35, and the world's gold mines were operating under a tightly controlled international agreement. It turned out that Fritz's take caused a serious imbalance in the yield of the precious metal compared to the daily estimates produced by the assay office.

So serious was the problem that the mine hired a private investigator, posing as an efficiency expert, to help them find the leak. It didn't take him long at all to make the acquaintance of our friend, who was chasing the rumour that the stranger was interested in acquiring some high-grade gold that might have fallen off the table. Fritz showed him a sample of his cache, bragging that there was a lot more where that came from. And so there was. When the police finally raided the house, they liberated several thousand dollars' worth of semi-refined gold.

Poor Fritz had to spend some time in jail before he was convicted of his crime, resulting in his deportation back to Germany. Even in this most serious infringement of the company's rules, his wife and kids were allowed to stay in the company house, rent free, until they could join him on his journey back to the Fatherland.

The second accident, near the end of our stay in Pioneer, came perilously close to putting me in Fritz's position.

I doubt that there is a piece of equipment that requires more skill and split-second timing than the operation of a hoist in a mine as deep as the one in Pioneer. The dual drums, driven by several-hundred-horsepower electric motors, were each wound with about 300 metres of steel cable as thick as a normal person's wrist. Even the slightest miscalculation in applying pressure to the brake levers would cause the elevator to behave as if it were mounted on the end of a rubber band.

The drums themselves were about three metres in diameter. Only a clock-like dial and some chalk markings on the drums aided the hoist man in bringing the equipment mounted on the end of the cables to within two or three inches of the station platforms underground. The elevators were coupled, so that the weight on one side would assist the lift on the other.

Given that the system was designed to carry both men and materials up and down the shafts, it was equipped with very elaborate monitors that controlled the speed and certain other operating limits. But these limits could become a nuisance on weekends, when the equipment was used exclusively to hoist the accumulated materials at the bottom of the shaft to the surface. That particular operation was also integrated into the production bonus regime, making speed and split-second timing of the essence. So it was necessary to override the limits to gain access to the headframe of the shaft, where the ore was dumped, and to the bins at the bottom, where it was loaded. It was also customary to eliminate the speed controls.

It was a recipe for disaster. On the day of the accident, we were in a hurry as usual, trying to improve on my own record for the number of

The hoist room at Pioneer, the scene of Frank's big accident.

tonnes of muck hoisted to the surface on a weekend shift. It was late in the shift and the prospect for another record day was looming large. Not a single mishap or hang-up at the chutes below had bothered us all day. Then it happened.

The dumping of ore, in particular, required split-second timing, so that the cable on the empty bucket was fully extended approaching the bottom of the shaft, assuring maximum counterweight, just as the other bucket disgorged its weight at the top. I was approaching the last 30 metres from the top at full speed when the brake lever controlling the right drum slipped out of my hand, causing the ore-filled bucket to crash through the headframe. At the same time, the empty lower bucket plummeted to the bottom of the shaft, with all the loose cable piling on top of the wreckage. The results were catastrophic. The damage to the shaft and the equipment could not have been worse.

My first concern was for the crew below who, much to my relief, reported that they had escaped injury. My next call was to Sid Simonds, the shift boss, who in turn alerted Rough on Rats Jack.

It was only minutes before I could hear him snorting up the steps at full steam. I swear he was puffing smoke out of his ears. As he navigated the last few steps up the covered stairs to the hoist room, his mouth spewed a torrent of obscenities, choking off the orderly flow of oxygen to his lungs and causing his eyes to bulge out of his head. He did not project the image of a well man.

"You are fired," he managed to gasp, using up the little breath he had left. "Get out of my sight before I throw you down the shaft with the rest of the shit you have managed to pile up down there." Fortunately Sid, as usual, had maintained his composure. He advised me to go home and wait for his phone call the following day, at which time he would have a better assessment of the damage and how it would affect my future with the company.

Because of the hoists' critical role in the safe operation of an underground mine, it was obligatory to report any major mishap involving them to the provincial authorities. They, in turn, ordered a formal inquiry. As promised, Sid Simonds called me the next day to tell me that I would be required to testify at the hearing and that I would be suspended with pay until that time. However, he did not hold out much hope regarding my future prospects with the company and suggested that I start looking for work elsewhere. He also suggested that I contact the Bralorne operation, where he was aware of an opening for a good hoist man. It never occurred to me at the time that he had already contacted his counterpart at Bralorne to recommend me for the position, and it was not until many years and several career changes later, when just by chance we met at a campground near Hudson's Hope, that I had the opportunity to thank him for his kindness and concern.

The next time I met Jack was at the inquiry. I was sitting on the steps outside the boardroom at the main office, waiting to be called, when he came out to tell me what was happening inside and what was expected of me. Needless to say, the Inspector of Mines, who was heading the inquiry, would likely have preferred to hear my testimony without my having been coached by the superintendent.

Jack's demeanour was almost friendly. He briefed me on the assessment of the damage I had caused; it would cost a staggering amount of money to repair. What was worse, depending on my testimony, the inspector might well order the mine shut down completely until certain modifications to the operation of the shafts could be carried out. Jack expected me to be questioned on the frequency of inspection and testing of both the electronic and mechanical devices controlling the operation of the equipment.

"You might recall," he suggested, "that we were doing that as required on a weekly basis during the weekend shifts when, in the main, you were on duty." I, of course, had no such recollection and was not surprised to learn that the safety devices I had overridden would not have worked to prevent the mishap anyway. Jack was asking me to commit perjury.

Sweating bullets, I entered the room, the last witness to be called. I was torn between loyalty to my employer and my fellow workers, who would obviously be affected by a shutdown, and the prospect of being charged with perjury, possibly resulting in my deportation back to Germany.

My face drained of the last drop of blood; the dilemma Jack had put me in must have been reflected in my eyes. There were about half a dozen people in the room, their eyes piercing my miserable body, none showing any sign of mercy. There was some shuffling of papers and documents, one of which I recognized as the logbook where I made my daily entries. After what seemed like an eternity, I was invited to sit down in front of the assembled gathering.

"I had expected someone older," the inspector finally said. "How old are you anyway?"

"Twenty-four, sir."

"How long have you been a hoist man?"

"One year, sir."

As if he didn't already know, he asked me to explain what happened and if I had any explanation why the safety provisions failed to function.

No sense skirting around the issue. I told him I had activated the override to facilitate access to the dump, and because the equipment was being used for the movement of materials, not people, I had felt justified to override the speed controls as well—but only after the two-man crew had been lowered to their work station at the bottom. Things weren't going well, but it was the next question that brought me to the edge of the abyss.

"You would, of course, be aware of the requirement to have the safety limits of the hoist tested on a weekly basis." (Indeed, I had been aware of it for at least the last 20 minutes.) Opening the logbook and paging through it, he asked me to explain why he could not find any entries relating to the procedure anywhere in the book.

This was it. My mouth was as dry as a popcorn fart, causing my voice to squeak out that I was unaware of the requirement to make a logbook entry of the event, unintentionally implying that the events had actually taken place. The damn fool never followed up on the comment to make certain of this critical point.

To this day I am unsure how I would have responded if he had.

The rest of the meeting was anticlimactic. Sid, the shift boss, caught up to me as I was making my way down the front steps of the building.

"You were brilliant," he declared. "I hope the management will appreciate what you have done to save their bacon."

I was just glad to go home to share my misery with Joan and make plans for an uncertain future. Jack Genest called me the following day with the good news that the inspector had left it to the discretion of management to decide whether or not I could resume my career, but a decision had not yet been made. For almost two weeks I heard nothing from the company, even though there was another paycheque waiting for me at the bank. It was on the same day that I received an invitation for an interview at Bralorne that I got a call from Jack.

"How soon can you get your sorry ass down here?" he demanded. "I need someone who can run this pile of shit before we wreck it completely and kill a few people in the process." As it happened, the work to rebuild the damaged shaft and rewind the cables, which the inspector had ordered replaced, was a challenge for even the most experienced and skilful operator of the hoist. Don Conn, my colleague on the opposite shift, had booked holidays when the accident happened, leaving it up to an inexperienced spare operator who, in Jack's words, "couldn't find his asshole in broad daylight using both hands."

With Isabell barely one year old and our financial resources hardly adequate to consider venturing into any kind of business, the sensible thing was to submit to another two years at the mine. I went back to work, but the experience left me feeling insecure. It served once again to reinforce our obsession with being liberated from dependence on others for a job or anything else. We began making plans in earnest for a new career where we would be our own bosses. As well, since we had never entertained the slightest thought of returning to Germany, it was time to apply for citizenship in our new homeland.

Preparing for the event spawned my interest in politics. After all, the manual that was handed out with the application form noted that basic knowledge was required of the institutions of Parliament and Canada's political system. It wasn't just the name of John George Diefenbaker (a common name in the Black Forest), but the message associated with it that caught my attention.

It seemed to be focussed less on the kind of fervent nationalism with which I had been indoctrinated in the past and more on individual rights and freedoms and equality of citizenship, regardless of ethnic origin, colour, and religion. Perhaps it could help me overcome my innate distrust derived from my previous experience with politics. There was to be an election within the next two years, and with any luck I might get a chance to vote.

I never had any regrets, but the experience of becoming a Canadian citizen was profoundly troubling.

The legendary Judge Henry Castillou was the presiding judge at the hearing, which was held in Lillooet. He was a mountain of a man with a booming voice that would rattle the windows within two blocks of the courthouse when he was presiding.

I had prepared well for what I thought was the most important decision I would make in my life. Unless one has experienced it, however, it would be difficult to understand the mix of emotions and rush of anxiety one feels when carrying through such a momentous undertaking.

Preceded by the local police constable in ceremonial uniform, the judge squeezed himself through the narrow doorway to fill half the room all by himself. The scene was intimidating and stifling. He was never known to be the most sensitive of the judges in the province, and he certainly made no effort to put anyone at ease on this occasion.

The first aspiring new Canadian was an old Swede. Apparently he had been in the country for most of his life and was pining to pay a visit to the land of his ancestors before the Grim Reaper called him to the other place. In order to get a passport he had to have proof of citizenship. Unfortunately, he could speak very little English, but he had brought a fellow countryman to interpret for him. The judge asked him a few questions, such as what the names of the prime minister of Canada and the premier of British Columbia were, but he soon became frustrated with the two old geezers and their insistence on arguing with each other as they tried to come up with the right answer.

"If Olli has been in Canada all these years, why can't he speak English?" his booming voice demanded.

"Well, Mister Judge," the friend timidly offered, "he work on the farm and only go into town once a month to drink beer."

"Is he a good drinking man?" His Honour wanted to know.

"*Ja, ja.* Olli is a very good drinking man."

"Well, if nothing else, that should qualify him to make a good Canadian."

I am sure he meant it to be funny, because everyone else in the room laughed, but I didn't find it so at all.

Another applicant was asked if, as a citizen of Canada, he would be ready to fight in a war for his new country. I felt the blood rushing to my head as my mind's eye scanned some of the scenes of horror that would never be erased from my subconscious. Fortunately, when it came my turn, he spared me from having to respond to this particular question. I doubt that I could have come up with the answer His Honour expected.

But I would not get off without another scar on my soul. The Federal Republic of Germany had chosen not to deny any right or privilege to which a German citizen was entitled, even if that person switched allegiance to another country. As a result, I would be required to formally renounce my German citizenship.

I knew I had ample reason to justify such a decision, but I was nevertheless totally unprepared for it. I felt the urge to check if Uncle Wilhelm or Lieutenant Boronovski were looking over my shoulder as I, my mind racing and my hand shaking, signed the form the clerk had laid in front of me. Strangely, I was in no mood at all to celebrate as I headed back to Pioneer in the 1946 Pontiac that we had acquired by then.

It would be a long time before I found the courage to confess to Joan that as the price for becoming a citizen of Canada and acquiring the privilege of being able to vote for John Diefenbaker in the 1957 election, I had cut off the last bridge linking me to my German heritage.

CHAPTER 17

A Town With a Milepost as Its Name

What is freedom? Freedom is the right to choose: the right to create for yourself the alternatives of choice. Without the possibility of choice and the exercise of choice a man is not a man but a member, an instrument, a thing.

—Archibald Macleish, American poet and public official

It was William James who said, "Man alone, of all the creatures of the earth, can change his own pattern. Man alone is the architect of his destiny." How easy it would have been to just float along in the artificial environment of the company town, without a worry in the world, without attempting any alterations to the pattern to which our lives in the mine had conformed.

Pioneer had been good to us and our friends. We would miss the natural beauty of the valley, the pristine forests, and the majestic mountains, even though they blocked out the sun in the valley from September to April every year. It had been a blissful existence for us once I had worked myself up to the position of hoist man, free of the danger and risks associated with working underground. The Pontiac wasn't much of a car, but it too had given us a certain freedom and added another dimension to our lives.

We even made a couple of trips to Vancouver during our last year in Pioneer to shop for clothes and necessities unavailable at the company store. These ventures always coincided with Dollar Day at the Army and Navy store on Hastings Street, where one could get a pair of shoes for one dollar, a sports jacket for four, and a five-dollar suitcase in one of the pawnshops nearby to fit it all in. Even today we seldom visit Vancouver without looking in on the Army and Navy, just for nostalgic reasons.

Frank and Joan at Pioneer with their first car.

But we were aspiring to greater things, and most great things don't happen by chance but by choice. The time had come for us to face the fact that the only thing that comes without risk and sacrifice is old age.

Several of our friends, the Winterfelds, the Hintereggers, and the Seebachers among them, had already left the mine for Vancouver, where they managed to establish themselves in small delicatessen stores catering to the ever-increasing demand for German sausages, French cheeses, and other culinary delights the multitudes of new Canadians from Europe were pining for. Rudi and Poldi Reibenschuh became proprietors of a beauty salon.

For Joan and me, dreaming of broader horizons, the city held few attractions. Why crowd together in a large city when the open spaces of such a large country offered so much more opportunity and the promise of so much more freedom, so much more independence? As well, we wanted to wean ourselves from the companionship of our fellow countrymen and avoid being caught in any ethnic ghetto.

Finally we decided, with considerable trepidation, that it was time to strike out in pursuit of better opportunities than those offered by the mine. We would embark on our first business career, a cattle ranch near 100 Mile House.

Compared to the risks and the sacrifices we had already made, the move was really no gamble at all. In fact, compared to some of our enterprises, this one was actually well thought out. Guenter, a boarder we had taken in at Pioneer, would be our partner in the enterprise. We had made a modest down payment on the ranch, knowing that the place would require some work and additional investment before it would show any return. The idea was that Joan and I would manage the farm while Guenter kept on working at the mine to earn the extra money needed to make it a viable enterprise.

We knew next to nothing about farming, but neither had I known much about being a logger or a miner, so this did not cause us any concern. In the spring of 1957 I quit the mine and we packed up and left Pioneer.

Some 30 years later, Joan and I made a nostalgic trip from Pemberton to Pioneer over the road that had been carved out of the mountains to gain access to the area and the timber along the way. As we drove in from the top of the valley, our old apartment building was the first place we came to. It had totally collapsed, and Mother Nature was making good progress reclaiming the site. Like so many of the little towns in British Columbia that once thrived, sustained by timber or minerals, Pioneer and nearby Bralorne had become ghost towns. All that remained of the church where Father Schweitzer had sanctioned our marriage was part of the roof and four walls that no longer had any windows or doors. God, too, had moved on, thinking perhaps that the church had served its purpose once Joan and I exchanged our vows.

The hospital where Isabell was born was relatively well preserved. It had a "For Sale" sign nailed to the front porch, with a price tag of $24,000, a bargain considering that the kitchen equipment was still in good repair and the first light Isabell saw as she came into this world was still hanging from the ceiling in the operating room.

We also found some of the old-timers still living in Bralorne and at Gun Lake, where we had spent so many happy weekends. They were dreaming about the mine reopening now that the price of gold was allowed to float to reflect its actual worth on the open market, but it remained just a dream.

Our new life in 100 Mile House, 450 kilometres north of Vancouver on the Cariboo Highway, did not get off to a great start. Even the best-laid plans can go awry. We ended up living in 100 Mile House just long enough to learn some valuable lessons about business and partnerships and for Joan to get pregnant again. I also found myself turning my hand to all kinds of new trades. Bartender, carpenter, janitor, hole digger, and insurance agent—in a few short months I did them all.

First of all, as we found out immediately, the ranch, because of its size and location, would never be anything more than a hobby farm, and we were hardly ready to think about acquiring a hobby.

Our past experience with partnerships should have been enough to resist the temptation to enter into another one, but on that subject I am a slow learner. Guenter's priorities were different from mine, and it didn't take more than a week before he was gone and we were left cleaning up the mess. It meant finding a place to live in town and finding another job.

Fortunately, it couldn't have happened at a better place. The people in 100 Mile House were of a different breed than those we had encountered so far. We were the only German immigrants, and we couldn't understand why people, total strangers, would take such an interest in us, offer us their friendship, help, and advice without asking a thing in return, and accept us in their town as if we had lived there all our lives. In no time at all, we had not one, but three jobs. Within days we invested our savings in a partly finished house, and I started working with Ed Williams, a building contractor who would teach me the skills I needed to complete the job myself.

There was not much to 100 Mile House. The status of any town in the hinterland is assessed by its amenities. By the time we arrived, a town of comparable size would have rated a liquor store, but this apparently was not very high on the list of priorities the Emissaries of Divine Light attached to the development of their town. The nearest dispensary of our spiritual needs, as well as other essential services, was in Williams Lake, another 100 kilometres to the north. A visit to the liquor store would usually be combined with a visit to the dentist, the lawyer, or the government agent.

However, 100 Mile House did have a hotel with a beer parlour. We got to know the proprietors of the Exeter Arms Hotel, the Brookses, who were chronically short of help. They saw no problem at all in offering a job to Joan, even though she still spoke very little English. Her good looks and European charm were needed to add some class to the coffee shop, where she started waiting tables. The most surly-looking characters—mill workers, truckers, and loggers who managed to accommodate a sizable wad of chewing tobacco in one cheek and a soft-boiled egg in the other, presumably without getting them mixed up—showed themselves to be kind and generous, even if the "eggs over easy" turned up scrambled or the bacon had turned into sausages on the way to the table. We were able to live on her tips alone, and when we added my earnings with Ed and our pay for cleaning the beer parlour after hours, we brought in more than double what I had been earning in the mine. Things were looking up.

Ed was a single man, the town's most eligible bachelor, and he made the most of it. He was part of Mr. Brooks' inner circle of friends, who on Saturday nights helped sling beer in the "Ladies and Escorts" section of the beer parlour. Occasionally, like all of us, he was pressed into service in the "Men Only" section as well, but only to assist the more experienced crew in keeping the upper hand in the occasional war that broke out. The rest of the time he was a good friend and an amazing carpenter.

Counting himself, Ed liked to work with just a three-man crew. He built complete houses without the help of any outside contractors, apart from the electrical services. Ed, I think, had never learned to walk. He ran all the time. I have never before, nor since, met a man more skilled or more efficient and better organized. Two of us perched on a roof, installing rafters in the most complex roof structures, had a hard time keeping up with Ed as he threw the individual pieces, each with a different, often compound, angle up the two-storey building. His Skil-saw and his carpenter's square seemed to be natural extensions of his arms. He insisted that in his time a man getting caught hitting a two-and-a-quarter-inch nail more than twice was chased off the job.

I know how frustrating it must have been for him to see me fumble through the day, but he always had a word of encouragement and some friendly advice to keep me going.

"Why," he wanted to know as he watched me using a fine-toothed handsaw for the first time, "do you think they would put over 200 teeth on this saw if you only needed 15?" Then he showed me just how easy it was to pull the saw through with long, even strokes instead of the jerking motions I had used.

With Joan and me both working, little time was left over for family or personal concerns. Besides the half-hour lunch break, I got two ten-minute coffee breaks in which I used to rush home to check on the kids. Ursula, at the ripe old age of five, was the babysitter. Joan, who never showed her pregnancies much, worked well into October and was reluctant to quit even then.

"After all, back home," she said, "women had their babies out in the fields, while making hay or hoeing potatoes, and hoped it would happen late in the afternoon so they could have the rest of the day to recuperate." Apparently Canadians were a bit backward in this regard. We found it strange that there were no midwives, particularly since doctors seemed to be restricted to practices in larger centres and were unavailable to make house calls, meaning that babies were born only in hospitals. We had a choice between the hospital at Williams Lake, 100 kilometres to the north, or at Ashcroft, 120 kilometres to the south. Since we had never been to Ashcroft, it was our natural choice.

I was standing on the scaffolding, sheeting a new house just a block away from home, making excellent time getting rid of a pile of "shiplap" lumber, hating to interrupt the rhythm Ed had set, setting the nail with one firm motion and driving it home with the other, when out of the corner of my eye I could see our neighbour's daughter running toward the site, waving her arms. "Mr. Oberle, you must come home right away, the water pipe has broken."

No further explanation was necessary. "You better get your ass in gear," Ed said as he reached into his pocket to toss me the keys to the new Jimmy—GM—pickup he had just bought a week earlier. "Let's not take a chance with your old jalopy. You might have to make some time."

For a moment I was miffed at the insult to my pride and joy, a 1952 fire-engine-red Ford convertible, for which we had traded the old Pontiac. But there was no time to argue. Mrs. Butterfield, our neighbour across the street, had taken charge of the situation.

"You better hurry," she said as I skidded the pickup to a halt in front of our house, "you might not make it in time." Her tone of voice and the expression on her face gave emphasis to what she was saying.

I didn't need to be told. The back wheels of the Jimmy were spewing gravel and sand before Joan could slam the door and wave goodbye to the girls, whom Mrs. Butterfield had offered to babysit. By the time we reached the top of the hill, moving south, I was clocking 100 miles an hour. At one point I could see the needle of the speedometer leaning over its maximum limit of 120 miles an hour.

The labour pains were already at regular intervals. Joan's fingernails were digging into my right arm every time she went into a spasm of pain. "Please stop," she kept pleading. "Please stop." At times she was delirious.

The road followed the contours of the terrain and was well endowed with bumps, potholes, and treacherous curves. It was torture.

As was customary during hunting season, the provincial game department was operating a monitoring station in Cache Creek, stopping all traffic filtering into the Fraser Canyon to register the game harvest for the season. I passed through the checkpoint, gas pedal to the floor, the horn blaring. Before I got to the first bend in the road, my rear-view mirror was filling up with the red lights of a cop car. I was sure he was about to give up the chase, but then he saw me take the Ashcroft turnoff, where the road, even more primitive, didn't allow for the same rate of speed. As a result, the pickup and the cop car skidded to a halt in front of the hospital at exactly the same time.

I bailed out, hitting the ground running, worried that my shaky knees might buckle under the strain. The flashing red lights outside helped convince the staff at the front desk that we might actually have an emergency here. When we came out with a wheelchair, the policeman himself was holding Joan's hand, needing no further explanation about why I had felt justified driving like I was possessed.

On our way to the delivery room, the nurse pushed me aside, declaring that she was now in charge, but there was about a one-inch bump in the hallway where a new addition had joined with the old, and I decided that the last thing we needed was one more bump. With a solid bodycheck, I bounced the poor woman off the wall as I grabbed hold of the handles on the wheelchair to ease the transition. Perhaps fortunately, that's as far as I got. It was unheard of in those days for a husband to attend the delivery. The nurse's firm hands and those of an orderly guided me into a room off to the side.

I had reached the end of my endurance. My knees were still shaking, and for the moment I had more reason to worry about Joan than the baby. With tears streaming down my face, I prayed again: "God, if you are listening and you think you owe me another favour, now is the time to cash it in. Please help us one more time, please save her, and don't let her suffer anymore."

Ah, the power of prayer. I was still struggling to regain my composure when the nurse came in to lead me to a recovery room, where Joan was struggling to stay conscious long enough to give me the good news before she allowed herself to succumb to her total exhaustion. Her face was swollen, but her cheeks were rosy and she had never looked more beautiful—as beautiful as the child.

They say that all babies look alike, but I would have been able to recognize my son anywhere. Frank's birth certificate was made out on October 27, 1957. Instead of listing Ashcroft, British Columbia, as the place of birth, it should have read, "A Jimmy pickup of the same vintage."

On the way back home, I stopped long enough to buy a box of cigars to give to my friends and the officers at the Cache Creek checkpoint, where the good news had preceded me via the police officer. There were handshakes and congratulations all around as I cranked up the pickup for the last stretch. The only dark cloud casting its shadow over the happy scene was an ominous noise coming from the motor, a sound that one of the attendants identified as a burnt-out exhaust valve.

I shouldn't have worried. Typically, Ed only commented that it was a good thing it happened while it was still under warranty, even though he was extremely proud of his new vehicle.

Mr. Brooks made it his practice to invite his battle-scarred crew for a drink after the bar had closed for the weekend. On one such occasion he was expounding on the virtues of the new Edsel car, of which he had just taken delivery, pointing to one particular feature that triggered an alarm any time the car exceeded a pre-set speed limit. Ed, not to be outdone, bragged about the Jimmy, which, he said, was equipped with a recorder that played "Nearer My God to Thee" if you went too fast.

Ed's joke got a good laugh at the time, but it wasn't nearly as funny when just a few days later we all sang this beautiful inspirational hymn at the first funeral I attended in Canada.

Ed had gone on a mission to Williams Lake to replenish his supply of beer and liquor. Naturally, the need for this vital lubricant often became too urgent to be postponed for a more convenient time. Such was the case when, on a certain bright sunny afternoon a few minutes before normal quitting time, Ed jumped into the pickup, now equipped with a new exhaust valve, with just enough time to get to the store before it closed at 6 p.m. I was home when Mrs. Brooks called to give me the shocking news. Ed had gotten to the store all right, and he even made it most of the way back. But coming down the 105 Mile hill he "failed to negotiate one of the curves," as the police put it, and spent the last seconds of his life flying 60 feet through the air to land in a cow pasture. He was dead at the scene.

The whole town was there to pay their last respects to an exceptional human being. I hadn't yet learned all the words to "Nearer My God to Thee," but it mattered little. My voice would have failed me in any event. The minister was right in his assertion that God, in His infinite wisdom, preferred only the best among us to die young. Apparently he was not fussy at all whether they died as soldiers on a battlefield or in a Jimmy pickup sailing into a cow pasture. I could not have been more devastated if I had lost one of my brothers or my sister. In the hall of fame where I honour my heroes, Ed occupies a prominent place.

Ed's untimely death spelled the end to my apprenticeship in carpentry and the construction business, although I had gained enough experience to finish the house we had bought and to benefit from what I had learned. It is still there today, the modest little one-storey house with less than a thousand square feet, situated on a corner lot just a block off the highway behind the hotel. It was our first home and a source of immense pride because we had done the bulk of the finishing work ourselves.

My next foray into entrepreneurship took me in a most unlikely direction. Like most people, Joan and I were constantly worried about becoming sick or suffering an accident without any insurance. I recall a weekend visit to a German family who had settled near Lac la Hache, about 30 kilometres north. We found them in a total state of panic. One of their children had swallowed a thumbtack that appeared to be lodged in the child's throat. I offered to drive them to the hospital in Williams Lake, but they refused because not only were they short on cash, but they also still owed a bill dating back to the delivery of the same child two years earlier. Finally we managed to persuade them to let us help out and pay whatever it would cost to treat the poor child.

When I expressed my concern for the health of my own family to Mr. Brooks, he offered to put me in touch with his own insurance agent to get some protection. At the end of my first meeting with Mr. Henderson, an agent with Canada Health and Accident Insurance, I had ample protection against any assault on our savings precipitated by one of the kids eating thumbtacks, and also had an offer to become an agent for his company.

There would be a two-week on-the-job training period, which he himself would conduct, after which I would be on my own. Only the sky was the limit to the amount of money I would earn, he said, depending on the time and effort I was prepared to contribute to the enterprise. "Take whatever time you need to think about it and let me know what you decide."

I took all the time it took to move from the kitchen table to the front door to make the decision. Two weeks later I was on a mission, bringing comfort and relief to the masses concerned about becoming sick or falling victim to an accident.

In the main, there were two problems that quickly dampened my enthusiasm for my new independent business career. The first had to do with the fact that none of the people I was visiting in remote logging camps and farmhouses all over the Cariboo were sick at the time, had swallowed any thumbtacks, or were making plans to meet with sudden death in the near future. The other, I discovered, was the difficulty I have trying to impose myself on people the way a Jehovah's Witness or a Fuller Brush salesperson would do, particularly to persuade them to spend their hard-earned money on something for which they saw no practical value or need.

Ironically, my very first solo sales trip proved exactly the opposite and almost got me into hot water.

I was spending a hot afternoon in a dusty little settlement near Horsefly, giving my sales pitch to a housewife with two little kids hanging on her apron. I sensed right away that she could not bring herself to say no, but on the other hand she lacked the courage to say yes. "Why don't you talk it over with your husband when he comes home, and I'll come back later in the evening?" I said.

Her husband, as it turned out, was operating a loader in a logging camp 30 kilometres away in the bush and wouldn't be home until the weekend.

"Would he mind if I drove out to see him?" I asked. She had no objection since the decision would be up to him anyway. I was on my way.

It wasn't the best venue to deliver a sales pitch, but he did give me his ear for a minute while he was waiting for another truck to pull up for a load of logs. Finally, spotting an opportunity to get rid of me, he agreed to my suggestion that I leave some pamphlets with his wife, together with an application form they could send in if they chose to buy the protection we were offering.

Now a good salesman would never let anyone off the hook that easily. Knowing full well that I would never hear from them again, I suggested an even better idea to the wife. Why couldn't we fill out and sign the form, without any risk or obligation, and give them the coverage while they thought about it some more? Then I would simply call back the following week to get their approval to proceed. No doubt more interested in getting rid of me than applying for insurance, she did as I suggested, warning me that her husband might not like what she was doing and making me promise that I would do nothing before he himself gave the approval.

Unfortunately, the poor guy never got the chance. He was strapping a cable on the last load of logs before going home for the weekend when something snapped, crushing him against his loader. He never made it to the hospital. One of the neighbours called me the following Sunday to inquire about the value of the insurance policy his friend's wife had bought from me earlier in the week. I was sweating bullets.

Apart from Mr. Henderson, I had never talked to, nor met, anyone from the insurance company, and it was only on the strength of a 30-day cancellation clause featured on the application form that I had made the commitment to my client. The problem was that the paper was still in my briefcase and should perhaps have been mailed in to be valid. I couldn't reach Mr. Henderson until the following day to give him the news. There would be an inquiry, he thought, but given that I was an official agent, he could see no reason why we would not pay. In fact, to my absolute surprise and to their credit, Canada Health and Accident did honour the policy, paying the widow $20,000.

After that, no doubt I could have found all kinds of new clients for Mr. Henderson in that little settlement, but I had lost interest in doing something I was not cut out for. I stuck with being an insurance salesman just long enough to find another job, which mercifully was not difficult at that time.

The telephone company hired a crew to extend its service to Lone Butte, about eight kilometres off the main highway south of 100 Mile House. The pay was good, but recruits for this type of back-breaking work were scarce. The postholes had to be dug by hand in advance of the line crews, who were setting the poles and stringing the wire. It was a temporary job, but for the moment it replaced the income I had lost.

While I was working on the line, an opportunity came up that almost sent us back to Vancouver. One of the senior company men who periodically checked the crew on the line had taken a liking to me. He asked me during a lunch break if I would be interested in a career with his company. He offered to inquire on my behalf at their recruiting office, which at the time was hiring trainees for middle-management positions. If I were successful, it meant relocating to Vancouver, at least for the training period.

It wasn't what we were looking for, but there were not a whole lot of other options available for us to consider. Our present situation forced us to submit to a reality check. We had avoided going into debt, but most of what we had managed to save had been invested in the house. It would likely be several more years before we could think about investing in a business. Furthermore, we now had three small children to fit into the equation. The prospect of a steady job with a large company started to look attractive.

However, before we could give up on part of our dream, another opportunity presented itself. Gordon Butterfield, the neighbour across the street and a good friend, happened to manage the local bulk station for Standard Oil. He invited the company's regional representative, Bud Harper, to join us for our customary Wednesday night beer at the hotel.

Another thing one needs to know about small northern communities is that the local beer parlour, in this case the "Men Only" section, fills in for the employment agency, the stockbroker, the business centre, and any of the other facilities one would have occasion to contact in larger places. The urinals are the town's mainstream of commercial and social activity. Joan found it difficult to understand that periodic visits to the beer parlour were essential—never more so than in this case.

In response to Gordon's elaborate and generous introduction, which included most of the salient parts of my life story, Mr. Harper mentioned the fact that his company was in the midst of a major expansion of service station facilities to serve their customers commuting between Alaska and the lower 49 states. Perhaps I might be interested in becoming a franchisee and taking on the proprietorship of one of the service outlets, three of which were in the final stages of construction.

After two more rounds, one of which I hosted myself, the deal was fairly well consummated. We would be required to invest in the neighbourhood of about $5,000 for start-up inventory, plus whatever we might need to sustain ourselves for the first month. After the third beer, he invited me to visit the sites and take my pick of whichever one we liked best. It was suggested that, in a pinch, the company might even be prepared to advance the necessary funds until the money we had invested in our house could be freed up.

"Why don't you and your missus take a trip up there next weekend and let me know if you are interested?" Mr. Harper suggested as we were navigating through the row of tables toward the front door.

Joan may have been more interested in spending a couple of days on our own (Mrs. Butterfield had offered to look after the kids) than she was in the prospect of being uprooted again. But knowing that this could be our best and perhaps last chance to realize our dream of becoming independent, it was worth investigating. The two available sites that interested us were at McLeod Lake and Little Prairie, and both were farther north and much more remote than even 100 Mile House.

It was a beautiful late-summer day, the air spiced with the aroma of fresh-cut hay, when we made our way past Williams Lake to explore new territory. The Fraser River from time to time lent its reflection of the sun to add sparkle to the natural beauty of the spectacular scenes that unfolded with every turn in the road. At noon we stopped outside Prince George, a city of about 35,000 people at the time, for a picnic before we tackled the next 160 kilometres along the Hart Highway to McLeod Lake, our first destination.

There were long stretches of road between Quesnel and Prince George that had not yet been hard-surfaced, and there was only a short distance on the other side of Prince George that was paved. For the rest of the way we had to pound our latest car, a 1956 Chevrolet, over what could best be described as a logging road that had been carved out of the bush to follow the path of least resistance. A sign over the new Standard Oil service station, the first substantial structure we came to, indicated we had reached our first goal.

There was only one other building of significance, a "lodge," which was located next door and was just a roadside restaurant and camping place. It shouldn't be said that the place was underpopulated. Quite the contrary. But we only counted 26 human beings—presumably these could be considered potential customers of the new service establishment. The other billion or so inhabitants were all dogs and blackflies. Even though we knew next to nothing about the service station business, we thought we had all the expertise needed to know that a skate-sharpening shop in the Canary Islands would be a far more viable proposition than what Standard Oil was expecting from their McLeod Lake establishment.

The sensible thing to do was to write off the experience as a wild goose chase and turn back, but it was only another 160 kilometres to Little

Prairie. Lured on by the mountains of the Hart Range towering in the distance, our blue Chevy was soon trailing a cloud of dust farther up the winding road, and just a short while later we reached the summit of 2,200-metre Pine Pass. The air was rich with the aroma of the conifers, the scenery breathtakingly beautiful. This had not been a wasted trip after all.

We followed the Pine River, which, after collecting the waters yielded by the snow-capped mountains and carving its way through the rugged terrain, now shared the space it had created with the road. After another few hours of torturous pounding, this brought us to our next destination. Late in the evening we pulled up in front of a modern hotel that, just recently built, was actually worthy of the name. The new service station, still in the final stages of construction, was beside it in the area that had been cleared off on the left side of the highway.

After we had checked into a comfortable room and treated ourselves to a hearty meal, we set out to survey the surroundings. Apart from a small post office, Little Prairie still lacked any of the other facilities by which its status could be assessed. There was only a mountain of sawdust from an abandoned sawmill where the government liquor store and the other downtown assets would eventually be positioned. But this place was full of life and bustling with activity. The patrons of the overcrowded beer parlour were washing down the dust they had swallowed on the construction site of a major new sawmill, which was being built by the Fort St. John Lumber Company.

Sig Schilling, who together with several of his brothers had come here from the prairies to work in the forest industry for the winter and had eventually decided to stay for good, was the first person we met. We could not have found anyone more accommodating and enthusiastic about the future prospects for this place. It required some imagination to make sense of the confusion, muck, and debris left behind by the construction crews, but Sig had enough imagination for the three of us.

He spoke of the railroad that was scheduled to arrive that fall. Little Prairie was to become the divisional point for the railway, which would branch out to serve Dawson Creek to the east and Fort St. John to the north. It would tap the vast resources of B.C.'s north, claiming the wealth that had previously found its way to the markets of the world via the Northern Alberta Railway. The town would also be connected to the natural gas line already built across the mountains, and there was talk of a giant hydroelectric project to be built on the Peace River near Hudson's Hope.

Now this sounded more like what we were looking for. The opportunities would be limitless. The fact that there was no place to rent or buy and that the town lacked even the most basic amenities seemed to us only a minor consideration.

It didn't hurt that Sig also spoke fluent German, his background being much like that of Bill Lekei. The family, originally from Sachsen, had emigrated to Russia, from which they came to help settle the prairies. We talked late into the night, generating enough interest for us to take a closer look at the situation in daylight.

"I'll be your first customer," Sig said when he left us with our heads spinning, tormented by the decisions that had to be made. If that wasn't enough to rob us of much-needed sleep, the familiar noises coming from the beer parlour below did the rest.

When we left about an hour after breakfast to tackle the 650-kilometre journey back to 100 Mile House, we had seen all there was to see of Little Prairie. Neither of us was courageous enough to venture an opinion, each wrestling with our own thoughts and emotions. No question, this was what we had dreamt about when we left Germany, but we were no longer as free and flexible as one would need to be to strike out on such an adventure. We now had three small children to think about, and both of us would have sold our souls to the devil to spare them anything like our own childhood.

On the other hand, how could we spend the rest of our lives tormented by the thought that we had missed an opportunity to break out of the stifling social class into which we had been born and to give our lives some real meaning? Our private thoughts were interrupted only by the cars we met going in the opposite direction, causing us to wonder how many of them would refuel and spend their money at the new service station.

Dead tired, we made it back safely late Sunday night. We had just gone to bed when the phone rang. "Hello, this is Bud Harper. I wonder if you took us up on the offer to visit some of our new stations in the north? Have you had time to think about it and reach a decision?"

Throughout our lives our children and friends often marvelled at Joan's immunity to shock and her tolerance for pain. She had a lot of conditioning.

"Well, Mr. Harper," she overheard me say on this occasion, "your timing is perfect. We have just come back and, yes, we have decided. We have settled on the one in Little Prairie."

As I hung up the phone she was beside me. Her eyes seemed to say, "Are you sure you know what you are doing?" Perhaps we should have talked about it some more. But we both knew this would be our last chance and if we failed, we failed together. Little did she know that her faith in my judgement, her trust, and her absolute loyalty would be tested on many other occasions. Yet there would never be any recriminations from her, even when things went wrong.

Three weeks later we had sold the house, quit our jobs, and were on our way to meet our destiny.

CHAPTER 18

Chetwynd

Small opportunities are often the beginning of great enterprises.
—Demosthenes, Athenian orator and statesman

On August 28, 1958, we coaxed our Chevy and all our worldly belongings north over the 100 Mile House hill to tackle the 650 kilometres of treacherous road for the third time in as many weeks. It was exactly 209 years after Wolfgang von Goethe's birth and five years before Martin Luther King's march on Washington to deliver his "I have a dream" speech.

The connection to the two historic titans is significant. Of all the dozens of poems and literary works our teachers obligated us to memorize verbatim, Goethe's were always my favourite. In "*Der Schatzgraeber*"—"The Treasure Hunter"—he pointed to poverty as the greatest evil, and wealth the greatest blessing. Unlike Father Dorer, who ruled out salvation in heaven for all the wealthy, Goethe legitimized the pursuit of wealth. He pointed to two ways it could be attained: hard work and dealing with the devil. I'd had my fill of being poor, and just like Martin Luther King, Joan and I had a dream that someday there would be a light at the end of the tunnel, even for us. Fortunately, neither of us was afraid of hard work, so for the moment at least we were prepared to take Goethe's advice to reject Satan as a passenger on our way to fame and fortune. Here in Little Prairie, we hoped we would find the financial stability and the freedom that were so much a part of the goals we had set for ourselves.

Our determination to reject Satan was severely tested almost at once. Never was a new beginning so unpromising. First, Simpson's department store had refused to extend us credit to purchase furniture for our home in 100 Mile. We had been unable to prove that we owned the house outright because the property on which it was built belonged to Lord Martin Cecil, a British peer and leader of the Emissaries of Divine Light. The Emissaries owned the entire town and exercised control over the area, allocating building lots under a 99-year lease to anyone willing to abide by their rules. The local manager of the Imperial Bank of Commerce had offered to advance us whatever we might deem to be necessary, but since we were seldom home to sit on a couch anyway and had gotten used to sleeping on the floor (no broken arms from falling out of bed in our family), we never took him up on it.

This meant we had little furniture and the move was very basic, which had its advantages. The biggest expense was the installation of a hitch at the tail end of the 1956 Chevrolet and the acquisition of a $75 homemade utility trailer to hook to it. Apart from a bag full of "Dollar Day" Army and Navy shoes (Joan never managed to subdue her instincts for frugality when it came to shoes), there were bags full of clothes, diapers (the washable kind), baby bottles, a box full of tools (I still have some of them), a kitchen table with four chairs, and a fridge.

Our good friend and neighbour Karl Klassen, a Free Evangelist minister, contributed a tarp to cover it all and a sermon invoking God to urge His only begotten son to come along for the ride to assure our safety. I recall wondering where he would sit, since every square inch inside the car was occupied, but Karl assured us that Jesus, resourceful as he was, would take up little space. In fact, we wouldn't even know he was there.

All went well at first. We stopped a few times for picnics and to check the gear. The climb to the summit at Pine Pass did challenge the horses under the Chevy's hood, but soon we were rewarded with the breathtaking panoramic view from the top. It would be all downhill from here. Soon the sky opened wide to invite us to a more gentle landscape that eventually flattened out to assume the characteristics of the great prairies. Our spirits were high as we worked through our extensive repertoire of German folk songs to keep ourselves entertained.

We came very close to reaching our destination—just 10 short kilometres to go—when disaster struck. I was making good time, perhaps too good, dodging potholes and boulders that had escaped the road-builder's crusher. Then I felt the rear of the car being pulled from side to side. Risking a look through the rear-view mirror, I was horror-struck to see the trailer, which had followed so obediently all day, suspended in mid-air. The hitch had broken and only the safety chain kept it attached to the car. Fortunately, it too broke, sending the trailer crashing to the ground and releasing the car as the trailer then passed it in a series of somersaults along the ditch to our right.

It took all my skills to tame the Chevy, which was veering from side to side, spewing rocks and gravel to cover the entire area in a cloud of dust that must have been visible for miles. When it settled, it exposed a scene of total devastation. The trailer had disintegrated. The impact had crushed every box and container, spilling the contents all over the landscape. Only the fridge appeared to have escaped with minor scratches and dents.

The use of seatbelts had not yet become customary, and our first concern was for the children, who were absolutely horrified by the experience. I was torn between releasing a stream of Panicky Bell-type obscenities at our divine passenger, who must have fallen asleep on the job, and praising him for saving us from serious injury. Once we regained control of our emotions, we scattered across the vicinity to retrieve some bits of paper and family pictures the wind had taken possession of. I also picked up my tools and left the rest until we could find a way to salvage it.

As we rolled over the last knoll on the road, behind which Little Prairie was hiding, I was exercising my vocal cords singing Julius Fucik's "Entrance of the Gladiators," causing Joan to speculate that I had lost the few marbles I might have had left. Anxious to get back to the scene of the accident, we installed the children at the service station, and Sig Schilling helped us find a truck to return for our belongings.

It was too late. Apart from the injured fridge, the site had been picked clean. Gone were the broken table and the chairs, boxes of books, my modest photo-lab equipment, our kitchen utensils, the children's toys, and everything else to which we had either a utilitarian or a nostalgic attachment. Someone among our future neighbours, we had to assume, had needed our worldly belongings more than we did, or else the neighbourhood had an overdeveloped sense of tidiness. We took just enough time to load the fridge before we rushed back to the village, now worried that whoever was cruel enough to profit from our misfortune in such a callous way might be inclined to kidnap our children as well.

We scrapped our initial plan of taking a room at the hotel for the first night, opting instead to camp out in the service station. It was now substantially complete, except for the grading of the entrance road, and despite the noxious odour of the freshly dried paint, it offered hot and cold running water, flushing toilets, and a central heating system.

Joan and I had to dig very deep that night to find words to comfort each other and the strength to face whatever the following day had in store for us. In the morning, never ones to accept defeat, but dejected, worried, and bleary-eyed from lack of sleep and the previous day's events, we stepped outside to be greeted by a bright sunny day—and our next couple of problems.

Since our first visit, workers had installed a huge sign above the station; the Chevron logo shared the space with big bold letters spelling "Chetwynd." Apparently the company, after being told that the new railway station would be named after Ralph Chetwynd, a former minister in the provincial government, had been persuaded to adopt the name as well. The newer element in town—the hotel and real estate developers— were promoting the idea of changing the name of the town to coincide with the railway's decision. It didn't take us long to discover that the original settlers were less than pleased with this idea and would resist any efforts toward that end.

The other problem was living quarters. It had not escaped our attention during the prior visit that Little Prairie was home to a sizable population of construction and mill workers with whom we had to compete for living accommodation. The place was scattered with makeshift trailers and tarpaper shacks, with only a few structures that could be described as houses. Again we called on our new friend Sig Schilling for advice on how to go about finding a place suitable to our needs. Much to our surprise, Sig, who had so recently infected us with his enthusiasm for moving to Little Prairie, was now the bearer of bad news.

"There is nothing to rent or buy in this place for love nor money," he declared. Further, commenting on the new sign over the service station, he warned us that the "old-timers" had already decided on a boycott of the new place as their first defensive move to save the much cherished name of their town.

The news was not getting any better.

Fortunately we had often been in situations where it seemed impossible to imagine how things could get worse. Looking on the bright side, we didn't have the money for renting a house anyway. It would be some time before we could expect to receive the proceeds from the sale of our home in 100 Mile House, and we had to replace some of the essentials we had lost the night before and pay out what we had committed to the oil company. Still, if someone had offered me a trip around the world for just a nickel's worth of my goodwill toward mankind, I couldn't have gotten out of sight.

Sig did suggest that I visit Norm Stirling, who was managing a hardware and supply store for the lumber company. So I trotted off to see Norm at his store.

He and his wife, Beverly, were newcomers as well. In fact, Beverly was the daughter of Gordon Moore, the owner of both the lumber company and the new hotel. It was he who had persuaded the oil company to build the service station. Norm and Beverly were curious to know who had been recruited to manage it. Danny, Beverly's younger brother, was to have been the proprietor as part of the plan, but he had changed his mind during a training session in Vancouver after a taste of what would be expected of him.

Norm was eager to help in any way he could, and the two of them are among our very best friends to this day. He couldn't offer much, but there was an old 8- by 20-foot bunkhouse, surplus to the company's needs, that we could have for a temporary residence. He even arranged to have it skidded behind the service station that very afternoon.

It would have been an understatement to call the bunkhouse primitive, but it had to do. Sure, the walls had no insulation or sheeting on the inside, there were no utilities, and the bunk beds were very basic, but it would serve the purpose. By day's end we had connected some power outlets to the place and were pleasantly surprised to find that the fridge, which we had strategically positioned in a corner to hide most of its scrapes and bruises, greeted us with its steady hum when we plugged in the cord.

Already things were looking up enough to expose some of the bright sides of our situation. We had a home, of sorts, which was close enough to the kids that we could keep an eye on them and avoid the cost of a babysitter. And soon we had customers. At about nine the following morning the first one pulled up to the gas pumps to help us launch our business career. An hour or so later the second customer was a young boy in need of having his bicycle tires inflated.

With only a few of the locals to patronize the enterprise, it was a slow start. The Native inhabitants, who made up about half the population, showed little interest in the political battle and did visit the station. Unfortunately, only a few of them had cars or pickup trucks needing our services, although there was usually a lineup at the entrance to the washroom at the side of the building as curious people stopped for their first experience with a flushing toilet.

Not all the old-timers joined the boycott, and Gordon Moore himself stopped in to promise us all his company's business, providing of course we gave good service. He never once reneged on his promise. Even though there were times when it was exceedingly difficult to carry his credit, Gordon became a good, reliable friend and steady customer.

We also had not miscalculated the volume of highway traffic, of which we were soon getting a major share. We had our first foothold in our new home.

Before the 1950s, Chetwynd, or Little Prairie, had just been a wide spot on the road, with a small service station, a store, and a post office catering to the rural farm population, mostly from the prairies, that had settled the area following the Great Depression. With the completion of the John Hart Highway in 1952, connecting Prince George to Dawson Creek and the timber and mineral resources along the way, new people moved in and created demand for additional and expanded services. But it wasn't until later in the decade that the town started to grow and prosper after Gordon Moore chose Little Prairie as the most central place to locate his company, Fort St. John Lumber, and, in anticipation of the railway's arrival, built a modern hotel, with the help of two partners.

Most of the Native people in the area lived around Moberly Lake, 25 kilometres to the north, but there was also a sizable number of Native and non-status Native people who had migrated to Little Prairie, drifting from job to job in some of the small sawmills and logging camps. Most came from northern Alberta, some having chosen to accept "scrip," a $3,000 payment for the surrender of their rights under Treaty No. 8, which covered all the territory east of the mountains in British Columbia, northern Alberta, and even some parts of Saskatchewan.

Little Prairie's old-timers had grown fond of their isolated rural way of living and, understandably, did not mix well with the newcomers, some of whom, like Joan and me, were looking for entrepreneurial opportunities and wanted to promote a faster pace of growth and development. The split between the two camps lasted for years and was sometimes bitter.

A classic example is the story of our missing stationery. Standard Oil had promised to have all the office supplies and stationery for the service station on site by the time of our arrival, but our inquiries at the post office were fruitless. Finally, after about two weeks, the company's representative arrived, insisting that several boxes of the material, including the credit card slips critical to doing business with American travellers, had been shipped in plenty of time to facilitate our opening. In an attempt to trace the errant shipment, we paid a personal visit to Ernie Pfanner, the postmaster.

"Maybe," Mr. Pfanner suggested, "it was addressed wrong"—something he had noted happening quite frequently lately. "Any mail addressed to Chetwynd instead of Little Prairie, for instance, goes directly into the wastebasket." Would he be so kind as to check his wastebasket to see if our shipments had by chance ended up there?

"No," he replied in his strong Austrian accent. "I wouldn't get anything done if I had to rummage through the wastepaper basket for every Tom, Dick, and Harry that comes in here."

Ernie had a change of heart and did discover the shipment—almost immediately after he received a phone call from his head office in Vancouver, where we had called to register a complaint. It was no more than half an hour after our visit that he came driving up to the front door of the station to deliver our mail personally, though not in any conventional way, of course. Using the soccer skills he must have acquired back in Austria, he kicked the pile of parcels off the back of his pickup into the dust of the as yet unpaved driveway.

It was the beginning of a long, less than harmonious relationship.

The winter was not exceptionally harsh that year, which was a good thing because the makeshift heaters we had installed in the bunkhouse were taxed to the limits, often forcing us to huddle together during the night to stay warm, establishing our own definition of a close-knit family. Fortunately, by spring the following year, one of the few small rental homes Don Titus, one of Gordon Moore's partners, had built to house employees became vacant, allowing Joan and me the luxury of once again sleeping in our own bedroom.

There was little time to miss any of the other conveniences one usually associates with a home. Both of us were manning the service station 16 hours a day, seven days a week, and volunteering the bulk of whatever "spare time" we had after caring for the kids to a vast array of community projects.

Joan and I soon learned that to survive and prosper in a community like Little Prairie, we had to get involved in its affairs. It's necessary to contribute to those volunteer efforts that fill the vacuum left by the lack of services and amenities only much larger, more established centres can afford. Most isolated northern resource towns are made up of young people whose extended families live elsewhere in faraway places. People therefore must rely for support in critical situations on the generosity of their friends and neighbours. We discovered that the personal benefits and rewards, the comfort and security one enjoys in such places are in direct proportion to the value of one's own contribution to the general welfare of the community. It was difficult at first to risk some of the independence we worked so hard to achieve in order to gain acceptance in the community and the refuge that it guaranteed, but the rich rewards that flowed from it far outweighed the sacrifices.

Among the benefits was the privilege of becoming acquainted with some truly fascinating characters. One of them, another of our early customers, was Father Jungbluth. Like Father Schweitzer from Lillooet, Father Jungbluth was an Oblate priest. His missionary career had brought him to the shores of Moberly Lake to minister to the needs of two Native bands there.

Unlike Father Schweitzer, Jungbluth was much more progressive, worldly, and innovative in his approach to God's work. He was a skilled electronics technician, able to build and repair his own radios, as well as his motorcycle or whatever motorized contraption the Lord was providing him with at the time.

He introduced himself in German with a somewhat rusty Alsace dialect, offering us his patronage in exchange for certain favours, such as the occasional use of space and the lift in our repair shop to lubricate and service his pickup.

At first I thought I had got by far the better of the bargain. He not only tutored me in my new vocation as an automotive mechanic, but also could be called upon to bail me out of a particularly complex or stubborn situation. However, in time the balance tilted much more in his direction. For one thing, he would not allow anyone but Joan to fill up his gas tank, knowing she would, more often than not, forget to ring the transaction through the cash register. He also reacquired a taste for German home cooking and baking, of which he had been deprived ever since he left his mother's house in the Strasbourg region, about 80 kilometres from Forchheim. Worst of all, he started to compete for Joan's time and talents to help with his own work.

She was promoted to president of the Catholic Women's League, charged with the responsibility of keeping an eye on God and substituting for Him on the all-too-frequent occasions when He failed to provide for Jungbluth's needs and those of his parishioners.

Father Jungbluth's exploits were legendary. In his early days, even before 1942, when the U.S. Army Corp of Engineers built the road from Dawson Creek, B.C., to Fairbanks, Alaska, presumably to repel a Japanese invasion of Alaska, he would venture as far as Fort Nelson, 480 kilometres to the north. Using not much more than game trails, he travelled by motorcycle in his quest to track down any Native heathens on the way so as to introduce them to the blessings and wonders of our civilization. Apart from an array of spare parts for his "iron pony," he only carried with him what was necessary to administer the Holy Sacraments.

Profiting from his familiarity with modern technology, he would, in rare cases, only after every conventional method had failed, devise the most ingenious ways to communicate with his faithful—via a direct link to God himself.

So it was that Napoleon, then chief of the Salteaux band, became the first beneficiary of an early version of what we know today as an "up-link." Napoleon, a hard-working, successful trapper and a highly respected leader among his people, was showing signs of drifting back to a spiritual universe more traditional to his culture. He no longer felt the urge to attend the house Father Jungbluth had built for his god. This situation called for extraordinary measures.

Heavily laden with the harvest his trap line had yielded, Napoleon was making his way on the familiar path along the shore of the lake. As it was mid-winter, darkness had descended early. The temperature was bitterly cold, and the little moisture in the air had formed an icy fog, giving the scene a ghost-like, surreal ambience. Just as he came to the vicinity of Father Jungbluth's quaint log church, Napoleon heard something. He could clearly discern, from somewhere directly above him, someone calling his name: "Napoleon."

He froze in his tracks. Cautiously, after a few seconds, he decided that his mind was playing tricks on him and took some tentative steps, but just as he had regained some of his composure and resumed his gait, there it was again, this time much more urgent: "N-a-p-o-l-e-o-n!"

Extricating himself from the bundle of furs strapped to his back, cold sweat drenching his body, he started running, but there was no escape. This time the voice was like roaring thunder that sent him crashing into a tree: "N-A-P-O-L-E-O-N!"

He could just make out the outline of the church as he picked himself off the ground. Throwing all caution to the wind, he made a wild dash for it. Miraculously, just as he stumbled up the front steps, the door opened wide, exposing Father Jungbluth, coal-oil lamp in hand, lending himself the appearance of a visitor from another dimension.

Napoleon, his whole body shaking, collapsed to his knees in front of him. "Forgive me, Father, I have sinned," he managed to say.

It took all of the good Father's not inconsiderable power of persuasion and some divine intervention to stabilize Napoleon's condition enough that he could find the courage to resume his way home.

Later on, he must have found it curious that God spoke in much the same accent and tone of voice as Father Jungbluth when he acted as the master of ceremonies at the local Moberly Lake rodeo and announced, through his loudspeaker, the names of the horses and riders who were entertaining the masses.

Regardless, Napoleon never missed another Sunday mass.

Likewise, Joan and I and the children seldom failed to attend the church Father Jungbluth's Little Prairie parishioners had built for him, even though I often thought that I could deliver a much better sermon.

Joan and I were God's partners in providing His earthly representative with transportation at greatly reduced prices. In all, we supplied Jungbluth with three cars (actually, one car and two pickups). These—plus the one Father Jungbluth was driving when we arrived—God, as His part of the bargain, had equipped with guiding angels. Jungbluth wrecked all of them totally, fortunately without killing anyone in the process and miraculously escaping every mishap without so much as a scratch.

On one occasion he called on me late in the evening, wondering whether I would have time to pick him up at Hudson's Hope, where he was giving a slide presentation to raise funds for one of his many projects.

"The pickup," he said, "slid off the side into a snowbank coming down the hill toward the Peace River, so we might need a winch to get it back on the road." It sounded simple. I arrived in time to catch the last of his presentation, and soon after we were on our way home. After no less than two hours driving up and down the Peace River hill, we hadn't found the slightest sign of either Father's pickup or, for that matter, any disturbance of the snowbank where it had "slipped off the road."

It wasn't till the next day that we found the pickup, revealing a much different scene than the one described to me the night before. Only part of the front bumper and one of the headlights were peeking out of the snow, no less than 40 metres off the road. Our sky pilot, as he was affectionately referred to by the locals, had lost control of the vehicle at what must have been a fair clip. Somehow it had somersaulted across the road, becoming airborne before it reached the bank and cleared the ditch on the other side. The price for the salvage of what was left of the pickup was not worth the effort to retrieve it. Guiding angels apparently have compassion only for the faithful pilgrims themselves, not for their pickups or for trailers behind old Chevys.

Jungbluth confessed he didn't remember much of the incident. Someone travelling close behind in the same direction had managed to bring his own car to a stop on the icy road, just in time to assist the good Father with his climb up the steep hill, up to his hips in snow, projector under one arm, the box of slides under the other, and mainly worried that he might be late for his presentation.

Jungbluth did help restore my faith in guiding angels and the power of the Lord, at least partially. It was the Lord acting in partnership with, among others, the Catholic Women's League, Gordon Moore, and Peter and Paul Demeulemeester, the logging contractors, who built the big youth centre at Moberly Lake.

Few were as concerned as Father Jungbluth by the deplorable living conditions of his Native parishioners settled near Little Prairie. All of them were living in poorly built houses and tarpaper shacks dotted around the fringes of the little community. They had no services or conveniences. I have known poverty and despair, but nothing—certainly not my Karl May-inspired interest in the North American Aboriginal people—had prepared me for some of our first encounters with our new Little Prairie neighbours. Their presence in the midst of a thriving, bustling community became for both Joan and me a source of profound interest and curiosity. We were deeply troubled and concerned, not only for the welfare of the many children, but also by the lack of concern or charity offered by the rest of the community. Most of the adults were alcoholics, spending much of their time in the beer parlour of the new hotel or walking around in a drunken stupor, sobering up only in time to attend Jungbluth's Sunday morning mass.

It was not long after we arrived that a particular incident gave us cause to wonder whether we could ever feel at home in the community where we had chosen to build our lives. We were visited by the only policeman, who had set up temporary quarters in a small trailer outside town, asking us to be on the lookout for a particular model of pickup. It had been involved in an accident on the previous night, causing the death of a Native couple. After a night of serious drinking in the "Ladies and Escorts" section of the local beer parlour, they had been making their way home along the highway when, apparently, they were struck by a vehicle. The impact had thrown them several metres into a ditch, where their children discovered their dead bodies the following morning.

Astoundingly, apart from Ron, the policeman, no one seemed to be overly alarmed or concerned by the situation. "Just a couple of drunken Indians staggering across the road, making it unsafe for decent folks to drive on."

Joan and I were somewhat surprised when, two days later, a prominent citizen—the son of his clan's patriarch, a wealthy farmer—steered his pickup under the big Chetwynd sign of our service station. It was exactly the kind of patron we had been told to watch out for. Eager to make the best of our first opportunity to win a customer from among the old-timers, and such an important one to boot, I was out beside the pump before he could shift his sizable wad of chewing tobacco to one side of his mouth, enabling him to say, "Hoooo," and get the old jalopy stopped.

"It needs about two dollars' worth," he said as I twisted off the filler cap and attached the nozzle.

Nobody ever left our place without a thorough cleaning of the windows. In this particular case it meant doing it more from the inside, which had been sheltered from the natural cleaning power of the rain that normally looked after the rest of it. Undeterred by the healthy smell of cow manure, Joan was at it in a flash.

I was hoping to lure our new customer to the inside of our establishment to show off its other impressive assets, but he could only be persuaded to let me check the air pressure in the tires.

"Tell me," he said. "I wonder if you could give me a sort of appraisal of what I might expect to get for this old hootenanny on a trade for a newer pickup." Not having the slightest idea, I nevertheless wrinkled my face to give it the appropriate expression of curiosity and expertise and followed him on a tour of inspection.

"There are a few dents as you can see," he offered, "but the engine and gears have been well looked after and are in mint condition." I was relieved to be excused from having to render an opinion on that at least, but pointed out that before a dealer could resell it, he would have to install a muffler. It seemed to be missing altogether. The "few dents" would have been more accurately described as the effects of a demolition derby. In fact, they may have been put there by the farm's cattle, using their horns to show affection for the pickup, the source of their daily rations of hay. I did notice just the slightest difference between the tone of the yellow paint on the right front fender and the rest of the wreck, but sensing by that time that my customer would prefer me to overlook it, I chose not to give it a second thought.

In the end, we both agreed that it would be unkind to the old beast to remove it from its familiar surroundings, leaving it to eke out what little life it might have left in a strange setting.

I invited him to please come again as he manoeuvred his big frame and cowboy hat back behind the steering wheel.

"What a relief," he offered as his way of saying thanks for cleaning his windows. "I thought I was going blind."

My first instinct was to contact the police with my suspicions that I had been set up as a witness to the soundness of the vehicle, which, two nights before, might have deposited parts of its headlights and right front fender in the bodies of the two unfortunate victims. I knew full well that by doing so I would forgo any chance of winning over some of the old-timers as patrons for our business. We decided to delay the decision until the following day when, luckily, other events intervened, sparing us from having to make it.

Our intrepid policeman, with the assistance of a light airplane, had solved the crime without my help. Overflying the ranch property, he had observed a crew of mechanics exchanging the front fender of an old forklift with that of a pickup of the suspected model. It would have been useless to deny the obvious any longer.

Our new customer's son and one of his friends had been on a bit of a tear and had decided to put the old pickup with the well-maintained engine and gears through its paces. Poor visibility and bad road conditions no doubt contributed to the mishap. As they cruised through town at what must have been a fair clip, the pair explained later, two ghostlike figures had appeared out of nowhere, throwing themselves in the path of the pickup and making it impossible to avoid the collision.

The commissioner for taking affidavits and oaths, who incidentally happened to be not only the driver's grandfather but also the magistrate, managed to muster enough sympathy for the two ghostbusters to reduce the much more serious charge contemplated by the police constable to one of simple misdemeanour, reasoning that having had the hell scared out of them was punishment enough. In Little Prairie, at that time at least, it seemed that it was less of a crime to drive a pickup recklessly in unsafe conditions, resulting in the deaths of two people, than it was to be plastered and walking on the side of the highway late at night, particularly if one happened to be Native.

Yet, paradoxically, there were ample occasions when our fellow citizens displayed the other side of their human traits, inspiring much more love and affection and making us proud to live among them.

House fires were a common occurrence. With so many flimsy wooden structures in and around the community, there were often tragic consequences, and people were lucky to escape with little else but their lives. Even the best efforts of the new volunteer fire department were no match against the raging fury of the fire, once unleashed.

Whenever this happened, the community quickly came together to help out. Even before the ashes were dry, Gordon Moore would have ordered a truckload of lumber delivered to the site. The manager of the hotel made sure that any volunteer who showed up to help build a new house wouldn't go thirsty, and the hardware store supplied the required nails and hardware to start with the reconstruction. Ray Rebagilatti, the railway superintendent, and Ned Stubberfield, one of his employees, would mobilize their "dance orchestra" and invite the town to the Legion Hall for a benefit performance. The hall was donated, as was a cut of the profits from the copious amounts of booze that were dispensed to fuel such benefit concerts. The proceeds, together with generous individual donations of furniture and other household articles, often restored a burned-out family to a situation better than the one they had sacrificed to the flames.

Such selfless displays of charity were at times a source of discord between Joan and me because she seldom invited me to share in the joy of giving away our own hard-earned wealth.

Once I found myself and the kids forced to operate an electric toy train, which we had built in the rec room, from a standing position only. This was because our domain had been stripped of its perfectly good chesterfield suite to help out an unsavoury character who may not only have been partially responsible for putting his family into their desperate situation, but was also definitely among the least deserving of the town's charity. We had vowed to each other that, as a general rule, we would avoid exposing our children to senseless arguments, so I had chosen the silent treatment as a means of dealing with my occasional displeasure.

It was after a particularly hard day's work, when I had just retired to bed, that I was summoned by the police to attend a potentially life-threatening situation 30 kilometres out on the highway, involving who else but the beneficiary of Joan's charity. The barometer mounted outside the garage window when I left on the "rescue mission" indicated more than −30°F.

It turned out not to be a serious situation at all. My friend, chauffeuring some of his buddies home after a hard night of serious drinking, had simply failed to negotiate an icy curve on the road and was lodged in a snowbank, plugging the vehicle's exhaust pipe.

No one inside the car made any move to help with the work of digging under their car to attach a chain and winch cable so as to dislodge them from their predicament. I was in less than a good mood. In my frozen state I walked up to the driver's window to inquire about the method of payment for my services. The subject of Joan's most charitable instincts moved to lower the window just enough to reveal the upper part of his overweight torso, which to my surprise was clad in the very same turtleneck sweater my dear mother had knitted for me when I left home and which had kept me warm during some of the colder days on the Queen Charlotte Islands.

As far as payment was concerned, that would have to wait until the following day because the festivities had rendered him a bit short on cash. In other words, if I expected to ever get paid, I would have to beat it out of him. It took all my willpower to restrain myself from doing just that, right there and then. Needless to say, there was an unpleasant encounter between Joan and me when I finally got home in the wee hours of the morning. But as is always the case, neither of us benefited from the experience, other than to lose whatever much-needed sleep we might have enjoyed for the rest of the night.

CHAPTER 19

Finding Home

A man's homeland is wherever he prospers.
—Aristophanes, Athenian playwright

My home is not a place, it is people.
—Lois McMaster Bujold, American science-fiction author

Joan and I never knew precisely what we were looking for, but it wasn't long before we knew we had found it: our new home. We became part of an exciting process of building a new town, part of a community of pioneers who would shape it and make it grow and prosper. Like most of the other small entrepreneurs who had settled in the community, we believed that helping to promote the town would enhance our own fortunes. There was never a shortage of demand for volunteers and money for the many causes that would make Chetwynd the special place we all wanted it to be.

Just as Sig Schilling had predicted, we witnessed the arrival of the first train at the "Chetwynd" station in the fall of 1958. The legendary W.A.C. Bennett, premier of British Columbia, and some of his cabinet were on it and helped us with the official opening of the first bank and the inauguration of the town's natural gas service. Bennett made a rousing speech comparing our part of British Columbia to the Ruhr region in Germany, predicting a boom in industrial development that would have no rival anywhere in the world. He spoke of projects on the drawing board that would soon bring the world's industrialists and financiers to our doorstep. If we had any doubt at all about our move to Little Prairie, it was removed then and there.

With the highway connection to the south and the expansion of the railway completed, the first part of Premier Bennett's big dream had been accomplished. Next his focus shifted to exploitation of the resources and development of the area that had previously been inaccessible from the lower part of British Columbia, thus sparking a period of growth and expansion in forestry, agriculture, and tourism. The railway would eventually carry on to Dawson Creek, connecting to the Northern Alberta Railway, and to Fort St. John and even farther north to Fort Nelson. Only Prime Minister Diefenbaker's vision extended farther north. He could see a vast storehouse of natural resources, which he sought to exploit with his railway from Edmonton all the way to Hay River in the Northwest Territories. Chetwynd was destined to become the gateway to all this activity, including the massive hydro power project on the Peace River, 60 kilometres to the north, and the rich coal deposits to the south.

Inspired by the premier's message and his infectious enthusiasm, some of us felt that no time should be wasted getting the town prepared for the arrival of all these industrialists and financiers. Even before the year was out we had organized a Chamber of Commerce, of which I became the first president. This eventually led to the thrust toward the first stage of local government and later the incorporation of the village, but there were more immediate priorities to address. We needed a variety of services, not the least of which was a fire department.

What was initially lacking in equipment was made up for by the enthusiasm of an army of volunteers willing to contribute their time and skills. Gordon Moore had donated an old truck, and there was a 500-gallon tank that Chevron, our landlord at the service station, had declared surplus to its needs. The overhaul of the engine and the fitting of the tank and an auxiliary pump, which took up much of the volunteers' time, provided me with a most valuable crash course in fundamental mechanics and automotive maintenance. I was fascinated by the expertise everyone was able to contribute to the enterprise. The people who had migrated to the area from the prairies, some with little more than a three-year exposure to a one-room school in a remote farming community, might have difficulty deciphering the letters on a stop sign, but they were absolute geniuses in fixing broken-down machinery and building or repairing anything to which they set their minds.

Meanwhile, the expansion of the sawmill spawned a variety of other smaller businesses, generating some diversity in the local economy. The town now had a bank; modern hardware, clothing, and variety stores; and several other new commercial establishments.

In my capacity as the president of the Chamber of Commerce, I had a visit from a Mr. Phillips. He was planning to move his grocery and variety store from a small farming town in northern Alberta to a place offering greater prospects for growth.

"Nothing like getting in on the ground floor of some place that is destined to become the hub not only of a thriving farming area, but also of a range of other industrial enterprises," I suggested.

As luck would have it, our own business was flourishing to the point where we could afford to hire the occasional help. Joan and I both enjoyed dealing with the public. We still had a lot to learn, but the rewards for our labour were generous enough for us to think about expanding our range of services to take advantage of some new opportunities, even if it meant postponing building our own home.

In less than an hour, Lee Phillips and I shook hands on a deal that was tailored to meet both our needs. I would put up a two-storey building that would suit his plans for a store on the ground floor and give me living quarters for my family on top. There would be a built-in option for him to buy the place at a later date if he so desired. During construction he would contribute not only his own labour, but also that of two full-time workers who were having trouble clearing up a charge account he had been carrying for them at his previous location. The value of their contribution would be charged against an equal amount of rent he would be paying during the initial period.

Selling the idea to Joan was somewhat more problematic. Sure, she was dreaming about her own home, but as she sensibly pointed out, this was much more than we should be biting off at a time when additional investment in the business could yield much better results. Furthermore, there would be no income from the tenant for some time, making it difficult to service a mortgage.

"You don't know these people from a hole in the ground. What guarantee would we have that they would actually carry through with the deal?"

I hated it every time she confronted me with such brutal logic and unassailable reason.

"Perhaps I should discuss the matter with the manager at the new bank," I offered, as a means of keeping the idea alive.

Eager to generate some business, Joe Engelman, young, ambitious, and himself an enthusiastic supporter of the Chamber of Commerce, could see no reason why the bank would not assist with financing the project, providing, of course, the amount required was in the range serviceable by our business. There was nothing wrong then in taking the idea a step further by getting a local contractor to give us an estimate. In the end, I managed to build a strong enough case to gain Joan's blessing.

True to his word, which was all I had for security, Mr. Phillips not only helped supervise the construction, but also, together with his two friends, contributed most of the labour.

The first building block toward Chetwynd's incorporated municipal government was the establishment of a water improvement district. Gordon Moore and his partners had built a modest dam at Windrem Creek to store some of the water flowing through the settlement on its way to the Pine River, but it was designed only to accommodate the needs of the hotel, the sawmill, and some of the houses they had built for their staff. The idea was to enlarge the facility to service emerging needs. The Chamber of Commerce sponsored the effort and dispatched a delegation to Victoria to invite the government into a partnership for the enterprise.

It was my first of many such trips and my first experience of this kind. For a time Bert Chatham, an electronics technician with the railway who had agreed to serve as the chairman of the committee, and I spent more time on this project than we did on our own duties. There were consultants to be hired, surveys to be taken, and reports to be submitted, only to end up where we first started once it was determined that Windrem Creek, as one consultant put it, "Will not make a living for a family of ducks."

Back to Victoria to promote tapping the underground aquifer with a system of wells, but that in the end proved impractical. Preliminary testing yielded more natural gas than water.

It seemed that the only secure source of water for a town that matched our ambitious dreams was the Pine River. Sourcing water from there, however, required an elaborate pumping system and a sizable storage tank placed high on the hill behind town, and that would require a public referendum and the establishment of a legal entity to underwrite the cost. But the base of ratepayers was much too small to service any debt the construction of such a large project would incur. So the project stalled again. In the end, it took a commitment from Gordon Moore and some of the other businesses to pay a hefty premium on their water rates during an initial amortization period to convince the government to give us permission to proceed.

The sanitary sewer would have to await a further stage in the evolution of local government, meaning that outdoor toilets remained a prominent feature on the skyline of Little Prairie. They were also a popular target for pranksters.

Someone, no doubt inspired by Father Jungbluth's innovative use of modern technology, targeted the wife of one of the more prominent citizens for one such prank. On an urgent visit to the biffy she had manoeuvred her ample posterior to the most comfortable position on the family's "two-holer" when she was startled by a voice coming from the abyss below: "Would you kindly move over to the other hole, please? I'm painting down here."

Joe Engelman, having earned himself enough notoriety to become a target as well, was on an urgent mission to respond to the call of nature late one night when he found himself knee-deep in the residue he and his staff had deposited in their outhouse over time. He had failed to note that the structure had been relocated several feet back from its original position. He was not a happy camper.

It was not pranksters but a brisk wind that provided Joan with a hilarious spectacle on another occasion. She was on her way to the shop, using the back lane that led her past the rather fancy outhouse Emil Breitkreitz had built for himself. Emil was the proprietor of the variety store next to our new building. No one in town had ever seen him without his cowboy hat.

Joan was just passing the facility when a gust of wind blew open the door, exposing Emil, pants down to his ankles, his hat loosely perched on his head. He instinctively reached for the door with one hand, using the other to pull up his pants. Unfortunately, the sudden movement dislodged the hat, sending it sliding down his back. Obviously Emil considered what was concealed under the hat to be even more private than, in Joan's assessment, the not inconsiderable assets of his anatomy residing in his pants. He let go of the door to retrieve the hat, allowing the wind to resume its mischief. Like a juggler in a circus, the cycle repeated itself several times until Joan, pretending to lose interest in the performance, abandoned the scene. When she got to the office, it took her some time to recapture the breath she had exhausted in her fits of laughter.

Another service Little Prairie lacked was a newspaper, and during one of its meetings, the Chamber of Commerce decided that we needed one. I undertook to contact the people at 100 Mile House who were publishing a weekly flyer that served as both an archive for the latest gossip and the means for local businesses to advertise their wares and services.

As luck would have it, the proprietor had just installed some new equipment to cope with his expanding business and made me an offer I could not refuse: his old Gestetner for a reasonable price. The plywood shack that had served as our living quarters during the first winter was shifted 90 degrees to face the road and outfitted with a sign identifying it as the office of the Chetwynd Chamber of Commerce and the newspaper.

Any Chamber of Commerce worth its salt would hardly be comfortable promoting a town with "little" as part of its name. As well, there were several towns in the region that had already identified with their prairie roots. There was Grande Prairie, High Prairie, Sunset Prairie, Lone Prairie, and perhaps a dozen others. The idea of finding an original name for our town was gaining momentum. Since we had already made the bold decision to name the Chamber after Ralph Chetwynd, why not call our first newspaper "The Chetwynd Chinook"? It would take the old-timers a bit longer to identify with it, but there was now an increasing number among them who could see the benefits to themselves and their families of the progress that was being registered.

With neither of us able to point to any degree of proficiency in English literature, Joan and I decided the role we would play in connection with the enterprise was in the main limited to its mechanical aspects. Ed Hoffman, who was an accountant with Gordon Moore's enterprises, became the first editor. There was no shortage of people—such as Bea Kuriata—who not only contributed their exceptional talents, but also gave generously of their time to make the effort look respectable.

In the end, though, only Joan was able to tame the stubborn monster we had hauled up from 100 Mile House to serve as the printing press. Only she knew how to synchronize the rhythm of the hand crank with the paper feed and the flow of the ink, a good portion of which ended up on her hands and her arms up to the elbows. It took her a whole week, the time between editions, to remove it.

It wasn't that we had a whole lot of spare time. Major construction projects to upgrade the highway and build a major pipeline to tap the natural gas fields north of Fort St. John were underway, adding a new dimension to our business. For a time we were boasting the biggest turnover of tires of any retail outlet north of Edmonton. There were signs that some of the schemes the premier had been talking about were coming to fruition. The Bennett Dam, just north of Hudson's Hope, would offer exciting prospects for other industries and was already attracting hordes of fortune seekers to the area.

It proved to be a constant struggle to balance our civic duties with our thriving business while finding some time to share with the children. When the news of our move from 100 Mile House to Little Prairie reached Berta back in Forchheim, she replied with a strongly worded letter suggesting that if it was our intention to continue to live like adventurers or gypsies, we should at least consider sending our children back home to have them raised properly. Her worry, no doubt, was more about the lack of a proper church than of a doctor or hospital.

While Forchheim would have been furthest from our minds as a place to send our children, we were conscious of depriving them of much of the time we would have liked to share with them. Our new home above the store was a major improvement. It was a happy place, even though we didn't allow ourselves nearly enough time to enjoy it and there were occasions when the stress of a particularly busy day affected our judgement in dealing with disciplinary matters at home. Joan did insist on some rigid rules regarding mealtimes. Only the most urgent business was allowed to interfere with spending our supper hour together.

During the building of the store, Frank Jr. had a serious accident. Even at the ripe old age of one and a half, just after he had started to be comfortable on his feet, he was curious enough to inspect the new building. He fell off a plank the painters had installed over the stairs, landing 10 feet below at the front entrance. He seemed all right at first, but when he refused to be touched or leave his bed the following day, Mrs. Phillips, trained as a nurse, suggested we take him to the hospital in Dawson Creek for X-rays.

The results were not good. Frank had broken his hip in a place that was impossible to treat with a cast. By the time we left the hospital, our son's lower body was suspended by a rope fastened around the heels of his feet, with only his shoulders touching the mattress of his bed. His screams, when we finally had to leave him to the care of his tormentors, rang in our ears all the way back to Little Prairie. He was still screaming when I visited him for the first time a few days later. Whatever pain he must have felt was hurting me more, but the doctor suggested we not visit, so that Frank could get used

The 1958 Chevron gas station.

The 1960 grocery and variety store Frank built for Mr. Phillips, with upstairs living quarters.

The 1962 RCMP detachment.

The 1964 Imperial Oil Esso station and Ford dealership.

Frank and Joan's 1965 residence.

to the place. Finally, after about a month, we were given permission to take him home.

"There have been some complications that will require some further treatment," the doctor, who was waiting for us in the ward, explained. Apparently the tape fastened around Frank's ankles had cut through the padding, causing some irritation, as he put it, at the back of his heel. He gave us some ointment and instructions on how to deal with the problem. What we discovered when we got home was a deep gash on the back of Frank's heel where the tape had eaten through the flesh, leaving him with a scar he would carry for the rest of his life.

I was on the phone to the doctor at once to find out if he had any idea of the torture to which he had subjected my son for the whole time Frank was under his care, but of course I got very little satisfaction.

"Things like that do happen from time to time, and fortunately for the child, he is young enough not to suffer any long-term effects from it," the doctor replied.

Meanwhile, Ursula had started school in the one-room building that was about to be converted to a modern facility so as to keep pace with the town's rapid population growth. Even at her young age, just six, she had been a real help in caring for her younger siblings, dressing and feeding them and even helping out with some of the household chores. With Ursula away at school, Frank and Isabell, now one and three years old, could more often than not be found tucked away behind the counter in the service station until Joan had time to break away to attend to her domestic duties.

In 1960, much to our surprise and great delight, we were informed that my parents had decided to pay us a visit. Ursula was their first grandchild and she had stolen her *oma's* heart before she left. That, together with Rösel's desire to meet her other two grandchildren, may explain why Adolf and Rösel mustered the courage to embark upon what was still—even with the advent of air travel—a gruelling 24-hour adventure.

For us, the timing was perfect. I had just hatched another deal that would keep our noses to the grindstone for some time to come, so the prospect of having Mom in the house to care for the kids was most enticing.

The Chamber of Commerce had launched an initiative to persuade the appropriate authorities to establish a permanent police presence in town. In response, we were told that the demand did not yet warrant the expense of building a facility to house a detachment, and a survey of the town indicated a lack of any suitable rental accommodations. The superintendent of the RCMP stationed in Prince George did offer to stop over in Little Prairie to discuss the situation with us.

When he did, he could not hold out hope for the foreseeable future, but he was more than happy to recommend the force enter into a long-term lease arrangement if someone were willing to build to their specifications. It didn't take me any longer than it had with Lee Phillips two years earlier to figure out who that someone would be.

The store was by now carrying itself, and the arrangement could not have worked out better. As well, Fugle Lumber, one of the area's smaller sawmill and logging enterprises, had gone out of business, leaving us holding the bag for a sizable amount of money that they could only repay with the lumber that was left in their inventory.

Even Joan could see the wisdom in fleshing out this opportunity. Our future tenants provided us with a blueprint of what they would require for an office, a holding facility for prisoners, and living quarters. As luck would have it, a pair of Swedish carpenters, who were regular customers at the service station and who had just finished a construction project to house railway employees, were eager to give us an estimate to build the place. The price was such that we could almost pay for the structural part of the building with our own resources, leaving only the interior finishing to be financed.

I always find it intriguing the way bankers phrase their responses to credit applications. As expected, our friend Joe Engelman at the bank, given the good record we had established, showed himself most generous. He could see no reason at all why he couldn't "help us out." Who would be helping whom in a transaction like this?

Mom and Dad arrived just as construction got underway. They were suitably impressed with our accomplishments thus far, and we of course were proud to show them off. Sure, the town was still in a primitive state of development. The streets had not been paved, sending clouds of dust into the air with every passing car. Mom found it hard to believe that people actually lived in some of the primitive shacks that dotted the landscape. With all the hustle and bustle, she likened the scenes she observed around town to those in some of the Wild West movies that had found their way from Hollywood to the German movie theatres after the war.

Dad, on the other hand, was fascinated by the clever, efficient, and practical building methods and, by Forchheim standards at the time, the comforts and conveniences they incorporated in the finished product. During breakfast one morning he offered, while he was here with little to do, to assume the responsibility of looking after whatever it was that heated the apartment. When I showed him how to turn up the thermostat in the hallway, he was most skeptical until I showed him the furnace room with its fully automated system. I don't think he ever quite believed that this small, simple-looking tin box heated both our apartment and the sizable store space below.

I made arrangements with my new Swedish friends at the construction site to accommodate Dad's desire to make himself useful during the day by letting him help them with their work. He was most fascinated by the experience. Unlike most Germans, who tend to lay claim to most of the world's patents and a monopoly on quality of workmanship and efficiency, Dad found that the German builders he knew would have had a lot to learn to get a job on our project.

Indeed, things did go exceptionally well. In no time at all we were putting up walls and tying them together with the roof trusses. Our business had even generated enough income during the summer to pay for roughing in the electrical, plumbing, and mechanical services. The new hardware and building supply centre offered us an attractive price for all the finishing materials required to complete the project. The future tenants were most pleased with the results and started paying rent several months before the building was ready for occupancy.

It all seemed too good to be true, and so it turned out to be when I presented the first bill for several thousand dollars' worth of finishing materials to the bank manager, a new man who had replaced Joe Engelman.

"There has unfortunately been a change in the bank's lending policy for the area," the new man told me, offering his sincere regret that he could not "help us out" after all. He arranged for me to meet with officials at the bank's regional headquarters in Edmonton, but considering the exposure they had accumulated during the first two years of operation and the number of delinquent loans on the books already, he held out little hope for a change in their position.

The trip would have been a total waste of time had it not taught me to never trust a banker. None of the banks in Dawson Creek would even look at an application from Chetwynd, leaving us at the mercy of the suppliers, who, like ourselves, had acted in good faith by extending us the credit.

Beaver Lumber, the main creditor, attached a lien to the finished building but offered to carry the debt, providing we could meet their terms. The monthly payments had to be structured to amortize the loan over just a two-year period, far exceeding what we could reasonably hope to generate with the rent from the two buildings and the business.

We had no other choice but to gamble and sign away our lives for at least two years. Making it through the first winter would be particularly tough since most of the lucrative highway business came from summer tourism. We became instant experts in juggling our trade accounts and pushing the limits of the marginal lines of credit the bank was "helping us out" with. Thanks to Mom and Dad, both Joan and I were free to apply ourselves to the business full time, saving the cost of at least one extra employee. The financial crunch of this period was hard on us. At times, after a long hard day with little to show in terms of profits, followed by trying to put on a brave face in front of my parents and the kids, the stress became almost unbearable. More often than not, Joan cried herself to sleep, tired, humiliated, angry, and frustrated, her body next to me convulsing to suppress the tears. At one point we had to impose on one of our friends, who had offered to loan us a small amount of money, to carry us through another month.

Mom and Dad left the following spring, eager to get home to share their experience and adventure with the rest of the family and their friends. In later years we often speculated that without their visit at such a critical time, we might well have lost contact with our past completely. But while Mom and Dad were here we got back in the habit of speaking German at home. It had become impractical when Ursula started school and found it more convenient to share her new experience with the rest of us in English. Likewise, Joan and I conversed only in English during the day, having acquired a business vocabulary for which we did not know the German equivalent.

My parents added another dimension to the lives of the children and sparked in us some curiosity about the Old Country: how might things have changed since we left? And might we find some comfort and peace in re-establishing contact with the past that was haunting us? Joan was reminded of the promise she had made on her departure: to come home for brother Rudi's ordination to the priesthood—the *Primiz*. So we tentatively started to make plans to keep that promise.

Meanwhile, perhaps a bit wiser and more humble, we emerged as winners financially. With more new businesses establishing themselves, the town continued to prosper, and us along with it. By the end of the two years, our own business had generated sufficient income to make the last few payments on the police facility, even leaving us with a marginal surplus. In fact the premises we were leasing under the Standard Oil franchise had become woefully inadequate for the business we were doing.

Most of the road between Prince George and Dawson Creek was still unpaved and spotted with potholes large enough to lose the little Volkswagens our Old Country compatriots began to ship to the North American markets. The road north was nothing more than a primitive logging trail that ended at Moberly Lake. The maximum lifespan for a tire under those conditions was no more than 10,000 miles. The average car or light truck, to be safe, required a regular alignment of the front wheel suspension.

Naturally, the oil company, even though it was taking 5 percent off the top of everything we sold, was interested only in selling its own products. Without a major expansion of the facilities and some investments in new machinery and equipment, we had reached the limit of any income our little business could generate. So I set out to convince the oil company to enlarge the premises to accommodate the additional services for which we had identified a demand.

A visit to the headquarters of Standard Oil in Vancouver earned me some condescending praise for the quality of my proposal, but no commitment to give it any serious consideration, causing me to doubt that I would ever hear from them on the subject.

After going to the expense of travelling to Vancouver anyway, I could see no harm in adding another day to the trip to execute a "Plan B" that Joan and I had been discussing. Without an appointment, I was able to arrange a meeting with senior personnel of Imperial Oil, whose offices were no more than a city block from their rivals. They needed no reminder that their brand was under-represented on the Alaska Highway, and I had no difficulty at all generating interest in the scheme I had hatched during the two-hour flight to Vancouver. Given a proper location across the highway from our present facility, and allowing for right-turn access for traffic from the south, I would no doubt take the bulk of local business and the lion's share of the highway trade with me to a new, much larger service facility. Buoyed by the positive tone of the initial discussion,

I boldly informed them that I would only be interested in a franchise arrangement based on a loan from their company to build and own the facility myself.

I was sure they were impressed when I showed not the slightest bit of intimidation at their suggestion to continue the discussions over lunch at the Vancouver Club with the regional vice president of the company.

When we got there, however, I had to reach very deep to draw on everything I had learned during my acting career in Forchheim to nonchalantly behave as if dining in such exclusive surroundings was an everyday occurrence. I followed my hosts to the lounge to freshen up, pretending, as they did, that my hands needed washing. I then dried them with the delicately embroidered towel that was tossed into a fancy hopper, even though it didn't appear to need cleaning. I even stuck the toes of my Army and Navy "Dollar Day" shoes into the mechanical rotary brush, pretending that they once had a shine.

The rules of the club did not allow for any business to be discussed in the main dining areas, so we were ushered into an anteroom three times the size of my first house in Little Prairie. There was enough cutlery on the table to supply the needs of the annual banquet of the Chetwynd Chamber of Commerce. My composure did suffer some minor cracks when, as the guest, I was invited to choose my preferred cocktail and to select from the menu that looked like something designed to guide one through the ritual of a High Mass in the Catholic Church.

All's well that ends well. "We'll have someone to see you within the next two weeks," Mr. Thompson, the VP, told me as we shook hands at the end of the ordeal. "If we find things the way you have outlined them to us, you can start making plans for your new business right away."

If I hadn't been in possession of an airline ticket, I could have made the return trip on Cloud 9, but as it was I needed the time to think. It was one thing to sell the deal to a bunch of hotshot corporate bureaucrats and quite another to get Joan to buy in to the brilliant scheme. I needn't have worried. She liked the idea that the project would be financed entirely with a loan from Imperial Oil, to be repaid through a levy on the sales of the company's products. We only had to use our own resources in securing the property. Unlike the present arrangement, the company would not be entitled a commission on any other products and services dispensed out of the new facility. To mitigate against any risk that was associated with the new venture, we would carry on with our present business at the Chevron station for as long as our present landlord would lease it to us.

True to their word, a representative of Imperial Oil, who was not at all hard to infect with my enthusiasm, soon paid us a visit. He suggested we secure the property and order some drawings to be made of what we had in mind for the building. The company, he offered, might be persuaded to pay for the actual blueprints.

We allowed our imagination to run free, knowing that our design, which included space for a modest car dealership complete with a parts department and a shop that could accommodate six work bays, might be more elaborate than what the oil company had in mind. To our surprise, Imperial suggested only minor changes to the layout. Soon afterward we received notification that the deal had been approved, granting us permission to proceed with construction.

At almost the same time we received a letter from Standard Oil, which informed us that they, too, were proceeding with an addition to their facility along the lines I had suggested. I could think of no gentle way to convey to them the news that we were no longer interested in what I had so passionately pleaded for them to consider, at least not without exposing the country to the spectacle of one of the major oil companies operating with a broken heart. We knew, however, that executing the plans we had for both businesses would be beyond our capacity to handle, so once again, and against our better judgement, we considered taking in a partner.

We offered a deal to Bert Chatham, a good friend, to manage the service station part of the new facility on a partnership basis, but the arrangement caused all of us more headaches than it was worth. To his credit, Bert tried hard to please both our customers and us. He was a highly skilled technician and entirely trustworthy. But because of his work experience in a big company environment, he was unaccustomed to dealing with the pressures, the demands, and the discipline of a small business. We all soon realized that the new enterprise would fall far short of our expectations and that it would take some time for the car dealership, at least, to show some return, so we parted company, thankfully on friendly terms.

For Joan and me, what should have been an easy sprint toward a relaxed work schedule, affording us more time to be with our children, turned into another marathon of digging ourselves out of the deep hole we had dug by the time both businesses were equipped with the necessary tools, equipment, and inventory. Naturally, we also had to increase our payroll to deliver the new services we were offering.

The townspeople identified our two businesses as "His" and "Hers," with Joan, looking after the old Chevron, winning out in terms of our local clientele's preference, whereas I, as expected, managed to attract most of the highway trade. Neither was enough to satisfy the bank, which as usual limited us to a line of credit barely sufficient for us to stay above water.

It was a year both of us, and perhaps more importantly our children, would rather forget. It came as a relief when Standard Oil discovered that it was in the bizarre situation of competing with its own lessee and served us notice that under the circumstances it was not inclined to renew our lease arrangement.

In the meantime, the new business showed some dramatic improvement. With Joan adding her expert touch to the operation, our fortunes once again began to improve. Despite his youth, Marshall Peters, who had trained as a parts salesman with Aspol Motors, our partners and suppliers of Ford automotive products in Dawson Creek, turned out to be our most reliable, trustworthy, and conscientious colleague. Better still, he was not shy about filling in for us on the odd weekend so we could have some precious time with the kids. Between us, we agreed that the towering Esso sign in front of the place stood for "Every Second Sunday Off."

We got further relief when our good friend Lee Phillips expressed an interest in purchasing the building that had served as our home. The proceeds from the sale helped to relieve some of the pressure at the bank and to build us a fine new home on the lot we had acquired next to the police station.

To make the most of this new-found freedom, we also managed to build a cabin at Moberly Lake where, equipped with a motorboat and other assorted toys, we spent many happy hours together as a family. It was around that time as well that we found the courage to revive our dormant dream to spend our later years in the ranching business. A couple of the original Little Prairie residents, Yvonne and Otto Elden, because of Otto's failing health, offered to sell us their farming enterprise on terms we were able to afford, providing the business lived up to its promise. We became the proud owners of 2,000 acres of fertile farmland in the Pine River valley, eight kilometres west of town.

Our workload had not lessened a great deal. During the summer months we felt obliged to operate the service station 24 hours a day, which often meant that Joan, with our trusty Alsatian dog King as a partner, had to man the night shift so as to spell off the person we had hired for that purpose. However, confident that we had committed to a path that would eventually satisfy our aspirations, the burden was made much lighter. The business would surely grow with the town and provide us with enough income to give our children a comfortable, secure home and the education we had been deprived of, and to give us the means to safeguard our independence beyond our active working career.

One after another the necessary building blocks that give a town its soul were put in place. The new schools, the post office, the library, a curling rink, the Legion Hall, and a ball diamond were each a source of immense civic pride to those who gave their time and effort to promote these important new assets.

The impetus leading to the village's incorporation stemmed from the now-urgent need to install sewers. Financing such an ambitious project required the support and guarantee of the provincial government; however, a giant leap of faith in the town's prospects would be needed to justify burdening its residents with the additional taxes the project would necessitate.

As far as the bureaucrats were concerned, the town would have to at least double in size before it could meet the established criteria for the government to endorse and underwrite the project. Luckily, some provincial politicians harboured their own ambitious dreams. Premier Bennett's minister responsible, Dan Campbell, was easily persuaded to allow the water district, under whose authority the water system was financed, to continue existing. This paved the way for a future, incorporated municipality to take over responsibility for the sewer. The bankers and bureaucrats (by their very nature, I suspect) never made the connection between the two entities, or that both of them taxed the same base. Again, businesses had to commit to paying premium rates for the service for however much time it would take to become viable.

So in 1962, Chetwynd was born. I had hoped that we could be designated as a town from the outset, because I was still having problems, so my "friends" told me, with properly pronouncing the "v" in village. Sadly, however, Chetwynd was classified as a village, and I found myself with a seat on the first village council. I was now Village Commissioner Frank Oberle and, although I didn't know it at the time, I had taken the first step toward my political career.

It was also at this time that Joan and I truly began to regard ourselves as true Canadians. I had made this discovery unexpectedly, during the promised visit to Germany. It took place in May 1962, just as we were planning the major expansion to our business. The dream of enlarging our prospects at the same location or, failing that, pursuing a new enterprise altogether was spinning in our heads as we started to arrange the trip. We had an appointment to keep with our past. In the immortal words of Robert Service: "A promise made is a debt unpaid." Rudi's *Primiz* was to be in May 1962, and everyone back home was insisting that if we came at all, we must bring the children.

First we hired Bert Chatham to manage the business, despite the cost on top of the price of the tickets. There was another hitch in the person of our son Peter, who was still living in another dimension. To say that this was by far the least opportune time for Joan to get pregnant again would be a gross understatement—but pregnant she was. Peter's siblings had chosen the advent of epic journeys as their time to be born, and he decided not only to follow the tradition, but also to become the main attraction of the show. He was born in 1962 on my own birthday, March 24, and so, with four children in tow and Peter just two months old, we set out on another incredible adventure.

Fortunately, the timing coincided with the introduction of the first commercial passenger jets. To add to the excitement, we were booked on a Boeing 707 scheduled to arrive at Orly Airport in Paris, just two months after one of the first of its series had crashed there. It was a major mistake to choose Paris over Amsterdam as the port of entering Europe. The French at that time made no distinction between English-speaking Canadians and Americans, who, for whatever reason, they hated with a passion. I presume the French considered it an affront to their honour that they had been liberated from the German occupation by a foreign power, particularly since that foreign power wreaked more devastation on their countryside than the German invaders had in the first place. Astonishingly, the memory span of the average Frenchman then must have been limited to about 20 years; by 1962 they seemed to have all but forgotten the humiliating defeat the Germans had inflicted on them in 1940. Had we been aware of that, our brief visit to Paris could have been turned into a much more pleasant experience by simply speaking German instead of English.

As it was, we were relieved to arrive at the German border, where we were greeted by a most friendly and accommodating customs agent. Soon the train was rushing us by the familiar vistas of the Black Forest and the countryside Joan and I had explored in our youth. Ursula and Isabell, old enough to share in the excitement of the moment, had their eyes glued to the windows, looking for familiar faces as the train got closer to our destination. Joan and I were troubled by the prospect of being reminded of our past, but full of anticipation and joy at the coming reunion with our brothers and sisters and the parents whose hearts were reaching out to us. We embraced to fight our emotions and suppressed bittersweet tears as the coach rolled into the station at Karlsruhe.

They were all there to greet us. There must have been 40 of them, waving, shouting, all of them speaking at once. Had it not been for Erich fighting his way toward us, past a rush of disembarking passengers, to remind us that the train would stop for two minutes exactly, we might have carried on to Heidelberg. (German trains were still running on time.) He started handing the kids through the open window into eager arms, while Joan and I gathered our belongings and made for the exit. The children were frightened at first, not knowing what to make of this sea of teary-eyed strangers speaking a strange language, their outstretched arms groping at them. It would take some time and a lot of patience and understanding before the outpouring of love everyone was showing could be reciprocated.

Driving through the city, our first impression was astonishment at the changes it had undergone while we were away. As if the war had never happened, there was no longer any visible evidence of the devastation it had caused. Even the *Schloss* and the other historic landmarks that are the city's soul and identity had been fully restored to their former splendour and in a way true to their historic character.

In Forchheim, too, people had been busy, not only removing signs that might have reminded them of the ugly past, but even managing to cleanse their collective memories of all the ugliness, the suffering, and the scars this dark chapter in their history had inflicted upon them. Everywhere one could see that profound and dramatic change in every sphere of human endeavour that only total chaos can foment. Through land reform the town was shedding its dependence on subsistence farming. There had been a major shift of the pre-war industrial centres in the north to the southern parts of the country, creating jobs and opportunities for smaller enterprises that catered to the pent-up demands of the local economy.

The refugees, seen at first as a heavy burden to the local communities and a threat to their culture and traditions, appeared now to be fully integrated and accepted. They had brought with them an iron will to rebuild their shattered lives and had combined their strong work ethic with government-provided financial assistance, in the form of equalization payments, to reach a level of prosperity comparable to the rest the population. They had contributed in a major way to the economy and had earned the respect and recognition of the original burghers for the diversity they brought, which enriched the community in a cultural sense as well.

Emil and Berta had remodelled and built onto their house to accommodate Cilli's photo shop and studio. The new place incorporated all the modern conveniences that it had been lacking. Joan and I soon realized that we were not the only ones whose lives had changed and who could point with pride and satisfaction to what we had accomplished during the last decade.

Before I was allowed to follow the throng of people into the house, where tables were decked with everything one's heart could desire—including lots of homemade sausage—Emil insisted on taking me out back behind the house. Where the potato fields had once been, he showed me the site he had reserved and selected for us to build our home.

"As proud as we are of what you two have accomplished, it's now time to bring your family home and end your gypsy life," he declared.

He did not react well when, sadly, I told him we had found another place that we now called home. We had, I said, grown roots in a world that nourished much more ambitious dreams and that offered us opportunities, freedom, and independence beyond anything we could ever aspire to here in Forchheim—a place where we could not escape being haunted by our past. I told him that to discuss this subject any further would only result in more heartache.

It should have felt good to get even with him for bombarding me with those rotten potatoes when I first came to date his daughter, but instead I felt pity. It was perhaps one of his own dreams to make up for the years during which he could not provide and care for his family. Now, with that dream in ruins, he looked very old and dejected as we walked back to the house to join the festivities and help the children get acquainted with their aunts, uncles, cousins, and grandparents, all of whom were so eager to make them feel welcome.

Word had gotten around the neighbourhood that no doubt we would be starved for the delights of Kneisel's sausages, and everyone, still remembering what it had been like to be deprived, donated whatever could be spared to help Berta stock up for the occasion. The inventory not only fed the whole assembly for all the time we were there, but also left us with copious quantities to be hidden in suitcases and baby clothes for the journey back home.

We chose to enjoy the limelight while it lasted, for all too soon someone else would become the centre of attention. Plans were well underway for a homecoming of another sort, one the whole town would celebrate and participate in. Prior to Rudi, the town had only produced two sons throughout its history who had committed to the priesthood. The First World War had claimed the life of one, World War Two the other. God had obviously required them to be at His side to bear witness to what was being done to His earthly creation and to ask what might have possessed the people He had created in His image to act in such a mindless, satanic fashion.

At least in the minds of the faithful congregation of St. Martin's in Forchheim, two inductees into the spiritual council within the precincts of St. Peter's domain were no substitute for a representative on earth whom they could trust to communicate their special interests and concerns to the higher authority directly. Much had changed, but the church was still the dominant force in the town, and it was now gearing up to celebrate Rudi's ordination with all the pomp and splendour only the Catholic Church could muster.

Rudi himself was still in retreat at St. Peter, a town high in the Black Forest, going through the final stages of induction into the life and career he, with Berta's help, had chosen. Joan, never quite convinced that the brother she knew would be a qualified candidate for such an important calling, felt the urge to visit him to be reassured. So, accompanied by the children and by Cilli, Leo, Erich, and Edith, we set out on a pilgrimage for an emotional reunion.

The time Rudi was allowed with us was restricted, of course, but therefore even more precious. He left us with no doubts about his deep commitment to the vow he was about to take. He spoke to us about the source of his inspiration: his confidence in his faith. He, too, had found a new home that would distance him from the past and his relationship to his natural family.

Besides the church hierarchs, only the immediate families were invited to the cathedral in Freiburg for the actual ordination ceremony, an experience to enrich one's memory for a lifetime. Then the new inductee arrived in Forchheim to be met at the town's square by the priest, the mayor and his council, a marching band, and literally the whole population. The forest had yielded wagonloads of greenery that were used to frame *die Hauptstrasse* all the way to the church. The street was paved with flower petals. Every home and building was brimming with flowers and adorned with happy, tearful faces as the solemn procession made its way to the place where the new priest would deliver his particularly potent first blessing.

He was allowed to be with his family until the next morning, when the townspeople assembled once more, this time in front of Emil and Berta's house. It had been decorated by Rudi's old schoolmates to become the backdrop for the special ceremony during which he received his mother's blessing and official farewell. Next, Father Danner, the successor to Father Dorer, and several visiting priests and church officials, now in full regalia, received him into their ranks and led another solemn procession, accompanied by a brass band, to the church for his first mass.

Flanked by the *Bürgermeister* [mayor] and the school principal, Berta and Emil led the rest of the family, bursting with pride and comfortably believing that this day was worth all the horrendous sacrifices leading to it and that God had forgiven any indiscretions that had been necessary in pursuing the eventual goal.

The bright sun even crowded out the shadow of the deadly sin with which Joan and I had burdened the family. Among the very first of the many emigrants ever to return, we too were treated with respect and adulation. And after liberating our troubled souls through the confession on which Emil had absolutely insisted, Joan and I felt worthy to share in the pride and humility befitting the occasion. So complete was the rapture that it included even Aunt Anna. When Joan had been in greatest need of her love and support, Anna had not been able to bring herself to visit her even once at the small clinic, a one-room affair at the midwife's home where Joan had borne our child. Now Anna could easily have been persuaded that our firstborn was the product of another Immaculate Conception.

Rudi's homecoming, the night before he celebrates his first mass.

Flanked by the mayor and school principal, Emil and Berta accompany their son on his way to celebrate his first mass. His sisters Cilli and Joan follow behind.

The town's marching band leads the parade.

Ursula and Isabell are among the principals in the parade.

To make sure that no person was left out, volunteers had produced mountains of cakes that were cut up and delivered to the town's elderly and sick, who were unable to attend the many banquets and public gatherings in the days following. There was coffee, too. Since it was still a scarce commodity, and expensive, Joan and I had raided Campbell's store in Chetwynd before we left. We had succeeded in smuggling the precious cargo through customs in Paris, and Berta put me in charge of guarding it while it was being ground through Aunt Anna's commercial machine and to make certain that none of it would "hang up" in the process.

Peter, because of his tender age, would remember little of the occasion, but relative to the price of his ticket, he played a pivotal role throughout it all—not only because he acted brilliantly as the main attraction, but also because of his special travel accommodation that he shared with the contraband we conspired to move in both directions. It was a rather larger than necessary basket equipped with sturdy enough handles to sustain not only his weight, but also whatever was stored under the mattress that served as a false bottom. On the way east the space was occupied with abundant quantities of coffee beans, and on the return trip it contained several metres and dozens of cans of different kinds of sausage, providing us for some time to come with the sustenance needed to tackle the rather serious problems we had left behind.

Customs agents dislike spending much time with small infants, particularly ones whose vocal cords emit the most primeval, blood-curdling screams as soon as the agents get near them. Peter, prompted by a firm pinch to his bottom at just the right time, was easily persuaded to act as such a specimen, affording us clear passage without even the most cursory inspection.

All in all, we spent six weeks away from our business at a time when perhaps we could least afford it, but in retrospect it may have been our only opportunity to reconnect with our families before it was too late. For Joan and me, the experience helped to expel at least some of the ghosts that still haunted our dreams, and for the children it provided a reference point to the other culture influencing their upbringing.

Aided by the Marshall Plan, Germany had risen like a phoenix from the ashes to become one of the most powerful nations on earth, in terms of both its industrial prowess and the political stability that manifested itself during the 18 years of the post-war period. There should have been ample cause to feel proud of what had been accomplished and to have faith and confidence in the future. Yet in the midst of the festive mood and the euphoria that Rudi's ordination and our visit had spawned in the little village, one could not help but sense an underlying fear and anxiety once again, this time over the deteriorating relationship between the powers of the Western alliance, of which Germany had now become a full partner, and the Soviet bloc in the east.

The Cuban Missile Crisis later that year gave substance to those fears and made the prospect of another war very real. The arsenal of nuclear weapons both sides had armed themselves with was more than sufficient to obliterate the entire planet—and Germany would of course be Ground Zero, the central battleground.

Unlike the farewell 12 years before, there was much less of the feeling of finality that had traumatized our earlier departure, even if there were just as many tears. The world had become a much smaller place. The British and the French were sponsoring the development of the Concorde, a supersonic aircraft that could travel from London to New York in just over three hours. "Who knows?" Mom ventured to say. "I liked it in Canada, and if things get out of hand again, Hanna and Franz might just find us a place to hide away."

Our visit helped us to reconcile some of the unpleasant memories that had led us to consider leaving the Fatherland in the first place. This time there was no uncertainty or anxiety about the future. Our children were homesick. We were not leaving for a far-off place where people were strangers and spoke a different language. This time we said goodbye to go home.

As much as we had enjoyed the visit, and despite the deep satisfaction Joan and I received from the spirit of kinship and family by which we felt embraced, in the end we were entirely at peace, satisfied with our decision to choose Canada as the place where we would raise our children and meet our destiny. In 1962, Canada was still lacking some of the essential elements that are the hallmark of a modern progressive, socially conscious nation, such as universal health care and a social security system coupled to a pension plan, but these were shortcomings that over time would be redressed. In the meantime, the journey back to our past turned out to be a stark reminder of the opportunities and the freedom our new homeland offered and of the recognition and respect that it afforded every individual citizen. These were things that we were not prepared to deprive our children of, things to which we had become accustomed ourselves.

At 30 years of age, we were already well established in business and had laid a solid foundation from which to pursue our future prospects. However, not even in our most daring dreams could we have anticipated the many twists and turns that were still ahead of us along the road our lives would take.

How, after all, could anyone with such humble beginnings ever anticipate the success and enjoyment we harvested from our various business ventures? How could we ever dream of being able to claim the rich rewards that are earned by playing an active role in the development of one's community and from service to one's fellow citizens? How indeed could anyone be so bold as to believe someone like me could be chosen by his peers as their representative in our Parliament and be elevated to one of the most exclusive and prestigious offices in the land, Her Majesty the Queen's Privy Council?

Perhaps God had made a mistake in targeting Joan and me for such utter pain, suffering, and punishment during our childhood and had decided to redress the oversight with rewards commensurate to the torment that had been visited upon us.

In the process, He acquainted us with people whose generosity of spirit and nobility of character helped restore our faith in humanity and whose kindness and own great daring inspired us to accept every challenge that came our way, giving us the courage to strive for ever higher achievement. They include the many friends we made among Canada's Native people; the people everywhere who shared our values and principles and contributed to our cause by inviting us to their homes and donating their time and efforts, without asking anything in return; the people in the north who elected me to six consecutive terms in Parliament; and those people in the highest offices in the land who invested in us their trust and confidence and offered us their friendship.

It is to all of them that the next and final volume of the story of our lives is dedicated.

After war and frontier living, Frank Oberle thought he was ready for anything life could throw at him, but nothing had prepared him for Ottawa or the realities of small-town politics. The second volume of Frank Oberle's memoirs (1-894384-83-0) continues his remarkable story, tracing his path from mayor of Chetwynd to member of Parliament for Prince George–Peace River. It was a post he held for 21 years, culminating in 8 years' service on the Privy Council as Prime Minister Brian Mulroney's Minister of Science and Technology and Minister of Forests.

Photo Credits

The Albecker family collection: page 20

The Oberle family collection: pages 23, 137, 166

The author's private collection: pages 25, 115, 127, 131, 141, 143, 159, 173, 206, 214, 234, 237, 257, 268, 276, 314, 329, 330

City of Karlsruhe Archives: pages 71

City of Rheinstetten Archives: front cover, back cover, page 111

Photo Studio Erich Bauer, Karlsruhe, pages 101, 109

Born in Forchheim, Germany, Frank Oberle survived the turmoil of Hitler's Germany and post-war chaos before immigrating to Canada in 1951. During his career he tried his hand at many jobs, including logger, gold miner, rancher, and town mayor, before serving six consecutive terms as a member of Parliament. In 1985 Frank became Canada's first German-born federal cabinet member when Prime Minister Brian Mulroney made him Minister of State for Science and Technology. Four years later, as Minister of Forests, his determination led him to confront the industry's clear-cutting practices and demand sustainable forest management. He received the Canadian Forestry Achievement Award in 1992 and was a founding member of the Canadian Institute for Advanced Research.

Frank lives near Nanoose, B.C., with his wife Joan. They have four children and seven grandchildren.